Other Books and Seri

1901-1907 Native American Census Seneca, Ottawa, Peoria, Quapaw, and Wyandotte Indi. Territory)

1932 Census of The Standing Rock Sioux Res. 1924-1932

Census of The Blackfeet, Montana, 1897- 1901 Expanded Edition

Eastern Cherokee by Blood, 1906-1910, Volumes I thru XIII

Choctaw of Mississippi Indian Census 1929-1932 with Births and Deaths 1924-1931 Volume I
Choctaw of Mississippi Indian Census 1933, 1934 & 1937, Supplemental Rolls to 1934 & 1935 with Births and Deaths 1932-1938, and Marriages 1936-1938 Volume II

Eastern Cherokee Census Cherokee, North Carolina 1930-1939 Census 1930-1931 with Births And Deaths 1924-1931 Taken By Agent L. W. Page Volume I
Eastern Cherokee Census Cherokee, North Carolina 1930-1939 Census 1932-1933 with Births And Deaths 1930-1932 Taken By Agent R. L. Spalsbury Volume II
Eastern Cherokee Census Cherokee, North Carolina 1930-1939 Census 1934-1937 with Births and Deaths 1925-1938 and Marriages 1936 & 1938 Taken by Agents R. L. Spalsbury And Harold W. Foght Volume III

Seminole of Florida Indian Census, 1930-1940 with Birth and Death Records, 1930-1938

Texas Cherokees 1820-1839 A Document For Litigation 1921

Choctaw By Blood Enrollment Cards 1898-1914 Volumes I thru XVII

Starr Roll 1894 (Cherokee Payment Rolls) Districts: Canadian, Cooweescoowee, and Delaware Volume One
Starr Roll 1894 (Cherokee Payment Rolls) Districts: Flint, Going Snake, and Illinois Volume Two
Starr Roll 1894 (Cherokee Payment Rolls) Districts: Saline, Sequoyah, and Tahlequah; Including Orphan Roll Volume Three

Cherokee Intruder Cases Dockets of Hearings 1901-1909 Volumes I & II

Indian Wills, 1911-1921 Records of the Bureau of Indian Affairs Books One thru Seven;
Native American Wills & Probate Records 1911-1921

Other Books and Series by Jeff Bowen

Turtle Mountain Reservation Chippewa Indians 1932 Census with Births & Deaths, 1924-1932

Chickasaw By Blood Enrollment Cards 1898-1914 Volume I thru V

Cherokee Descendants East An Index to the Guion Miller Applications Volume I
Cherokee Descendants West An Index to the Guion Miller Applications Volume II (A-M)
Cherokee Descendants West An Index to the Guion Miller Applications Volume III (N-Z)

Applications for Enrollment of Seminole Newborn Freedmen, Act of 1905

Eastern Cherokee Census, Cherokee, North Carolina, 1915-1922, Taken by Agent James E. Henderson   Volume I (1915-1916)
Volume II (1917-1918)
Volume III (1919-1920)
Volume IV (1921-1922)

Complete Delaware Roll of 1898

Eastern Cherokee Census, Cherokee, North Carolina, 1923-1929, Taken by Agent James E. Henderson   Volume I (1923-1924)
Volume II (1925-1926)
Volume III (1927-1929)

Applications for Enrollment of Seminole Newborn Act of 1905 Volumes I & II

North Carolina Eastern Cherokee Indian Census 1898-1899, 1904, 1906, 1909-1912, 1914 Revised and Expanded Edition

1932 Hopi and Navajo Native American Census with Birth & Death Rolls (1925-1931) Volume 1 - Hopi
1932 Hopi and Navajo Native American Census with Birth & Death Rolls (1930-1932) Volume 2 - Navajo

Western Navajo Reservation Navajo, Hopi and Paiute 1933 Census with Birth & Death Rolls 1925-1933

Cherokee Citizenship Commission Dockets 1880-1884 and 1887-1889 Volumes I thru V

Other Books and Series by Jeff Bowen

Applications for Enrollment of Chickasaw Newborn Act of 1905
Volumes I thru VII

Cherokee Intermarried White 1906 Volume I thru X

Applications for Enrollment of Creek Newborn Act of 1905
Volumes I thru XIV

Applications for Enrollment of Choctaw Newborn Act of 1905
Volume I, II, III, IV, V, VI, VII, VIII, IX, X, XI, XII & XIII

Visit our website at **www.nativestudy.com** to learn more about these
and other books and series by Jeff Bowen

APPLICATIONS FOR ENROLLMENT OF CHOCTAW NEWBORN ACT OF 1905

VOLUME XIV

TRANSCRIBED BY
JEFF BOWEN

NATIVE STUDY
Gallipolis, Ohio
USA

Originally published:
Baltimore, Maryland
2013

Reprinted by:

Native Study LLC
Gallipolis, OH
www.nativestudy.com
2020

Library of Congress Control Number: 2020918113

ISBN: 978-1-64968-107-2

Made in the United States of America.

This series is dedicated to the descendants of the Choctaw newborn listed in these applications.

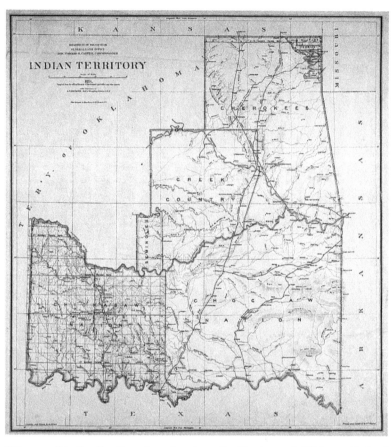

This map of Indian Territory shows how large the Choctaw and Chickasaw Nations' land base was that contained huge deposits of asphalt and coal. Just the size and territory involved was flooded with the "Grafters".

DEPARTMENT OF THE INTERIOR.

Commissioner to the Five Civilized Tribes.

NOTICE.

Opening of Land Office at Wewoka,

IN THE SEMINOLE NATION, INDIAN TERRITORY.

Notice is hereby given that on Monday, September 4, 1905, the Commissioner to the Five Civilized Tribes will establish a land office at Wewoka, in the Seminole Nation, Indian Territory, for the purpose of allowing citizens and freedmen of the Seminole Nation to select allotments of land for their minor children enrolled under the Act of Congress approved March 3, 1905 (33 Stat. L 1060), and for the further purpose of allowing citizens and freedmen of the Seminole Nation, whose allotments are incomplete, to select additional land in order to bring the value of their allotments up to the standard of $309.09, as nearly as may be practicable.

Each child whose enrollment in accordance with the Act of March 3, 1905, has been duly approved by the Secretary of the Interior, is entitled to receive an alllotment of forty acres without regard to the character or value of the land selected.

Selection of allotments for minor children must be made by their citizen or freedmen parents or by a duly appointed guardian, or curator, or by a duly appointed administrator.

TAMS BIXBY,
Commissioner.

Muskogee, Indian Territory,
July 29, 1905.

This particular notice for the Seminole and Creek Newborn makes mention of the Act of 1905. It is likely that a similar notice was posted in the Choctaw and Chickasaw Nations for the registration of newborn children.

DEPARTMENT OF THE INTERIOR,
Commission to the Five Civilized Tribes.

Rules and Regulations Governing the Selection of Allotments and the Designation of Homesteads in the Choctaw and Chickasaw Nations.

1. Selections of allotments and designations of homesteads for adult citizens and selections of allotments for adult freedmen must be made in person except as herein otherwise provided.

2. Applications to have land set apart and homesteads designated for duly identified Mississippi Choctaws must be made personally before the Commission to the Five Civilized Tribes. Fathers may apply for their minor children and if the father be dead the mother may apply. Husbands may apply for wives. Applications for orphans, insane persons and persons of unsound mind may be made by duly appointed guardian or curator, and for aged and infirm persons and prisoners by agents duly authorized thereunto by power of attorney, in the discretion of said Commission.

3. At the time of the selection of allotment each citizen and duly identified Mississippi Choctaw shall designate as a homestead out of said selection land equal in value to one hundred and sixty acres of the average allottable land of the Choctaw and Chickasaw Nations, as nearly as may be.

4. Each Choctaw and Chickasaw freedman, at the time of selection shall designate as his or her allotment of the lands of the Choctaw and Chickasaw Nations, land equal in value to forty acres of the average allottable land of the Choctaw and Chickasaw Nations.

5. Citizens, freedmen and identified Mississippi Choctaws who are married, whether they have attained their majority or not, will be regarded as of age for the purpose of making selections.

6. Selections may be made by citizen and freedman parents for unmarried male children under twenty-one years of age and for unmarried female children under eighteen years of age, and a male citizen or freedman may make selection for his wife, if she is entitled to make selection, unless she shall, at the time or previously thereto, protest in writing.

7. Where the father of an unmarried minor citizen, freedman or identified Mississippi Choctaw is a non-citizen, the citizen, freedman or identified Mississippi Choctaw mother of such children must make selection in person in behalf of said children.

8. Selections of allotments and designations of homesteads for minor citizens and selections of allotments for minor freedmen may be made by the citizen father or mother or freedman father or mother, as the case may be, or by a guardian, curator, or an administrator having charge of their estate, in the order named.

9. Selections of allotments and designations of homesteads for citizen, and selections of allotment for freedmen, prisoners, convicts, aged and infirm persons and soldiers and sailors of the United States on duty outside of Indian Territory, may be made by duly appointed agents under power of attorney, and for incompetents by guardians, curators, or other suitable person akin to them.

10. Selections may be made and homesteads designated by duly identified Mississippi Choctaws, who have, within one year after the date of their identification as such, made satisfactory proof of bona fide settlement within the Choctaw-Chickasaw country, at any time within six months after the date of their said identification.

11. Persons authorized to make selections by power of attorney, as provided in rules 2 and 9 hereof, must be the husband or wife, or a relative not further removed than a cousin of the first degree of the person for whom such selection is made.

12. It shall be the duty of the Commission to the Five Civilized Tribes to see that selections of allotments and designations of homesteads for the classes of persons mentioned in rules 2, 6, 7, 8 and 9 hereof, are made for the best interests of such persons.

13. Selections of allotments for citizens, freedmen and identified Mississippi Choctaws who have died subsequent to September 25, 1902, and before making a selection of allotment, shall be made by a duly appointed administrator or executor. If, however, such administrator or executor be not duly and expeditiously appointed, or fails to act promptly when appointed, or for any other cause such selections be not so made within a reasonable and practicable time, the Commission to the Five Civilized Tribes shall designate the lands thus to be allotted.

14. In determining the value of a selection the appraised value of the land selected shall be increased by the appraised value of such pine timber on such land as has heretofore been estimated by the Commission to the Five Civilized Tribes.

15. Selections of allotments may be made only by citizens and freedmen whose enrollment has been approved by the Secretary of the Interior, and by persons duly identified by the Commission to the Five Civilized Tribes as Mississippi Choctaws, and by none others.

16. When a selection of land has been made by a citizen, freedman or identified Mississippi Choctaw, and the land so selected is claimed by a person whose rights as a citizen or freedman have not been finally determined, contest for the land so selected may be instituted by the person claiming the land, formal application for the land being first made as is required by the Rules of Practice in Choctaw and Chickasaw allotment contest cases.

THE COMMISSION TO THE FIVE CIVILIZED TRIBES.
Tams Bixby, Chairman.

Muskogee, Indian Territory, March 24, 1903.

The above statement published prior to 1905, was established for what was supposed to be a set of guidelines when it came to allotments. But with supplemental agreements and Congressional legislation, time frames as well as rules and regulations often changed and were not the same for every tribe.

INTRODUCTION

The *Applications for Enrollment of Choctaw Newborn Act of 1905*, National Archive film M-1301, Rolls 50-57, are found under the heading of Applications for Enrollment of the Commission to the Five Civilized Tribes. For this series, I have transcribed the application forms filled out by individuals applying for enrollment in the Five Civilized Tribes under the Dawes Commission. These applications contain considerably more information than stated on the census cards found in series M-1186. M-1301 possesses its own numerical sequence, separate from M-1186. To find each party's roll number you would have to reference M-1186.

The Choctaw as well as the Chickasaw allotments were likely some of the most sought after properties in Indian Territory. There was supposed to be a 25-year restriction on the sale or lease of any Indian lands so as to insure that the owners wouldn't be swindled, but that isn't what happened. This fact is borne out in the Dawes Commission General Allotment Act, of February 8, 1887, Section 5, which "Provides that after an Indian person is allotted land, the United States will hold the land 'in trust [1] for the sole use and benefit of the Indian' (or his heirs if the Indian landowner dies) for a period of 25 years. (Land held in trust by the United States government cannot be sold or in anyway alienated by the Indian landowner, since the United States government considers the underlying ownership of the land held by itself and not the tribe. After the period of trust ends, the Indian landowner is free to sell the land and is free from any encumbrance from the United States.)"[1] Instead, Native Americans were exploited by the devious. The Choctaw and Chickasaw Districts both had huge asphalt and coal deposits, so there was pressure from outsiders to acquire them from the minute they were discovered. After repeated attacks throughout the years and many legislative changes, President "Roosevelt finally signed the Five Tribes Bill at noon on April 26, 1906, the forces seeking to end all restrictions were disappointed. Section 19 removed restrictions from the sale of all inherited land but directed that no full-bloods could sell their land for twenty-five years. The Act also prohibited leases for more than one year without the approval of the Secretary of the Interior."[2]

Angie Debo described the opportunists that wanted these Native American allotments as, "Grafters". The parents of the newborns enumerated within this series would no sooner receive the approval for their child's allotment than there would be someone there with cash in hand holding a new deed or lease for the parents to sign their child's birthright away. Angie Debo said it best, "As the business incapacity of the allottees became apparent, a horde of despoilers fastened themselves upon their property." According to Debo, "The term 'grafter' was applied as a matter of course to dealers in Indian land, and was frankly accepted by them. The speculative fever also affected Government employees so that it was almost impossible to prevent them from making personal investments."[3]

---

[1] General Allotment Act, Act of Feb. 8, 1887 (24 Stat. 388, ch. 119, 25 USCA 331)
[2] The Dawes Commission and the Allotment of the Five Civilized Tribes, 1893-1914 by Kent Carter, pg. 173
[3] And Still the Waters Run, Angie Debo, p. 92.

INTRODUCTION

According to the Department of Interior in 1905, "It is estimated that there will be added to the final rolls of the citizens and freedmen of the Choctaw and Chickasaw nations the names of 2,000 persons, including 1,500 new-born children to be enrolled under the provisions of the act of Congress approved March 3, 1905."[4]

The quote below explains, in detail, the requirements for qualifying as a newborn Choctaw, "By the act of Congress approved March 3, 1905 (H.R. 17474), entitled 'An act making appropriations for the current and contingent expenses of the Indian Department and for fulfilling treaty stipulations with various Indian tribes for the fiscal year ending June 30, 1906, and for other purposes,' it was provided as follows:

'That the Commission to the Five Civilized Tribes is hereby authorized for sixty days after the date of the approval of this act to receive and consider applications for enrollment of infant children born prior to September twenty-fifth, nineteen hundred and two, and who were living on said date, to citizens by blood of the Choctaw and Chickasaw tribes of Indians whose enrollment has been approved by the Secretary of the Interior prior to the date of the approval of this act; and to enroll and make allotments to such children.'

'That the Commission to the Five Civilized Tribes is authorized for sixty days after the date of the approval of this act to receive and consider applications for enrollment of children born subsequent to September twenty-fifth, nineteen hundred and two, and prior to March fourth, nineteen hundred and five, and who were living on said latter date, to citizens by blood of the Choctaw and Chickasaw tribes of Indians whose enrollment has been approved by the Secretary of the Interior prior to the date of the approval of this act; and to enroll and make allotments to such children.'

"Notice is hereby given that the Commission to the Five Civilized Tribes will, up to and inclusive of midnight, May 2, 1905, receive applications for the enrollment of infant children born prior to September 25, 1902, and who were living on said date, to citizens by blood of the Choctaw and Chickasaw tribes of Indians whose enrollment has been approved by the Secretary of the Interior prior to March 3, 1905."[5]

Following is the scope of these transcriptions: Besides the applications themselves, researchers will find the identities of other individuals within these applications -- doctors, lawyers, mid-wives, and other relatives -- that may help with you genealogical research.

Jeff Bowen
Gallipolis, Ohio
NativeStudy.com

---

[4] Annual Reports of the Department of the Interior For the Fiscal Year Ended June 30, 1905, p. 609.
[5] Annual Reports of the Department of the Interior For the Fiscal Year Ended June 30, 1905, p. 593.

Applications for Enrollment of Choctaw Newborn
Act of 1905   Volume XIV

Choc New Born 961
<u>   Edith Goings[sic]   b.   12-30-03</u>

BIRTH AFFIDAVIT.

DEPARTMENT OF THE INTERIOR.
COMMISSION TO THE FIVE CIVILIZED TRIBES.

IN RE APPLICATION FOR ENROLLMENT, as a citizen of the   Choctaw   Nation, of
Edith Going   , born on the   30th   day of December   , 1903

Name of Father: Ben Going   a citizen of the   Choctaw   Nation.
Name of Mother: Sophie Going   a citizen of the   Choctaw   Nation.

Postoffice   Goodwater, Ind. Ter.

AFFIDAVIT OF MOTHER.

UNITED STATES OF AMERICA, Indian Territory, ⎱
    Central   DISTRICT. ⎰

   I,   Sophie Going   , on oath state that I am   19   years of age and a citizen by
blood   , of the   Choctaw   Nation; that I am the lawful wife of   Ben Going   ,
who is a citizen, by blood   of the   Choctaw   Nation; that a   female   child
was born to me on   30th   day of   December   , 1903; that said child has been named
Edith Going   , and was living March 4, 1905.

                                                her
                                  Sophie   x   Going
Witnesses To Mark: mark
  ⎧ Robert Anderson
  ⎩ Vester W Rose

   Subscribed and sworn to before me this   10th   day of   April   , 1905

                              Wirt Franklin
                                    Notary Public.

AFFIDAVIT OF ATTENDING PHYSICIAN OR MID-WIFE.

UNITED STATES OF AMERICA, Indian Territory, ⎱
    Central   DISTRICT. ⎰

   I,   Sissy Going   , a   mid-wife   , on oath state that I attended on
Mrs.   Sophie Going   , wife of   Ben Going   on the   30th   day of   December   ,

1

1903; that there was born to her on said date a   female   child; that said child was living March 4, 1905, and is said to have been named Edith Going

Sissy Going

Witnesses To Mark:

{

Subscribed and sworn to before me this   10th day of   April   , 1905

Wirt Franklin
Notary Public.

NEW-BORN AFFIDAVIT.

Number.............

...Choctaw Enrolling Commission...

IN THE MATTER OF THE APPLICATION FOR ENROLLMENT, as a citizen of the Choctaw   Nation, of   Edith Going

born on the 30th day of   December   190 3

Name of father   Ben Going   a citizen of   Choctaw
Nation final enrollment No. 3026
Name of mother   Sophie Hudson   a citizen of   Choctaw
Nation final enrollment No. 1619

Postoffice   Goodwater I.T.

AFFIDAVIT OF MOTHER.

UNITED STATES OF AMERICA
INDIAN TERRITORY
   Central   DISTRICT

        I   Sophie Hudson   , on oath state that I am
   19   years of age and a citizen by   blood   of the   Choctaw   Nation, and as such have been placed upon the final roll of the   Choctaw Nation, by the Honorable Secretary of the Interior my final enrollment number being   1619 ; that I am the lawful wife of   Ben Going   , who is a citizen of the   Choctaw   Nation, and as such has been placed upon the final roll of said Nation by the Honorable Secretary of the Interior, his final enrollment number being   3026   and that a   female   child was born to me on the 30th day of   December   190 3; that said child has been named   Edith Going   , and is now living.

Sophie Hudson

Witnesseth.

Must be two
Witnesses who
are Citizens. } Wilson E Frazier

Arlington King

Subscribed and sworn to before me this   14   day of   March   190 5

W A Shoney

Notary Public.

My commission expires: Jan 10, 1909

Affidavit of Attending Physician or Midwife

UNITED STATES OF AMERICA,
  INDIAN TERRITORY,
  Central   DISTRICT }

I,   Sissie Going   a   midwife
on oath state that I attended on Mrs. Sophie Hudson Going   wife of   Ben Going
on the 30th   day of   December , 190 3, that there was born to her on said date a   female
child, that said child is now living, and is said to have been named Edith Going

Sissie Going   ~~M. D.~~

Subscribed and sworn to before me this the   14   day of   march   1905

W.A. Shoney

Notary Public.

WITNESSETH:

Must be two witnesses
who are citizens and
know the child. { Wilson E Frazier

Arlington King

We hereby certify that we are well acquainted with   Sissie Going
a   midwife   and know   her   to be reputable and of good standing in the
community.

Must be two citizen
witnesses. { Wilson E. Frazier
Arlington King

3

<u>Choc New Born 962</u>
     Eva Battice b. 3-9-03

NEW-BORN AFFIDAVIT.

          Number.............

...Choctaw Enrolling Commission...

          IN THE MATTER OF THE APPLICATION FOR ENROLLMENT, as a citizen of the
Choctaw   Nation, of   Eva Battiest[sic]

born on the 9 day of ___March___ 190 3

Name of father   Thompson Battiest[sic]   a citizen of   Choctaw
Nation final enrollment No...............
Name of mother Sallie Battiest   a citizen of   Choctaw
Nation final enrollment No. ....

                              Postoffice   Idabel I.T.

AFFIDAVIT OF MOTHER.

UNITED STATES OF AMERICA
INDIAN TERRITORY
   Central   DISTRICT

          I   Sallie Battiest   , on oath state that I am
     26   years of age and a citizen by blood   of the   Choctaw   Nation,
and as such have been placed upon the final roll of the   Choctaw   Nation, by the Honorable
Secretary of the Interior my final enrollment number being ....; that I am the lawful wife
of   Thompson Battiest   , who is a citizen of the   Choctaw   Nation, and as such
has been placed upon the final roll of said Nation by the Honorable Secretary of the Interior,
his final enrollment number being .... and that a   female   child was born to me on
the   9th   day of   March   190 3; that said child has been named   Eva Battiest   ,
and is now living.
                                        her
                              Sallie x Battiest
Witnesseth.   mark
   Must be two   ⎫   Keith Shaw
   Witnesses who ⎬
   are Citizens. ⎭   Frank McAfee

     Subscribed and sworn to before me this 21   day of Jan   190 5

                    W A Shoney
                              Notary Public.
My commission expires: Jan 10, 1909

                    4

Applications for Enrollment of Choctaw Newborn
Act of 1905   Volume XIV

AFFIDAVIT OF ATTENDING PHYSICIAN OR MIDWIFE

UNITED STATES OF AMERICA
INDIAN TERRITORY
Central   DISTRICT

I,   Bessie Shaw   a   Midwife
on oath state that I attended on Mrs. Sallie Battiest   wife of   Thompson Battiest
on the 9th day of March   , 190 3 , that there was born to her on said date a   female
child, that said child is now living, and is said to have been named   Eva Battiest

                                                    Bessie Shaw
                        Subscribed and sworn to before me this, the   21st   day of
                        Jan   190 5

WITNESSETH: W A Shoney   Notary Public.
   Must be two witnesses ⌠ Keith Shaw
   who are citizens   ⌡
                          Frank McAfee

         We hereby certify that we are well acquainted with   Bessie Shaw
a   midwife   and know   her   to be reputable and of good standing in the
community.

         Keith Shaw   _____

         Frank McAfee   _____

BIRTH AFFIDAVIT.
DEPARTMENT OF THE INTERIOR.
COMMISSION TO THE FIVE CIVILIZED TRIBES.

IN RE APPLICATION FOR ENROLLMENT, as a citizen of the   Choctaw   Nation, of
Eva Battice   , born on the 9th   day of March , 1903

Name of Father: Thompson Battice   a citizen of the   Choctaw   Nation.
Name of Mother: Sallie Battice   a citizen of the   Choctaw   Nation.

                        Postoffice   Idabel, Ind. Ter.

5

Applications for Enrollment of Choctaw Newborn
Act of 1905   Volume XIV

AFFIDAVIT OF MOTHER.

UNITED STATES OF AMERICA, Indian Territory, ⎫
Central   DISTRICT. ⎭

I,   Sallie Battice   , on oath state that I am   25   years of age and a citizen by blood   , of the   Choctaw   Nation; that I am the lawful wife of   Thompson Battice   , who is a citizen, by blood   of the   Choctaw   Nation; that a female   child was born to me on   9th   day of   March   , 1903; that said child has been named   Eva Battice   , and was living March 4, 1905.

her
Sallie x Battice
mark

Witnesses To Mark:
⎧ Robert Anderson
⎩ Vester Rose

Subscribed and sworn to before me this   10th   day of   April   , 1905

Wirt Franklin
Notary Public.

AFFIDAVIT OF ATTENDING PHYSICIAN OR MID-WIFE.

UNITED STATES OF AMERICA, Indian Territory, ⎫
Central   DISTRICT. ⎭

I,   Bissy[sic] Shaw   , a   mid-wife   , on oath state that I attended on Mrs.   Sallie Battice   , wife of   Thompson Battice   on the 9th   day of   March , 1903; that there was born to her on said date a   female   child; that said child was living March 4, 1905, and is said to have been named   Eva Battice

her
Bissy x Shaw
mark

Witnesses To Mark:
⎧ Robert Anderson
⎩ Vester Rose

Subscribed and sworn to before me this   10th   day of   April   , 1905

Wirt Franklin
Notary Public.

6

Choc New Born 963
Davis James   b.   1-3-04

NEW BORN AFFIDAVIT

No ....

CHOCTAW ENROLLING COMMISSION

IN THE MATTER OF THE APPLICATION FOR ENROLLMENT as a citizen of the Choctaw
Nation, of   Davis James   born on the   3rd day
of   January   190 4

Name of father   Moses James   a citizen of   Choctaw   Nation,
final enrollment No.   2234
Name of mother   Sophie Dennis   a citizen of   Choctaw   Nation,
final enrollment No.   2914

Garvin I.T.   Postoffice.

AFFIDAVIT OF MOTHER

UNITED STATES OF AMERICA
    INDIAN TERRITORY
DISTRICT   Central

    I   Sophie Dennis   , on oath state that I am   20   years of age and a
citizen by   blood   of the   Choctaw   Nation, and as such have been placed upon
the final roll of the   Choctaw   Nation, by the Honorable Secretary of the Interior my final
enrollment number being   2914   ; that I am the lawful wife of Moses James   , who is
a citizen of the   Choctaw   Nation, and as such has been placed upon the final roll of
said Nation by the Honorable Secretary of the Interior, his final enrollment number being
2234   and that a   Male   child was born to me on the   3rd   day of   January   190 4;
that said child has been named Davis James   , and is now living.

                        her
WITNESSETH: Sophie x Dennis
  Must be two witnesses { Byington Williams   mark
  who are citizens   { Wilson Jackson

Subscribed and sworn to before me this, the 15 day of   Feb   , 190 5

W.A. Shoney
Notary Public.
My Commission Expires: Jan 10, 1909

7

___

BIRTH AFFIDAVIT.

DEPARTMENT OF THE INTERIOR.
COMMISSION TO THE FIVE CIVILIZED TRIBES.

___

IN RE APPLICATION FOR ENROLLMENT, as a citizen of the   Choctaw   Nation, of
Davis James   , born on the 3rd   day of   January   , 1904

Name of Father: Moses James   a citizen of the   Choctaw   Nation.
Name of Mother: Sophie James   a citizen of the   Choctaw   Nation.

Postoffice   Garvin, Ind. Ter.

___

AFFIDAVIT OF MOTHER.

UNITED STATES OF AMERICA, Indian Territory, ⎤
        Central   DISTRICT. ⎦

I,   Sophie James   , on oath state that I am   20   years of age and a citizen by
blood   , of the   Choctaw   Nation; that I am the lawful wife of   Moses James,
deceased   , who is a citizen, by   blood   of the   Choctaw   Nation; that a
male   child was born to me on   3rd   day of   January   , 1904; that said child has
been named   Davis James   , and was living March 4, 1905.

her
Sophie x James
mark

Witnesses To Mark:
⎧ Robert Anderson
⎩ Vester W Rose

Subscribed and sworn to before me this   10th   day of   April   , 1905

Wirt Franklin
Notary Public.

___

AFFIDAVIT OF ATTENDING PHYSICIAN OR MID-WIFE.

UNITED STATES OF AMERICA, Indian Territory, ⎤
        Central   DISTRICT. ⎦

I,   Viney James   , a   mid-wife   , on oath state that I attended on
Mrs.   Sophie James   , wife of   Moses James   on the 3rd day of   January   ,
1904; that there was born to her on said date a   male   child; that said child was living
March 4, 1905, and is said to have been named   Davis James

                                        her
                                Viney x James
Witnesses To Mark: mark
   ⎰ Robert Anderson
   ⎱ Vester W Rose

     Subscribed and sworn to before me this 10th   day of   April   , 1905

                                Wirt Franklin
                                        Notary Public.

AFFIDAVIT OF ATTENDING PHYSICIAN OR MIDWIFE

UNITED STATES OF AMERICA
INDIAN TERRITORY
   Central   DISTRICT

     I,   Winey James   a   midwife
on oath state that I attended on Mrs.   Sophie Dennis   wife of Moses James
on the 3rd day of January   , 190 4 , that there was born to her on said date a   male
child, that said child is now living, and is said to have been named   Davis James

                                        her
                                Winey x James
                                        mark
     Subscribed and sworn to before me this, the   15   day of
     Feb   190 5

WITNESSETH: W.A. Shoney   Notary Public.
   Must be two witnesses ⎰ Byington Williams
   who are citizens   ⎱ Wilson Jackson

     We hereby certify that we are well acquainted with   Winey James
a   midwife   and know   her   to be reputable and of good standing in the
community.

     Byington Williams   _____

     Wilson Jackson   _____

Applications for Enrollment of Choctaw Newborn
Act of 1905 Volume XIV

<u>Choc New Born 964</u>
Sissy Washington b. 1-23-04

BIRTH AFFIDAVIT.

DEPARTMENT OF THE INTERIOR.
COMMISSION TO THE FIVE CIVILIZED TRIBES.

IN RE APPLICATION FOR ENROLLMENT, as a citizen of the   Choctaw   Nation, of
Sissy Washington   , born on the 23rd day of January , 1904

Name of Father: Ben Washington   a citizen of the   Choctaw   Nation.
Name of Mother: Acy Washington   a citizen of the   Choctaw   Nation.

Postoffice   Harrington, Ind. Ter.

AFFIDAVIT OF MOTHER.

UNITED STATES OF AMERICA, Indian Territory, ⎱
       Central   DISTRICT. ⎰

I,   Acy Washington   , on oath state that I am   30   years of age and a citizen
by   blood   , of the   Choctaw   Nation; that I ~~am~~ *was* the lawful wife of   Ben
Washington, deceased   , who ~~is~~ *was* a citizen, by   blood   of the   Choctaw
Nation; that a   female   child was born to me on 23rd   day of   January , 1904;
that said child has been named   Sissy Washington   , and was living March 4, 1905.
                                        her
                              Acy x Washington
Witnesses To Mark: mark
  ⎰ Robert Anderson
  ⎱ Vester W Rose

Subscribed and sworn to before me this 10th day of   April   , 1905

                    Wirt Franklin
                    Notary Public.

AFFIDAVIT OF ATTENDING PHYSICIAN OR MID-WIFE.

UNITED STATES OF AMERICA, Indian Territory, ⎱
       Central   DISTRICT. ⎰

I,   Silvia Harley   , a   mid-wife   , on oath state that I attended on
Mrs.   Acy Washington   , wife of   Ben Washington   on the 23rd day of

10

January   , 1904; that there was born to her on said date a   female   child; that said child was living March 4, 1905, and is said to have been named Sissy Washington

Witnesses To Mark:

      her

Silvia x Harley

      mark

{ Robert Anderson
{ Vester W Rose

Subscribed and sworn to before me this 10th   day of   April   , 1905

Wirt Franklin
Notary Public.

Choc New Born 965
    Wilson Lewis   b. 10-4-03

Ida Lewis may be on final roll as Ida Wallace. Her father was Dixon Wallace (Dec'd). Her mother was Becky Wallace (Dec'd).

NEW-BORN AFFIDAVIT.

Number............

...Choctaw Enrolling Commission...

    IN THE MATTER OF THE APPLICATION FOR ENROLLMENT, as a citizen of the Choctaw   Nation, of   Wilson Lewis

born on the   4 day of ___October___ 190 3

Name of father   Jamison Lewis   a citizen of   Choctaw
Nation final enrollment No. 5797
Name of mother   Ida Bohanan   a citizen of   Choctaw
Nation final enrollment No............

Postoffice   Beach I.T.

Applications for Enrollment of Choctaw Newborn
Act of 1905   Volume XIV

AFFIDAVIT OF MOTHER.

UNITED STATES OF AMERICA
INDIAN TERRITORY
Central   DISTRICT

I   Ida Bohanan   , on oath state that I am
20   years of age and a citizen by Blood   of the   Choctaw   Nation,
and as such have been placed upon the final roll of the   Choctaw Nation, by the Honorable
Secretary of the Interior my final enrollment number being ....; that I am the lawful wife
of   Jamison Lewis   , who is a citizen of the   Choctaw   Nation, and as such has
been placed upon the final roll of said Nation by the Honorable Secretary of the Interior, his
final enrollment number being   5797   and that a   Male   child was born to me on the
4 day of October   190 3; that said child has been named Wilson Lewis   , and is
now living.

                                                    her
                                        Ida x Bohanan
Witnesseth.   mark

Must be two ⎱ Earl Samuel
Witnesses who ⎰
                                        wife of J. M. Lewis
are Citizens.   Arsihill McGee

Subscribed and sworn to before me this 28   day of   Jan   190 5

                                        C L Lester
                                                Notary Public.
My commission expires: Oct 15 1905

AFFIDAVIT OF ATTENDING PHYSICIAN OR MIDWIFE

UNITED STATES OF AMERICA
INDIAN TERRITORY
Central   DISTRICT

I,   Artie Samuels   a   midwife
on oath state that I attended on Mrs. Ida Lewis   wife of   Jamison Lewis
on the 4   day of   Oct   , 190 3 , that there was born to her on said date a   mail[sic]
child, that said child is now living, and is said to have been named   Wilson Lewis

            Subscribed and sworn to before me this, the   28   day of
            Jan   190 5

WITNESSETH: C L Lester   Notary Public.
Must be two witnesses ⎰ Earl Samuel
who are citizens   ⎱
                         Arsihill McGee

We hereby certify that we are well acquainted with   Artie Samuel
a   midwife   and know her   to be reputable and of good standing in the
community.

12

Earl Samuel	her Artie x Samuels mark
Arsihill McGee	_____

BIRTH AFFIDAVIT.

DEPARTMENT OF THE INTERIOR.
COMMISSION TO THE FIVE CIVILIZED TRIBES.

IN RE APPLICATION FOR ENROLLMENT, as a citizen of the   Choctaw   Nation, of
Wilson Lewis   , born on the 4th   day of   October   , 1903

Name of Father: Jamison Lewis   a citizen of the   Choctaw   Nation.
Name of Mother: Ida Lewis   a citizen of the   Choctaw   Nation.

Postoffice   Beach, Ind. Ter.

AFFIDAVIT OF MOTHER.

UNITED STATES OF AMERICA, Indian Territory, ⎫
   Central   **DISTRICT.** ⎭

     I,   Ida Lewis   , on oath state that I am   20   years of age and a citizen by
blood   , of the   Choctaw   Nation; that I am the lawful wife of   Jamison Lewis   ,
who is a citizen, by   blood   of the   Choctaw   Nation; that a   male   child
was born to me on   4th   day of   October   , 1903; that said child has been named
Wilson Lewis   , and was living March 4, 1905.

                 her
             Ida x Lewis
Witnesses To Mark: mark
   ⎰ Robert Anderson
   ⎱ Vester W Rose

Subscribed and sworn to before me this 5th   day of   April   , 1905

           Wirt Franklin
           Notary Public.

Applications for Enrollment of Choctaw Newborn
Act of 1905   Volume XIV

AFFIDAVIT OF ATTENDING PHYSICIAN OR MID-WIFE.

UNITED STATES OF AMERICA, Indian Territory, ⎱
Central   DISTRICT. ⎰

I,   Artie James   , a   mid-wife   , on oath state that I attended on Mrs.   Ida Lewis , wife of   Jamison Lewis   on the   4th day of   October , 1903; that there was born to her on said date a   male   child; that said child was living March 4, 1905, and is said to have been named   Wilson Lewis

Her
Artie   x   James
mark

Witnesses To Mark:
⎰ Thompson Taylor
⎱ Noel J Samuels

Subscribed and sworn to before me this 8   day of   April   , 1905

C L Lester
Notary Public.

Choc New Born 966
     Myrtle Zula Johnson   b.   6-1-04

BIRTH AFFIDAVIT.
DEPARTMENT OF THE INTERIOR.
COMMISSION TO THE FIVE CIVILIZED TRIBES.

IN RE APPLICATION FOR ENROLLMENT, as a citizen of the   Choctaw   Nation, of Myrtle Zula Johnson   , born on the 1st   day of   June , 1904

Name of Father: Elam J Johnson   a citizen of the   Choctaw   Nation.
Name of Mother: Frances Johnson   a citizen of the   Choctaw   Nation.

Postoffice   Smithville, Ind. Ter.

AFFIDAVIT OF MOTHER.

UNITED STATES OF AMERICA, Indian Territory, ⎱
Central   DISTRICT. ⎰

I,   Frances Johnson   , on oath state that I am   38   years of age and a citizen by   blood   , of the   Choctaw   Nation; that I am the lawful wife of   Elam J

14

Johnson   , who is a citizen, by blood   of the   Choctaw   Nation; that a
female   child was born to me on   1st   day of   June   , 1904; that said child has
been named   Myrtle Zula Johnson   , and was living March 4, 1905.

                                              Frances Johnson
Witnesses To Mark:

    Subscribed and sworn to before me this 7th   day of   April   , 1905

                                      Wirt Franklin
                                              Notary Public.

AFFIDAVIT OF ATTENDING PHYSICIAN OR MID-WIFE.

UNITED STATES OF AMERICA, Indian Territory,
    Central   DISTRICT.

    I,   Bettie Bowen   , a   mid-wife   , on oath state that I attended on
Mrs.   Frances Johnson   , wife of   Elam J Johnson   on the 1st day of June   ,
1904; that there was born to her on said date a   female   child; that said child was
living March 4, 1905, and is said to have been named Myrtle Zula Johnson

                                              Bettie Bowen
Witnesses To Mark:

    Subscribed and sworn to before me this   7th day of   April   , 1905

                                      Wirt Franklin
                                              Notary Public.

Choc New Born 967
    Eveline Elliott b. 7-15-04

BIRTH AFFIDAVIT.

DEPARTMENT OF THE INTERIOR.
COMMISSION TO THE FIVE CIVILIZED TRIBES.

_____

IN RE APPLICATION FOR ENROLLMENT, as a citizen of the   Choctaw   Nation, of
Eveline Elliott   , born on the   15th   day of   July   , 1904

Name of Father: Abbott Elliott   a citizen of the   Choctaw   Nation.
Name of Mother: Bicey Elliott   a citizen of the   Choctaw   Nation.

Postoffice   Eagletown, Ind. Ter.

_____

AFFIDAVIT OF MOTHER.

UNITED STATES OF AMERICA, Indian Territory, ⎱
    Central   DISTRICT. ⎰

I,   Bicey Elliott   , on oath state that I am   about 30   years of age and a
citizen by   blood   , of the   Choctaw   Nation; that I am the lawful wife of
Abbott Elliott   , who is a citizen, by blood   of the   Choctaw   Nation; that
a   female   child was born to me on   15th   day of   July   , 1904; that said child
has been named   Eveline Elliott   , and was living March 4, 1905.

                                        her
                                Bicey x Elliott
Witnesses To Mark: mark
⎰ Robert Anderson
⎱ Vester W Rose

Subscribed and sworn to before me this   12th day of   April   , 1905

                        Wirt Franklin
                                Notary Public.

_____

AFFIDAVIT OF ATTENDING PHYSICIAN OR MID-WIFE.

UNITED STATES OF AMERICA, Indian Territory, ⎱
    Central   DISTRICT. ⎰

I,   Adeline Watt   , a   mid-wife   , on oath state that I attended on
Mrs.   Bicey Elliott   , wife of   Abbott Elliott   on the 15th day of   July   ,
1904; that there was born to her on said date a   female   child; that said child was
living March 4, 1905, and is said to have been named   Eveline Elliott

                                        her
                                Adeline x Watt
                                        mark

16

Witnesses To Mark:
   { Robert Anderson
     Vester W Rose

    Subscribed and sworn to before me this   12th   day of   April   , 1905

                            Wirt Franklin
                                Notary Public.

<u>Choc New Born 968</u>
    Herbert Dendy   b. 9-7-03

                    ————

BIRTH AFFIDAVIT.

DEPARTMENT OF THE INTERIOR.
COMMISSION TO THE FIVE CIVILIZED TRIBES.

————

IN RE APPLICATION FOR ENROLLMENT, as a citizen of the   Choctaw   Nation, of
Herbert Dendy   , born on the 7th   day of Sept , 1903

Name of Father: Daniel B. Dendy   a^citizen of the   Choctaw   Nation.
Name of Mother: Annie L. Dendy   a citizen of the   Choctaw   Nation.

                   Postoffice   Pauls Valley, Ind. Ter.

————

AFFIDAVIT OF MOTHER.

UNITED STATES OF AMERICA, Indian Territory, }
    Southern   **DISTRICT.** }

      I, Annie L. Dendy   , on oath state that I am   27   years of age and a citizen
by   blood   , of the   Choctaw   Nation; that I am the lawful wife of   Daniel B.
Dendy   , who is a citizen, by .... of the   United States   ~~Nation~~; that a
male   child was born to me on 7th   day of September   , 1903; that said child
has been named   Herbert Dendy   , and was living March 4, 1905.

                          Annie L. Dendy
Witnesses To Mark:
   {

Subscribed and sworn to before me this   23rd   day of march   , 1905

JW Shumate
Notary Public.

AFFIDAVIT OF ATTENDING PHYSICIAN OR MID-WIFE.

UNITED STATES OF AMERICA, Indian Territory, ⎫
  Southern   DISTRICT. ⎭

I,   W. C. Threlkeld   , a physician   , on oath state that I attended on
Mrs.   Annie L Dendy   , wife of   Daniel B Dendy   on the 7th   day of
September   , 1903; that there was born to her on said date a   male   child; that said
child was living March 4, 1905, and is said to have been named Herbert Dendy

W.C. Threlkeld M.D.
Witnesses To Mark:

{

Subscribed and sworn to before me this 24 day of   March   , 1905

WW Jones
Notary Public.
My com. ex Jan 8, 1907

Choc New Born 969
  Walter Howel Buckholts b. 10-24-03

DEPARTMENT OF THE INTERIOR,
Commission to the Five Civilized Tribes.
FILED
APR 18 1905
Tams Bixby CHAIRMAN.

NEW BORN
In the matter of the
application for the
enrollment of
Walter Howel Buckholts
as a citizen by blood
of the
Choctaw Nation
Born Oct. 24, 1903

Applications for Enrollment of Choctaw Newborn
Act of 1905   Volume XIV

Department of the Interior.

Commission to the Five Civilized Tribes.

IN Re Application for Enrollment, as a citizen of the   Choctaw   Nation of   Walter Howel*l* Buckholts   , born on the   24   day of   October, 1903.

Name of Father   Adelbert L. Buckholts   , a citizen of the   Choctaw   Nation.
Name of Mother   Carrie L. Buckholts   , a citizen of the Choctaw Nation, by inter-marriage.

AFFIDAVIT OF MOTHER.

United States of America,
    Indian Territory,   SS.
Southern District,

I, Carrie L. Buckholts, on oath state that I am, 20 years of age past, and a citizen by inter-marriage of the Choctaw Nation, that I am the lawful wife of Adelbert L. Buckholts, who is a citizen by blood of the Choctaw Nation; that a male child was born to me on the 24th day of October, 1903; that said child has been named Walter Howel Buckholts, and is now living.

Carrie L. Buckholts

Subscribed and swron[sic] to before me this   3   day of   April   A.D. 1905.

JP Gibson
Notary Public.
My commission expires 2/24/09.

Affidavit of Attending Physician.

UNITED STATES OF AMERICA,
INDIAN TERRITORY,
SOUTHERN DISTRICT,   I, Dr. W.T.Howell, a Physician, on oath state that

I attended on Mrs. Carrie L. Buckholts, wife of Adelbert L. Buckholts, on the 24th day of October, 1903; that there was born to her on the said date a male child; that said child is now living and is said to have been named Walter Howel Buckholts.

W.T. Howell M.D.

Subscribed and sworn to before me this the   30th   d ay of   March   1905.

R.L. March
Notary Public.

<u>Choc New Born 970</u>
Rosie Jackson   b. 6-4-04

_____

7-NB-970.

Muskogee, Indian Territory, June 8, 1905.

Joseph Jackson,
Lodi, Indian Territory.

Dear Sir:

Referring to the application for the enrollment of your infant child, Rosie Jackson, born June 4, 1904, it is noted from the affidavits heretofore filed in this office that you claim to be a citizen by blood of the Choctaw Nation.

If this is correct you are requested to state when, where and under what name you were listed for enrollment, the names of your parents and other members of your family for whom application was made at the same time, and if you have selected an allotment, please give your roll number as the same appears upon your allotment certificate.

This matter should receive your immediate attention, as no further action can be taken until this information is furnished to the Commission.

Respectfully,

Chairman.

_____

(The letter below typed as given.)

Lodi, I.T.
7/21/05

Commision[sic] to the Five Civilized tribes, Muskogee, I.T.
Dear sir By Request of yours of June the eight to my being a Citizen by Blood and want name I was enrolled under name of father Ralin Jackson, Brothers Willis and Arthur Jackson.

Roll No 8878

Yours very Resp

Joseph Jackson

Lodi, Ind. Ter.

_____

7-NB-970

Muskogee, Indian Territory, July 27, 1905.

Joseph Jackson,
Lodi, Indian Territory.

Dear Sir:

Receipt is hereby acknowledged of your letter of July 21, 1905, giving your roll number and the names of your parents, in the matter of the enrollment of your child Rosa Jackson as a citizen by blood of the Choctaw Nation.

In reply to your letter you are advised that this information has enabled this office to identify you as an enrolled citizen by blood of the Choctaw Nation and has been made a matter of record.

Respectfully,

Commissioner.

BIRTH AFFIDAVIT.

DEPARTMENT OF THE INTERIOR.
COMMISSION TO THE FIVE CIVILIZED TRIBES.

IN RE APPLICATION FOR ENROLLMENT, as a citizen of the   Choctaw   Nation, of
Rosie Jackson   , born on the 4th   day of   June   , 1904

Name of Father: Joseph Jackson   a citizen of the   Choctaw   Nation.
roll #8789
Name of Mother: Lizzie Jackson - nee Jacobs -   a citizen of the   Choctaw   Nation.

Postoffice   Lodi, Ind Ter

AFFIDAVIT OF MOTHER.

UNITED STATES OF AMERICA, Indian Territory, ⎱
          Central   **DISTRICT.** ⎰

I,   Lizzie Jackson - nee Jacobs - *roll #8789* , on oath state that I am   24   years of age and a citizen by   blood   , of the   Choctaw   Nation; that I am the lawful wife of   Joseph Jackson   , who is a citizen, by blood   of the   Choctaw Nation; that a   female   child was born to me on   4th   day of   June   , 1904; that said child has been named Rosie Jackson   , and was living March 4, 1905.

21

her
Lizzie x Jackson - nee Jacobs
mark

Witnesses To Mark:
⌠ JM Homer
⌡ A.J. Gardenhire

Subscribed and sworn to before me this 10th day of   April   , 1905

Lacey P. Bobo
Notary Public.

AFFIDAVIT OF ATTENDING PHYSICIAN OR MID-WIFE.

UNITED STATES OF AMERICA, Indian Territory, ⎫
Central   **DISTRICT.** ⎭

I,   Winnie Jackson   , a mid-wife   , on oath state that I attended on Mrs.   Lizzie Jackson - nee Jacobs , wife of   Joseph Jackson   on the 4th   day of June   , 1904; that there was born to her on said date a   female   child; that said child was living March 4, 1905, and is said to have been named Rosie Jackson

her
Winnie x Jackson
mark

Witnesses To Mark:
⌠ JM Homer
⌡ A.J. Gardenhire

Subscribed and sworn to before me this 10th day of   April   , 1905

Lacey P. Bobo
Notary Public.

Choc New Born 971
Mary Wesley   b. 2-22-05

BIRTH AFFIDAVIT.

DEPARTMENT OF THE INTERIOR.
COMMISSION TO THE FIVE CIVILIZED TRIBES.

IN RE APPLICATION FOR ENROLLMENT, as a citizen of the   Choctaw   Nation, of
Mary Wesley   , born on the 22nd   day of February   , 1905

Name of Father: Elias Wesley   a citizen of the   Choctaw   Nation.
Name of Mother: Matsy Wesley   a citizen of the   Choctaw   Nation.

Postoffice   Eagletown, Ind. Ter.

AFFIDAVIT OF MOTHER.

UNITED STATES OF AMERICA, Indian Territory, ⎱
      Central   DISTRICT. ⎰

I,   Matsy Wesley   , on oath state that I am   about 20   years of age and a
citizen by   blood   , of the   Choctaw   Nation; that I am the lawful wife of Elias
Wesley   , who is a citizen, by blood   of the   Choctaw   Nation; that a
female   child was born to me on   22nd   day of   February   , 1905; that said child
has been named   Mary Wesley   , and was living March 4, 1905.

                                      her
                                Matsy x Wesley
Witnesses To Mark: mark
    ⎰ Robert Anderson
    ⎱ Vester W Rose

Subscribed and sworn to before me this   10th day of   April   , 1905

                        Wirt Franklin
                              Notary Public.

AFFIDAVIT OF ATTENDING PHYSICIAN OR MID-WIFE.

UNITED STATES OF AMERICA, Indian Territory, ⎱
      Central   DISTRICT. ⎰

I,   Juisy Cooper   , a mid-wife   , on oath state that I attended on
Mrs. Matsy Wesley   , wife of Elias Wesley   on the 22nd day of   February   ,
1905; that there was born to her on said date a   female   child; that said child was
living March 4, 1905, and is said to have been named Mary Wesley
                                      her
                                Juisy x Cooper
                                      mark

Witnesses To Mark:
 { Robert Anderson
 { Vester W Rose

Subscribed and sworn to before me this   10th day of   April   , 1905

Wirt Franklin
Notary Public.

Choc New Born 972
         Harry L Denison   b. 10-12-03

NEW-BORN AFFIDAVIT.

Number...............

Choctaw Enrolling Commission.

IN THE MATTER OF THE APPLICATION FOR ENROLLMENT, as a citizen of the
Choctaw   Nation, of   Harry Denison

born on the   12th day of   Oct   190 3

Name of father   Ben L. Denison   a citizen of   United States
Nation final enrollment No...............
Name of mother   Sue Denison *(nee Susan M Oakes)*   a citizen of   Choctaw
Nation final enrollment No   4104

Postoffice   Garvin, Ind. Ter

AFFIDAVIT OF MOTHER.

UNITED STATES OF AMERICA, ⎫
    INDIAN TERRITORY,   ⎬
    Central   DISTRICT   ⎭

I   Sue Denison   on oath state that I
am   26 years of age and a citizen by   blood   of the   Choctaw   Nation, and as such
have been placed upon the final roll of the   Choctaw   Nation, by the Honorable
Secretary of the Interior my final enrollment number being   4104   ; that I am the lawful
wife of   Ben L Denison   , who is a citizen of the   United States   Nation,
and ~~as such~~ has been placed upon ~~the final roll~~ of said ~~Nation~~ by ~~the Honorable~~ Secretary of the
~~Interior~~, his ~~final enrollment number being~~ ——and that a   Male   child was born to me on

the 12   day of   Oct   190 3 ; that said child has been named   Harry Denison   ,
and is now living.

Sue Denison

WITNESSETH:

Must be two ⎫ Joel Spring
Witnesses who ⎬
are Citizens. ⎭ Henry Spring

Subscribed and sworn to before me this   19   day of   Jan   190 5

Chas. G. Shull
Notary Public.

My commission expires   Dec 14 1906

Mrs Denison was Susan M Oakes
whos (sic) enrollment no is 4104

Affidavit of Attending Physician or Midwife

UNITED STATES OF AMERICA, ⎫
   INDIAN TERRITORY, ⎬
Central   DISTRICT ⎭

I,   Ben L. Denison   a   Physician
on oath state that I attended on Mrs. Sue Denison   wife of   Ben L Denison
on the   12th   day of   Oct , 190 3, that there was born to her on said date a   male   child,
that said child is now living, and is said to have been named   Harry Denison

Ben L Denison   M. D.

Subscribed and sworn to before me this the   19   day of   Jan   1905

Chas. G. Shull
Notary Public.

WITNESSETH:

Must be two witnesses ⎧ Joel Spring
who are citizens and ⎨
know the child. ⎩ Henry Spring

We hereby certify that we are well acquainted with   Ben L Denison
a   **Physician**   and know   him   to be reputable and of good standing in
the community.

Must be two citizen ⎧ Joel Spring
witnesses.   ⎩ Henry Spring

Affidavit of Attending Physician or Midwife.

UNITED STATES OF AMERICA ⎫
INDIAN TERRITORY   ⎬
Central   DISTRICT ⎭

I,   Mrs Mary Schultze   a..
on oath state that I attended on Mrs.   Sue Denison   wife of   Ben L Denison
on the   12ᵗʰ   day of   October   , 190 3 , that there was born to her on said date a
Male   child, that said child is now living, and is said to have been named   Harry L. Denison

Mrs Mary Schultze   ~~M.D.~~

Subscribed and sworn to before me this, the   10ᵗʰ   day of   April   190 5

T.G. Carr

My com expires Sept. 8, 1908   Notary Public.

WITNESSETH:
   Must be two witnesses ⎧ ....
   who are citizens and   ⎨
   know the child.   ⎩ ....

We hereby certify that we are well acquainted with...
a............................ and know .... to be reputable and of good standing in
the community.

⎧ ....
⎨
⎩ ....

Affidavit of Attending Physician or Midwife.

UNITED STATES OF AMERICA ⎫
INDIAN TERRITORY   ⎬
Central   DISTRICT ⎭

I,   Mrs T.J. Barnes   a..
on oath state that I attended on Mrs.   Sue Denison   wife of   B L Denison
on the   12ᵗʰ   day of   October   , 190 3 , that there was born to her on said date a
male   child, that said child is now living, and is said to have been named   Harry L. Denison

Mrs T.J. Barnes   ~~M.D.~~

Subscribed and sworn to before me this, the   10ᵗʰ   day of   April   190 5

T.G. Carr

My com expires Sept. 8, 1908   Notary Public.

WITNESSETH:
   Must be two witnesses ⎧ ....
   who are citizens and   ⎨
   know the child.   ⎩ ....

Applications for Enrollment of Choctaw Newborn
Act of 1905   Volume XIV

We hereby certify that we are well acquainted with..
a..and know ....to be reputable and of good standing in the community.

{ ....
  ....

BIRTH AFFIDAVIT.

DEPARTMENT OF THE INTERIOR.
COMMISSION TO THE FIVE CIVILIZED TRIBES.

IN RE APPLICATION FOR ENROLLMENT, as a citizen of the   Choctaw   Nation, of
Harry L. Denison   , born on the 12th   day of   October   , 1903

Name of Father: B.L. Denison   a citizen of the United States Nation.
Name of Mother: Sue Denison   a citizen of the   Choctaw   Nation.

Postoffice   Garvin, Ind. Ter.

AFFIDAVIT OF MOTHER.

UNITED STATES OF AMERICA, Indian Territory, }
    Central   DISTRICT.

I,   Sue Denison   , on oath state that I am   27   years of age and a citizen by blood   , of the   Choctaw   Nation; that I am the lawful wife of   B.L. Denison   , who is a citizen, ~~by~~ ....of the   United States   ~~Nation~~; that a   male   child was born to me on 12th   day of   October   , 1903; that said child has been named Harry L Denison   , and was living March 4, 1905.

                              Sue Denison
Witnesses To Mark:
{

Subscribed and sworn to before me this 10th   day of   April   , 1905

                    Wirt Franklin
                    Notary Public.

27

Applications for Enrollment of Choctaw Newborn
Act of 1905   Volume XIV

AFFIDAVIT OF ATTENDING PHYSICIAN OR MID-WIFE.

UNITED STATES OF AMERICA, Indian Territory, }
Central   DISTRICT. }

I, B. L. Denison , a physician , on oath state that I attended on
Mrs. Sue Denison , ~~wife of~~ *my wife* on the 12th day of October , 1903;
that there was born to her on said date a   male   child; that said child was living
March 4, 1905, and ~~is said to have~~ *has* been named Harry L Denison

B.L. Denison

Witnesses To Mark:

{

Subscribed and sworn to before me this 10th day of   April   , 1905

Wirt Franklin
Notary Public.

Choc New Born 973
Calvin Ballaio[sic] Clay   b. 9-12-03

United States of America,   )
)
Indian Territory,   )   ss.
)
Central District.   )

I, William A. Durant, Indian Territory on oath state that I am thirty-four years of
age and a citizen by blood of the Choctaw Nation; that my post office address is Garvin,
Indian Territory; that I was personally acquainted with Agnes Clay, nee John, formerly
the wife of Abner H. Clay; that I lived within four miles of said parties and knew them
well, and often passed their house; that I know of my own knowledge that on or about the
12th day of September, 1903, there was born to the said Agnes Clay a male child; that
said child is now living and has been named Calvin Ballaid Clay; and that the said Agnes
Clay died on July 13, 1904.

William A Durant

Subscribed and sworn to before me this 12th day of April, 1905.

Wirt Franklin
Notary Public.

United States of America,   )
)
Indian Territory,   )   ss.
)
Central District.   )

    I, Phoebe Thomas, on oath state that I am about sixty-five years of age and a citizen by blood of the Choctaw Nation; that my post office address is Lukfata, Indian Territory; that I was personally acquainted with Agnes Clay, nee John, formerly the wife of Abner H. Clay; that the said Agnes Clay came to my house in January 1904, and brought with her a little boy about four months old, whom I have always understood to be the son of said Agnes Clay and her husband Abner H. Clay; that said child's name is Calvin Ballaid Clay; that said child is now living; that the said Agnes Clay and Calvin Ballaid Clay remained at my house from the time of their arrival there in January, 1904, until the death of the said Agnes Clay on the 13th day of July, 1904.

her
Phoebe x Thomas
mark

Subscribed and sworn to before me this 12th day of April, 1905.

Wirt Franklin
Notary Public.

Witnesses to mark.
    Vester Rose
    Robert Anderson

BIRTH AFFIDAVIT.

DEPARTMENT OF THE INTERIOR.
COMMISSION TO THE FIVE CIVILIZED TRIBES.

    IN RE APPLICATION FOR ENROLLMENT, as a citizen of the   Choctaw   Nation, of Calvin Ballaid Clay   , born on the 12th   day of September , 1903

Name of Father: Abner H Clay   a citizen of the   Choctaw   Nation.
Name of Mother: Agnes Clay   a citizen of the   Choctaw   Nation.

Postoffice   Lukfata, Ind. Ter.

AFFIDAVIT OF MOTHER.

UNITED STATES OF AMERICA, Indian Territory, ⎫
Central   DISTRICT. ⎭

I,   Abner H Clay   , on oath state that I am   33   years of age and a citizen by blood   , of the   Choctaw   Nation; that I ~~am~~ *was* the lawful ~~wife~~ *husband* of   Agnes Clay, deceased   , who ~~is~~ *was* a citizen, by   blood   of the   Choctaw   Nation; that a   male   child was born to me on   12th   day of   September   , 1903; that said child has been named   Calvin Ballaid Clay   , and was living March 4, 1905.

Abner H Clay

Witnesses To Mark:

{

Subscribed and sworn to before me this   12th   day of   April   , 1905

Wirt Franklin
Notary Public.

Choc New Born 974
Florence Going   b. 10-20-03

_____

United States of America,   )
)
Indian Territory,   )   ss.
)
Central District.   )

I, Sophia Going, on oath state that I am thirty-five years of age and a citizen by blood of the Choctaw Nation; that my post office address is Smithville, Indian Territory; that I am personally acquainted with Sophie Going, wife of Osborne Going, and have known said parties for about four years; that on or about the 20th day of October, 1903, there was born to the said Sophie Going a female child; that said child is now living and has been named Florence Going; that I know of my own knowledge the circumstances attending the birth of said child for I was at their house and saw said child about a half hour after her birth.

                                        her
                        Sophia x Going
                                        mark

Subscribed and sworn to before me this 7th day of April, 1905.

Wirt Franklin
Notary Public.

Witnesses to mark.
> Robert Anderson
> Vester W Rose

AFFIDAVIT OF ATTENDING PHYSICIAN OR MIDWIFE

UNITED STATES OF AMERICA
INDIAN TERRITORY
  Central   DISTRICT

  I,   Osborne Going   a _____
on oath state that I attended on Mrs. Sophie Going   wife of Osborne Going
on the   28 day of   Oct , 190 3 , that there was born to her on said date a   female   child,
that said child is now living, and is said to have been named   Florence Going

> Subscribed and sworn to before me this, the   21   day of
> Jan   190 5

WITNESSETH: C L Lester   Notary Public.
  Must be two witnesses ⎰ *(Name Illegible)*
  who are citizens   ⎱ Peter Going

  We hereby certify that we are well acquainted with   Osborne Going
a _____ and know   him   to be reputable and of good standing in the
community.

> *(Name Illegible)*   Osborne Going

> Peter Going   _____

7-NB-974

Muskogee, Indian Territory, July 18, 1905.

Osborn[sic] Going,
  Smithville, Indian Territory.

Dear Sir:

  Receipt is hereby acknowledged of your letter of July 10, 1905, in which you ask to be informed when the enrollment of your child is approved, so that you can select an allotment for her.

  In reply to your letter you are advised that the name of your child is now being placed upon a schedule of citizens by blood of the Choctaw Nation prepared for forwarding to the Secretary of the Interior for approval.   You will be notified when her enrollment is approved.

Respectfully,

Commissioner.

_____

(The letter below typed as given.)

(Copy)

Smithville, I. T.

Commission to the Five Civilized Tribes

Dear Sir

In replying to your communication I will inform you Florence Going my daughter who has been enrolled as Choctaw by blood her mother former name is Sophia Harrison her present Marriage name is Sophia Going

Sophia Harrison No 5567   Florence Going is her daughter   If this is satisfactory I will appreciate your early reply

Yours truly

O. G. Going

_____

7 NB 974

Muskogee, Indian Territory, May 5, 1905.

Osborn Going,
Smithville, Indian Territory.

Dear Sir:

Receipt is hereby acknowledged of your letter of April 26, 1905, transmitting affidavit of Sophia Going to the birth of Florence Going, daughter of Osborn and Sophie Going, October 20, 1903, and the same have been filed with our records as an application for the enrollment of said child.

Receipt is also acknowledged of certificate of allotment issued to Sophia Harrison who is the mother of Florence Going from which it appears that her roll number upon the approved roll of citizens by blood of the Choctaw Nation is 5567.

The certificate of allotment inclosed with your letter is herewith returned.

Respectfully,

EB 2-5

Commissioner in Charge.

_____

7--NB--974

Muskogee, Indian Territory, June 2, 1905.

Osborne Going,
      Smithville, Indian Territory.

Dear Sir:

Referring to the application for the enrollment of our infant child, Florence Going, it is noted from the affidavits heretofore filed in this office that you were the only one in attendance upon your wife at the time of the birth of the applicant.

In this event it will be necessary that the affidavits of two persons, who are disinterested and not related to the applicant, who have actual knowledge that the child was born, the date of her birth; that she was living on March 4, 1905, and that Sophie Going is her mother be filed in this office.

There is also enclosed herewith affidavit to be executed by Sophie Going, mother of the applicant. In the affidavits executed January 21, 1905, the date of the birth of this applicant is given as October 28, 1903, while in the affidavits dated April 7, 1905, this date is given as October 20, 1903. In the enclosed affidavits the date of birth has been left blank. Please insert the correct date and when the affidavits have been properly executed return to this office.

In having the affidavits executed care should be exercised to see that all names are written in full, as they appear in the body of the affidavits and in the event that either of the persons signing the affidavit are unable to write, signatures by mark must be attested by two witnesses. Each separate affidavit must be executed before a Notary Public and the notarial seal and signature of the officer attached thereto.

This matter should receive your immediate attention as no further action can be taken relative to the enrollment of said child until the Commission has been furnished these affidavits.

Respectfully,

Commissioner in Charge.

Enc-FVK-19

_____

33

Applications for Enrollment of Choctaw Newborn
Act of 1905   Volume XIV

Choctaw N B 974

Muskogee, Indian Territory, June 28, 1905.

Osborne Going,
      Smithville, Indian Territory.

Dear Sir:

Receipt is hereby acknowledged of your affidavit and the affidavits of Sophie Going, Edson Jefferson and Wilkin Wall to the birth of Florence Going, daughter of Osborne and Sophie Going, October 28, 1903, and the same have been filed with the record in the matter of the enrollment of said child.

Respectfully,

Chairman.

United States of America
Indian Territory
Central District

Affidavit of Acquaintance

I Wilkin Wall on oath state that I am 41 years of age and a citizen by blood of the Choctaw Nation, that my post office address is Smithville, Indian Territory, that I am not related to the applicant who is a citizen by blood of the Choctaw Nation, that I am personally acquainted with Sophie Going, wife of Osborne Going, who is a citizen by blood of the Choctaw Nation, and that a female child was born to Sophie Going on the 28th day of October 1903, and that said female child has been named Florence Going and that said Florence Going was living on the 4th day of March 1905; and I have personal knowledge that Sophie Going is the mother of said Florence Going.

Wilkin Wall

Subscribed and sworn to before me this 19th day of June 1905

W.H. McKinney
Notary Public.

My commission expires March 30-1909

34

Applications for Enrollment of Choctaw Newborn
Act of 1905   Volume XIV

BIRTH AFFIDAVIT.

DEPARTMENT OF THE INTERIOR.
COMMISSION TO THE FIVE CIVILIZED TRIBES.

IN RE APPLICATION FOR ENROLLMENT, as a citizen of the   Choctaw   Nation, of
Florence Going   , born on the 28   day of   October   , 1903

Name of Father: Osborne Going   Roll 1093   a citizen of the   Choctaw   Nation.
                                        Roll
Name of Mother: Sophie Going nee Harrison 5567 a citizen of the   Choctaw   Nation.

                              Postoffice   Smithville I.T.

AFFIDAVIT OF MOTHER.

UNITED STATES OF AMERICA, Indian Territory, ⎫
    Central   DISTRICT. ⎰

        I,   Sophie Going, nee Harrison   , on oath state that I am   19   years of age
and a citizen by   blood   , of the   Choctaw   Nation; that I am the lawful wife of
Osborne Going   , who is a citizen, by blood   of the   Choctaw   Nation;
that a   female   child was born to me on 28   day of   October   , 1903; that said
child has been named   Florence Going   , and was living March 4, 1905.

                              Sophie Going

Witnesses To Mark:
    ⎧
    ⎨
    ⎩

        Subscribed and sworn to before me this 19 day of   June   , 1905

My commission expires March 30-1909   W.H. McKinney
                                              Notary Public.

AFFIDAVIT OF ATTENDING PHYSICIAN OR MID-WIFE.

UNITED STATES OF AMERICA, Indian Territory, ⎫
    Central   DISTRICT. ⎰

        I,   Osborne Going   , *23 years of age*   , on oath state that I attended on
Mrs. Sophie Going   *my* wife ~~of   Osborne Going~~ on the 28 day of   October ,
1903; that there was born to her on said date a   female   child; that said child was
living March 4, 1905, and is said to have been named   Florence Going

                              Osborne Going

35

Witnesses To Mark:

{

Subscribed and sworn to before me this   19 day of   June   , 1905

My commission expires March 30-1909   W.H. McKinney
                                             Notary Public.

United States of America
Indian Territory
Central District

Affidavit of Acquaintance

I, Edson Jefferson on oath state that I am 35 years of age and a citizen by blood of the Choctaw Nation, that my post office address is Smithville, Indian Territory, that I am not related to the applicant, who is a citizen by blood of the Choctaw Nation, that I am personally acquainted with Sophie Going, wife of Osborne Going, who is a citizen by blood of the Choctaw Nation, and that a female child was born to Sophie Going on the 28th day of October 1903, and that said female child has been named Florence Going and that said Florence Going was living on the 4th day of March 1905, and I have personal knowledge that Sophie Going is the mother of said Florence Going.

Edson Jefferson

Subscribed and sworn to before me this 19th day of June 1905.

                                             W.H. McKinney
My commission expires March 30 1909.   Notary Public.

BIRTH AFFIDAVIT.
DEPARTMENT OF THE INTERIOR.
COMMISSION TO THE FIVE CIVILIZED TRIBES.

IN RE APPLICATION FOR ENROLLMENT, as a citizen of the   Choctaw   Nation, of
Florence Going   , born on the 20th   day of October   , 1903

Name of Father: Osborne Going   a citizen of the   Choctaw   Nation.
Name of Mother: Sophie Going   a citizen of the   Choctaw   Nation.

Postoffice   Smithville, Ind. Ter.

Applications for Enrollment of Choctaw Newborn
Act of 1905   Volume XIV

AFFIDAVIT OF MOTHER.

UNITED STATES OF AMERICA, Indian Territory, }
Central   DISTRICT. }

I,   Sophie Going   , on oath state that I am   19   years of age and a citizen by blood   , of the   Choctaw   Nation; that I am the lawful wife of   Osborne Going   , who is a citizen, by blood   of the   Choctaw   Nation; that a   female   child was born to me on   20th   day of   October   , 1903; that said child has been named Florence Going   , and was living March 4, 1905.

Sophie Going

Witnesses To Mark:
{ Vicy James
{ Simpson Wilson

Subscribed and sworn to before me this   26   day of   April   , 1905

A. W. James
Notary Public.

BIRTH AFFIDAVIT.

DEPARTMENT OF THE INTERIOR.
COMMISSION TO THE FIVE CIVILIZED TRIBES.

IN RE APPLICATION FOR ENROLLMENT, as a citizen of the   Choctaw   Nation, of Florence Going   , born on the 20th   day of October   , 1903

Name of Father: Osborne Going   a citizen of the   Choctaw   Nation.
Name of Mother: Sophie Going   a citizen of the   Choctaw   Nation.

Postoffice   Smithville, Ind. Ter.

AFFIDAVIT OF ATTENDING PHYSICIAN OR MID-WIFE.

UNITED STATES OF AMERICA, Indian Territory, }
Central   DISTRICT. }

I,   Osborne Going   , a ...., on oath state that I attended on Mrs.   Sophie Going   , ~~wife of~~ *my wife*   on the 20th   day of   October   , 1903; that there was born to her on said date a   female   child; that said child was living March 4, 1905, and ~~is said to have~~ *has* been named   Florence Going   *and that no one else was present when said child was born*

Osborne Going

37

Witnesses To Mark:

{

Subscribed and sworn to before me this   7th day of   April   , 1905

Wirt Franklin
Notary Public.

NEW-BORN AFFIDAVIT.

Number..................

...Choctaw Enrolling Commission...

IN THE MATTER OF THE APPLICATION FOR ENROLLMENT, as a citizen of the
Choctaw   Nation, of   Florence Going

born on the 28   day of ___Oct___ 190 3

Name of father   Osborne Going   a citizen of   Choctaw
Nation final enrollment No. 1093
Name of mother   Sophie Harrison   a citizen of   Choctaw
Nation final enrollment No. 5567

Postoffice   Smithville

AFFIDAVIT OF MOTHER.

UNITED STATES OF AMERICA
INDIAN TERRITORY
Central   DISTRICT

     I   Sophie Harrison   , on oath state that I am
19   years of age and a citizen by Blood   of the   Choctaw   Nation,
and as such have been placed upon the final roll of the   Choctaw   Nation, by the Honorable
Secretary of the Interior my final enrollment number being   5567 ; that I am the lawful wife
of Osborne Going   , who is a citizen of the   Choctaw   Nation, and as such has
been placed upon the final roll of said Nation by the Honorable Secretary of the Interior, his
final enrollment number being   1093   and that a   Female   child was born to me on
the   28   day of   October   190 3; that said child has been named   Florence Going
, and is now living.   her
Sophie x Harrison
Witnesseth.   mark

Must be two   } (Name Illegible)
Witnesses who
are Citizens.   (Name Illegible)

38

Subscribed and sworn to before me this   21   day of   Jan   190 5

C L Lester

Notary Public.

My commission expires: Oct 15-1905

Choc New Born 975
Edwin Billy   b. 9-19-04

BIRTH AFFIDAVIT.

DEPARTMENT OF THE INTERIOR.
COMMISSION TO THE FIVE CIVILIZED TRIBES.

IN RE APPLICATION FOR ENROLLMENT, as a citizen of the   Choctaw   Nation, of
Edwin Billy   , born on the 19th   day of September   , 1904

Name of Father: Always Billy   a citizen of the   Choctaw   Nation.
Name of Mother: Easter Billy   a citizen of the   Choctaw   Nation.

Postoffice   Eagletown, Ind. Ter.

AFFIDAVIT OF MOTHER.

UNITED STATES OF AMERICA, Indian Territory, ⎫
    Central   DISTRICT. ⎭

I,   Easter Billy   , on oath state that I am   23   years of age and a citizen by
blood   , of the   Choctaw   Nation; that I am the lawful wife of Always Billy   ,
who is a citizen, by blood   of the   Choctaw   Nation; that a   male   child
was born to me on 19th   day of September   , 1904; that said child has been named
Edwin Billy   , and was living March 4, 1905.

                        her
                Easter   x   Billy
Witnesses To Mark: mark
  ⎰ Robert Anderson
  ⎱ Vester W Rose

Subscribed and sworn to before me this 10th   day of   April   , 1905

Wirt Franklin
Notary Public.

AFFIDAVIT OF ATTENDING PHYSICIAN OR MID-WIFE.

UNITED STATES OF AMERICA, Indian Territory, ⎫
    Central   **DISTRICT.** ⎰

I,   Selina Hotubbee   , a   mid-wife   , on oath state that I attended on
Mrs.   Easter Billy   , wife of Always Billy   on the 19th day of   September ,
1904; that there was born to her on said date a   male   child; that said child was living
March 4, 1905, and is said to have been named   Edwin Billy

her
Selina x Hotubbee
mark

Witnesses To Mark:
 ⎧ Robert Anderson
 ⎩ Vester W Rose

Subscribed and sworn to before me this 10th   day of   April   , 1905

Wirt Franklin
Notary Public.

Choc New Born 976
    Lucy Charles   b. 2-29-04

NEW BORN AFFIDAVIT

No ....

CHOCTAW ENROLLING COMMISSION

IN THE MATTER OF THE APPLICATION FOR ENROLLMENT as a citizen of the Choctaw
Nation, of   Lucy Charles   born on the 29 day
of   February   190 4

Name of father   William Charles   a citizen of   Choctaw   Nation,
final enrollment No.   3142
Name of mother   Sayanis Willie   a citizen of   Choctaw   Nation,
final enrollment No. 13481

Garvin, I.T.   Postoffice.

Applications for Enrollment of Choctaw Newborn
Act of 1905   Volume XIV

AFFIDAVIT OF MOTHER

UNITED STATES OF AMERICA ⎫
    INDIAN TERRITORY   ⎬
DISTRICT   Central   ⎭

    I   Sayanis Willie   , on oath state that I am 36   years of age and a citizen by blood of the   Choctaw   Nation, and as such have been placed upon the final roll of the Choctaw   Nation, by the Honorable Secretary of the Interior my final enrollment number being 13481   ; that I am the lawful wife of William Charles   , who is a citizen of the   Choctaw   Nation, and as such has been placed upon the final roll of said Nation by the Honorable Secretary of the Interior, his final enrollment number being 3142 and that a female child was born to me on the 29 day of Feb   190 3; that said child has been named Lucy Charles   , and is now living.

                                             her

WITNESSETH: Sayanis x Willie

  Must be two witnesses ⎰   mark
  who are citizens ⎱

    Subscribed and sworn to before me this, the 10 day of   Feb , 190 5

                              W.A. Shoney
                                  Notary Public.
My Commission Expires: Jan 10-1909.

Affidavit of Attending Physician or Midwife.

UNITED STATES OF AMERICA ⎫
INDIAN TERRITORY   ⎬
  Central   DISTRICT ⎭

    I,   Rampsay Hall   a   attendant on oath state that I attended on Mrs. Sayanis Charles Willie   wife of William Charles on the 29   day of Feb   , 190 4 , that there was born to her on said date a   female child, that said child is now living, and is said to have been named Lucy Charles

                                his
                        Rampsay x Hall   M.D.
                              mark

    Subscribed and sworn to before me this, the 10 day of   Feb   190 5

                            W.A. Shoney
                                  Notary Public.

WITNESSETH:
  Must be two witnesses ⎰ ....
  who are citizens and ⎨
  know the child.   ⎱ ....

41

We hereby certify that we are well acquainted with..
a..and know ....to be reputable and of good standing in the community.

{ ....
....

NEW-BORN AFFIDAVIT.

Number....................

...Choctaw Enrolling Commission...

IN THE MATTER OF THE APPLICATION FOR ENROLLMENT, as a citizen of the Choctaw   Nation, of   Lucy Charles

born on the 29th day of February   190 4

Name of father William Charles   a citizen of   Choctaw
Nation final enrollment No. 3142
Name of mother Sayanis Willie   a citizen of   Choctaw
Nation final enrollment No. 13481

Postoffice   Garvin I.T.

AFFIDAVIT OF MOTHER.

UNITED STATES OF AMERICA
INDIAN TERRITORY
Central   DISTRICT

I   Sayanis Willie   , on oath state that I am
35   years of age and a citizen by blood of the Choctaw   Nation,
and as such have been placed upon the final roll of the   Choctaw Nation, by the Honorable
Secretary of the Interior my final enrollment number being   13481 ; that I am the lawful
wife of William Charles   , who is a citizen of the   Choctaw   Nation, and as such
has been placed upon the final roll of said Nation by the Honorable Secretary of the Interior,
his final enrollment number being   3142   and that a   female   child was born to me on
the 29 day of February   190 4; that said child has been named   Lucy Charles   ,
and is now living.   her
                                   Sayanis x Willie nee Charles
Witnesseth.   mark

Must be two } Wilson Jackson
Witnesses who }
are Citizens.   Willis Willie

42

Subscribed and sworn to before me this   24   day of   Feb   190 5

W.A. Shoney
Notary Public.

My commission expires: Jan. 10, 1909

BIRTH AFFIDAVIT.

DEPARTMENT OF THE INTERIOR.
COMMISSION TO THE FIVE CIVILIZED TRIBES.

IN RE APPLICATION FOR ENROLLMENT, as a citizen of the   Choctaw   Nation, of
Lucy Charles   , born on the   29th   day of   February , 1904

Name of Father: William Charles   a citizen of the   Choctaw   Nation.
Name of Mother: Sayanis Charles   a citizen of the   Choctaw   Nation.

Postoffice   Garvin, Ind. Ter.

AFFIDAVIT OF MOTHER.

UNITED STATES OF AMERICA, Indian Territory, ⎫
   Central   **DISTRICT.** ⎭

I,   Sayanis Charles   , on oath state that I am   35   years of age and a citizen
by   blood   , of the   Choctaw   Nation; that I am the lawful wife of   William
Charles   , who is a citizen, by blood   of the   Choctaw   Nation; that a
female   child was born to me on   29th   day of   February   , 1904; that said child
has been named   Lucy Charles   , and was living March 4, 1905.

                                                            her
                                              Sayanis x Charles
Witnesses To Mark: mark
   ⎰ Robert Anderson
   ⎱ Vester W Rose

Subscribed and sworn to before me this 10th   day of   April   , 1905

                                      Wirt Franklin
                                      Notary Public.

Applications for Enrollment of Choctaw Newborn
Act of 1905 Volume XIV

AFFIDAVIT OF ATTENDING PHYSICIAN OR MID-WIFE.

UNITED STATES OF AMERICA, Indian Territory, ⎱
  Central   DISTRICT. ⎰

I,   Sally Charles   , a mid-wife   , on oath state that I attended on Mrs. Sayanis Charles   , wife of   William Charles   on the 29th   day of February   , 1904; that there was born to her on said date a   female   child; that said child was living March 4, 1905, and is said to have been named Lucy Charles

her

Sally x Charles

Witnesses To Mark: mark
    ⎰ Robert Anderson
    ⎱ Vester W Rose

Subscribed and sworn to before me this 10th day of   April   , 1905

Wirt Franklin
Notary Public.

<u>Choc New Born 977</u>
     Willie Henry McCoy   b. 10-6-04

Choctaw 2392 /[sic]

Muskogee, Indian Territory, April 14, 1905.

Holman McCoy,
     Talihina, Indian Territory.

Dear Sir:

Receipt is hereby acknowledged of the affidavits of Emaline Pike McCoy and Littie Beams Willie to the birth of Willie Henry McCoy, October 6, 1904, son of Holman and Emaline McCoy, and the same have been filed with our records as an application for the enrollment of said child.

Respectfully,

Commissioner in Charge.

Emeline Pike Roll #6930 Choc by blood

BIRTH AFFIDAVIT.

DEPARTMENT OF THE INTERIOR.
COMMISSION TO THE FIVE CIVILIZED TRIBES.

IN RE APPLICATION FOR ENROLLMENT, as a citizen of the   Choctaw   Nation, of
Willie Henry McCoy   , born on the   6   day of   October   , 1904

Name of Father: Holman McCoy   a citizen of the   Choctaw   Nation.
Name of Mother: Emeline[sic] (Pike) McCoy   a citizen of the   Choctaw   Nation.

Postoffice   Talihina I.T.

AFFIDAVIT OF MOTHER.

UNITED STATES OF AMERICA, Indian Territory,
   Central   **DISTRICT.**

   I,   Emeline McCoy, on oath state that I am   26   years of age and a citizen by
Blood   , of the   Choctaw   Nation; that I am the lawful wife of   Holman McCoy ,
who is a citizen, by   Blood   of the   Choctaw   Nation; that a   male   child
was born to me on   6   day of   October   , 1904, that said child has been named
Willie Henry McCoy   , and is now living.

                                        Emaline Pike McCoy
Witnesses To Mark:

   Subscribed and sworn to before me this 11 day of   April   , 1905.

                              Sam T. Roberts Jr
                              Notary Public.

Joe Willie Interpreter

AFFIDAVIT OF ATTENDING PHYSICIAN OR MID-WIFE.

UNITED STATES OF AMERICA, Indian Territory,
   Central   **DISTRICT.**

   I, Littie Beams Willie   , a   midwife   , on oath state that I attended on
Mrs. Emeline McCoy   , wife of   Holman McCoy   on the 6   day of   October ,
1904; that there was born to her on said date a   male   child; that said child is now
living and is said to have been named   Willie Henry McCoy

her
Littie x Beams Willie
mark

Witnesses To Mark:
⎰ Joe Willie
⎱ T.B. Lunsford

Subscribed and sworn to before me this 11 day of   April   , 1905.

Sam T. Roberts Jr
Notary Public.

Choc New Born 978
Robert Lee Pugh   b. 2-10-04

———————

Choctaw 2187.

Muskogee, Indian Territory, April 14, 1905.

A. Pearl Pugh,
Talihina, Indian Territory.

Dear Sir:

Receipt is hereby acknowledged of the affidavits of Ada Pugh and Elizabeth Horn to the birth of Robert Lee Pugh, son of A. Pearl and Ada (Wilson) Pugh, February 10, 1904.

It appears from the affidavits that the child is not now living and for the purpose of making his death a matter of record there is enclosed herewith a blank which please have executed showing the correct date of the death of this child.

Respectfully,

Commissioner in Charge.

———————

(The letter below typed as given.)

(COPY)

Talihina I T
April 25 1905

The Commission to the Five Civilized Tribes.
Muscogee[sic] Ind Ty

Gentlemen:-

Mr. A Pearl Pugh called at my office this morning in reference to the application made for the enrollemtn of Robert Lee Pugh and referred to your letter of the 14th, (Choctaw 2187) in which it appears that from the affidavits the child is dead. None of the parties to the affidavit can explain the matter as the child is living and was shown to me this morning, it may have been that I used an obsolete form and in making change to conform caused the error Enclosed please find a new affidavit on blank furnished me by your commission, trusting this may enable you to locate the error I remain

Very respectfully,

Sam T. Roberts.

(The letter, above, given again.)

Choctaw 2187.

Muskogee, Indian Territory, May 1, 1905.

Sam T. Roberts,
Talihina, Indian Territory.

Dear Sir

Receipt is hereby acknowledged of your letter of April 25, stating that Robert Lee Pugh, child of A. Pearl Pugh, is now living and that you forward an amended application for his enrollment.

In reply you are advised that the affidavits of Ada Pugh and Eliza Harris to the birth of Robert Lee Pugh, son of A. Pearl and Ada (Wilson) Pugh, Fenruary[sic] 10, 1904, have been filed with our records in the matter of the enrollment of said child.

Respectfully,

Chairman.

47

for Identification Ada Wilson Choc by blood #6330

BIRTH AFFIDAVIT.

DEPARTMENT OF THE INTERIOR.
COMMISSION TO THE FIVE CIVILIZED TRIBES.

IN RE APPLICATION FOR ENROLLMENT, as a citizen of the   Choctaw   Nation, of
Robert Lee Pugh   , born on the   10   day of   February   , 1904

Name of Father: A Pearl Pugh   a citizen of the United States Nation.
Name of Mother: Ada (Wilson) Pugh   a citizen of the   Choctaw   Nation.

Postoffice   Talihina I.T.

AFFIDAVIT OF MOTHER.

UNITED STATES OF AMERICA, Indian Territory, }
    Central   DISTRICT.

    I,   Ada Pugh   , on oath state that I am   18   years of age and a citizen by
Blood   , of the   Choctaw   Nation; that I am the lawful wife of   A Pearl Pugh ,
who is a citizen, ~~by~~ _of the United States_ ~~Nation~~; that a   Male   child was born
to me on   10   day of   February   , 1904, that said child has been named   Robert Lee
Pugh   , and is now living.

                                    Ada Pugh
Witnesses To Mark:
{

    Subscribed and sworn to before me this   8   day of   April   , 1905.

                        Sam T Roberts Jr
                            Notary Public.

AFFIDAVIT OF ATTENDING PHYSICIAN OR MID-WIFE.

UNITED STATES OF AMERICA, Indian Territory, }
    Central   DISTRICT.

    I,   Eliza Harris   , a   midwife   , on oath state that I attended on
Mrs.   Ada (Wilson) Pugh   , wife of   A Pearl Pugh   on the   10   day of   Feby ,
1904; that there was born to her on said date a   Male   child; that said child ~~is now~~
was living _March 4-1905_ and is said to have been named   Robert Lee Pugh

Applications for Enrollment of Choctaw Newborn
Act of 1905   Volume XIV

Eliza Harris

Witnesses To Mark:

{

Subscribed and sworn to before me this 10 day of   April   , 1905.

Sam T. Roberts Jr
Notary Public.

Amended affidavit

BIRTH AFFIDAVIT.

DEPARTMENT OF THE INTERIOR.
COMMISSION TO THE FIVE CIVILIZED TRIBES.

Ada Wilson Pugh Choc by blood #6330

IN RE APPLICATION FOR ENROLLMENT, as a citizen of the   Choctaw   Nation, of
Robert Lee Pugh   , born on the 10   day of   February , 1904

Name of Father: A. Pearl Pugh   a citizen of the United States Nation.
Name of Mother: Ada (Wilson) Pugh   a citizen of the   Choctaw   Nation.

Postoffice   Talihina I T

AFFIDAVIT OF MOTHER.

UNITED STATES OF AMERICA, Indian Territory, }
        Central   **DISTRICT.** }

        I,   Ada (Wilson) Pugh   , on oath state that I am   18   years of age and a
citizen by   Blood   , of the   Choctaw   Nation; that I am the lawful wife of A
Pearl Pugh   , who is a citizen, by   of the United States   of the ....
Nation; that a   Male   child was born to me on   10   day of   February   , 1904;
that said child has been named   Robert Lee Pugh   , and was living March 4, 1905.

Ada Pugh

Witnesses To Mark:

{

Subscribed and sworn to before me this   25 day of   April   , 1905

Sam T. Roberts Jr
Notary Public.

49

Applications for Enrollment of Choctaw Newborn
Act of 1905   Volume XIV

AFFIDAVIT OF ATTENDING PHYSICIAN OR MID-WIFE.

UNITED STATES OF AMERICA, Indian Territory, ⎤
Central   DISTRICT. ⎦

I,   Eliza Harris   , a   Midwife   , on oath state that I attended on Mrs.   Ada (Wilson) Pugh   , wife of   A Pearl Pugh   on the   10   day of February   , 1904; that there was born to her on said date a   male   child; that said child was living March 4, 1905, and is said to have been named   Robert Lee Pugh

Eliza Harris

Witnesses To Mark:

{

Subscribed and sworn to before me this   25   day of   April   , 1905

Sam T. Roberts Jr
Notary Public.

Choc New Born 979
    Willie Wilkin   b. 2-1-03

DEPARTMENT OF THE INTERIOR,
COMMISSIONER TO THE FIVE CIVILIZED TRIBES.

Chickasha, Indian Territory, January 31, 1907.

_____OoooO_____

In the matter of the application for the enrollment, as a citizen by blood of the Choctaw Nation, of Willie Gibson, whose name appears on Choctaw New Born Card Number 979 as Willie Wilkin.

Testimony taken at Chickasha, Indian Territory, January 31, 1907.

JACOB HOMER, being duly sworn by Lacey P. Bobo, Notary Public in and for the Southern District of the Indian Territory, testified as follows:

BY THE COMMISSIONER:

Q What is your name? A Jacob Homer.
Q What is your age? A About 30.
Q What is your post office address? A Atoka, I. T.

50

Witness is a regular employee of the Commissioner to the Five
Civilized Tribes in the capacity of Choctaw Interpreter.

Q Are you acquainted with Wilmon Gibson? A Yes, I am acquainted with him, and I
have also known him by the name of Wilmon Wilkins; he goes by both names.
Q Are you likewise acquainted with his wife? A I am.
Q Do you know her given name? A When I was first acquainted with her she was
known as Lucy Wilkins.
Q When you first became acquainted with he she was the wife of Wilmon Gibson or
Wilkin? A Yes.
Q Are Wilmon Gibson and Lucy Gibson Choctaws by blood? A Yes.
Q Do you know this woman to be the mother of a New Born Choctaw by blood? A
Yes.
Q What is the name of the child? A Its name is Willie Gibson or Wilkin.
Q What is the sex of the child? A Boy.
Q Do you know when the child was born? A I do not.
Q Do you know the child to have been born prior to March 4, 1905? A Yes, sir.
Q State why you know this? A Because when I first saw the child it was walking, and
that was before I was assigned to field duty by the Commissioner to the Five Civilized
Tribes in December 1904. Some time in the year 1904 the mother of the child was filing
land in the Chickasaw Nation and they came to my home in Atoka and Stayed about a
month, there were at my house when I took the field in December 1904. Afterwards I
heard Wilmon and Lucy separated and the grandmother of the child took it and has it yet.
Q Do you know as a matter of fact that this child Willie Gibson was living March 4,
1905?
A Yes, sir, it is still living, if it was dead they would let me know, because the child is
kin to my wife. I was at my home in Atoka about 15 days ago and the grandmother of
the child was visiting my home and had the child with her.

Witness Excused.

W. P. Covington, being duly sworn, states that the above and foregoing is a
full, true and correct transcript of his stenographic notes taken in said case on
said date.

W P Covington

Subscribed and sworn to before me this 1st   day of Feby   1907.

Lacey P Bobo
Notary Public.

(The letter below typed as given.)

July 2 195

Commission to the five civilized Tribes.

Muskogee Ind. Ter.

Dear Sir I Rite to you few line about my Infant child Willie Wilkin my wife name Lucy James, and my neme wes Wilmon Gibson my wife meke applicetion the meskmestek.

Wilmon Roll No. 1662
my wife Roll No. 2055

this me Be oright Ife don isand you certificate.

Right wey

Right me Ardmor I. T.

thet Be my Posoffece

Wilmon Wilkin Ardmor

I. T.

7-NB-979.

Muskogee, Indian Territory, June 9, 1905.

Wilmon Wilkin,
    Bethel, Indian Territory.

Dear Sir:

Referring to the application for the enrollment of your infant child, Willie Wilkin, born February 1, 1903, it is noted in the affidavits heretofore filed in this office that you claim to be a citizen by blood of the Choctaw Nation.

If this is correct, you are requested to state when, where and under what name you were listed for enrollment, the names of your parents and other members of your family who made application at the same time, and if you have selected an allotment please give your roll number as the same appears upon your allotment certificate.

This matter should be given your immediate attention as no further action can be taken until this information is furnished the Commission.

Respectfully,

Chairman.

_____

<u>Sub</u>

7-NB-979

Muskogee, Indian Territory, July 11, 1905.

Wilmon Gibson,
    Ardmore, Indian Territory.

Dear Sir:

Receipt is hereby acknowledged of your letter of July 2, 1905, in which you state that at the time your wife made application to the Commission to the Five Civilized Tribes, for the enrollment of your infant child, Willie, born February 1, 1903, she made a mistake in giving the surname as Wilkin. You further state that your correct name if Wilmon Gibson, and that your roll number is 1662.

Replying to your letter there is inclosed herewith application to be executed for the enrollment of your infant child, Willie Gibson, born February 1, 1903.

In having these affidavits executed care should be exercised to see that all names are written in full, as they appear in the body of the affidavit, and if either of the persons signing the affidavits are unable to write, signatures by make must be attested by two witnesses. Each affidavit must be executed before a Notary Public and the notarial seal and signature of the officer must be attached to each separate affidavit.

This matter should receive you immediate attention as no further action can be taken relative to the enrollment of your child until the evidence requested is supplied.

Respectfully,

LM 11-1

Commissioner.

_____

7-NB-979.

Muskogee, Indian Territory, August 19, 1905

Wilmon Gibson (or Wilkin),
    Ardmore, Indian Territory.

Dear Sir:

On July 11, 1905, this office acknowledged receipt of your letter of July 2, 1905, in which you stated that at the time your wife made application to the Commission to the Five Civilized Tribes for the enrollment of your infant child Willie, born February 1, 1903, she made a mistage[sic] in giving the surname as Wilkin. You further stated that your correct name is Wilmon Gibson and that your roll number is 1662. With said letter of July 11, 1905, there was forwarded you for execution blank for proof of birth which had been properly filled out and you were requested to have the same executed and return it to this office. No response has been received to said letter.

You are again requested to have said application properly executed and return the same to this office, and are advised that until the same is received nothing further can be done in the matter of the enrollment of your said child Willie Gibson as a citizen by blood of the Choctaw Nation.

Respectfully,

Acting Commissioner.

––––––––––

BIRTH AFFIDAVIT.
DEPARTMENT OF THE INTERIOR.
COMMISSION TO THE FIVE CIVILIZED TRIBES.

––––––––––

IN RE APPLICATION FOR ENROLLMENT, as a citizen of the   Choctaw   Nation, of
Willie Gibson   , born on the 1st day of February , 1903

Name of Father: Wilmon Gibson A-1662 Roll   a citizen of the   Choctaw   Nation.
Name of Mother: Lucy Gibson   a citizen of the   Choctaw   Nation.

Postoffice   Bethel Ind Ter

––––––––––

Applications for Enrollment of Choctaw Newborn
Act of 1905   Volume XIV

AFFIDAVIT OF MOTHER.

UNITED STATES OF AMERICA, Indian Territory, ⎞
    Central   DISTRICT. ⎠

I,   Lucy Gibson (now Noahuby)   , on oath state that I am   23   years of age and a citizen by   blood   , of the   Choctaw   Nation; that I ~~am~~ *was* the lawful wife of   Wilmon Gibson   , who is a citizen, by blood   of the   Choctaw Nation; that a   male   child was born to me on 1st   day of   February   , 1903; that said child has been named Willie Gibson   , and was living March 4, 1905.

her
Lucy x Gibson
mark

Witnesses To Mark:
⎰ W.P. Covington
⎱ Jacob Homer

Subscribed and sworn to before me this 23rd day of   June   , 1906

A.W. James
Notary Public.

AFFIDAVIT OF ATTENDING PHYSICIAN OR MID-WIFE.

UNITED STATES OF AMERICA, Indian Territory, ⎞
    Central   DISTRICT. ⎠

I,   Elmia[sic] Whale   , a   mid wife   , on oath state that I attended on Mrs. Lucy Gibson   , wife of Wilmon Gibson   on the 1 day of February , 1903; that there was born to her on said date a   male   child; that said child was living March 4, 1905, and is said to have been named Willie Gibson

her
Elmia x Whale
mark

Witnesses To Mark:
⎰ Vicey James
⎱ *(Name Illegible)*

Subscribed and sworn to before me this 29   day of   June   , 1906

A.W. James
Notary Public.

55

BIRTH AFFIDAVIT.

DEPARTMENT OF THE INTERIOR,
COMMISSIONER TO THE FIVE CIVILIZED TRIBES.

ENROLLMENT OF MINORS.   ACT OF CONGRESS, APPROVED APRIL 26, 1906.

IN RE APPLICATION FOR ENROLLMENT, as a citizen of the   Choctaw   Nation,
of   Willie Gibson   , born on the 1st day of Feby , 1903

Name of Father: Wilmon Gibson   a citizen of the   Choctaw   Nation.
Name of Mother: Lucy Gibson nc James   a citizen of the   Choctaw   Nation.

Tribal enrollment of father A-1662   Tribal enrollment of mother A-2055

          Postoffice   Atoka IT - fathers
             "   Bethel IT - mothers

_____

AFFIDAVIT OF MOTHER.

UNITED STATES OF AMERICA, Indian Territory,
....District.

I, Wilmon Gibson , on oath state that I am 22 years of age and a citizen by
blood , of the Choctaw Nation; that I ~~am~~ *was* the lawful ~~wife~~ *husband* of Lucy James ,
who is a citizen, by blood of the Choctaw Nation; that a male child was born to me
on 1st day of Feb , 1903, that said child has been named Willie Gibson , and was
living March 4, 1906.

                    Wilmon Gibson
WITNESSES TO MARK:

Subscribed and sworn to before me this 18th   day of Jany , 1907

                    Lacey P Bobo
                        Notary Public.

_____

BIRTH AFFIDAVIT.

DEPARTMENT OF THE INTERIOR.
COMMISSION TO THE FIVE CIVILIZED TRIBES.

_____

IN RE APPLICATION FOR ENROLLMENT, as a citizen of the   Choctaw   Nation, of
Willie Wilkin   , born on the 1st day of February , 1903

Name of Father: Wilmon Wilkin   a citizen of the   Choctaw   Nation.
Name of Mother: Lucy Wilkin   a citizen of the   Choctaw   Nation.

Postoffice   Bethel Ind Ter

AFFIDAVIT OF MOTHER.

UNITED STATES OF AMERICA, Indian Territory, ⎫
Central   DISTRICT. ⎰

   I,   Lucy Wilkin   , on oath state that I am   22   years of age and a citizen by blood   , of the   Choctaw   Nation; that I am the lawful wife of   Wilmon Wilkin   , who is a citizen, by   blood   of the   Choctaw   Nation; that a   male   child was born to me on   1st   day of   February   , 1903; that said child has been named Willie Wilkin   , and was living March 4, 1905.

her
Lucy x Wilkin
mark

Witnesses To Mark:
 ⎰ Robert Anderson
 ⎱ Vester W Rose

   Subscribed and sworn to before me this   6th day of   April   , 1905

Wirt Franklin
Notary Public.

AFFIDAVIT OF ATTENDING PHYSICIAN OR MID-WIFE.

UNITED STATES OF AMERICA, Indian Territory, ⎫
Central   DISTRICT. ⎰

   I,   Elmira Whale   , a   mid-wife   , on oath state that I attended on Mrs. Lucy Wilkin   , wife of   Wilmon Wilkin   on the 1st   day of   February   , 1903; that there was born to her on said date a   male   child; that said child was living March 4, 1905, and is said to have been named   Willie Wilkin

her
Elmira x Whale
mark

Witnesses To Mark:
 ⎰ Robert Anderson
 ⎱ Vester W Rose

   Subscribed and sworn to before me this   6th day of   April   , 1905

Wirt Franklin
Notary Public.

BIRTH AFFIDAVIT.

DEPARTMENT OF THE INTERIOR,
COMMISSIONER TO THE FIVE CIVILIZED TRIBES.

ENROLLMENT OF MINORS. ACT OF CONGRESS, APPROVED APRIL 26, 1906.

IN RE APPLICATION FOR ENROLLMENT, as a citizen of the   Choctaw   Nation,
of   Willie Gibson   , born on the   1st day of   Feby   , 1903

Name of Father: Wilmon Gibson   a citizen of the   Choctaw   Nation.
Name of Mother: Lucy Gibson formerly James   a citizen of the   Choctaw   Nation.

Tribal enrollment of father .... Tribal enrollment of mother ....

Postoffice   Mother: Bethel I.T.

AFFIDAVIT OF MOTHER.

UNITED STATES OF AMERICA, Indian Territory, ⎤
   Central   District. ⎦

I,   Holton Hayes   , on oath state that I am   23   years of age and a citizen by blood, of the   Choctaw   Nation; that I ~~am~~ am *personally acquainted with Lucy Gibson, formerly James, who was* the lawful wife of   Wilmon Gibson   , who is a citizen, by blood of the   Choctaw   Nation; that a   male   child was born to ~~me~~ *her* on   or about 1st day of February   , 1903 , that said child has been named   Willie Gibson   , and was living March 4, 1906.

Holton Hayes

WITNESSES TO MARK:
{

Subscribed and sworn to before me this   12th day of   *(Illegible)*   , 190**7**

WA Martin
Notary Public.

AFFIDAVIT OF ATTENDING PHYSICIAN OR MID-WIFE.

UNITED STATES OF AMERICA, Indian Territory, ⎤
   Central   District. ⎦

I,   Almon Carterby   , ~~a~~ , on oath state that I *am personally acquainted with Lucy Gibson, formerly James* ~~attended on~~   , wife of *Wilmon Gibson & know that* on *or about* the   1st day of   Feby   , 1903 ; ~~that~~ there was born to her ~~on said date~~ a   male   child; that said child was living March 4, 1906, and is said to have been named   Willie Gibson

Almon Carterby

WITNESSES TO MARK:

{

Subscribed and sworn to before me this   12th   day of   *(Illegible)* , 190**7**

WA Martin
Notary Public.

Choc New Born 980
Clorine Curry   b. 5-9-04

Choctaw N B 980

Muskogee, Indian Territory, May 19, 1905.

B. P. Curry,
Newcastle, Indian Territory.

Dear Sir:

Receipt is hereby acknowledged of your letter of May 13, stating that you made application for the enrollment of your child, Clorine Curry while the Commission was at Chickasha but have heard nothing in regard thereto and you ask if the same has been received.

In reply to your letter you are advised that the affidavits heretofore forwarded to the birth of your child, Clorine Curry, have been filed with our records as an application for the enrollment of said child. In the event further evidence is necessary to enable us to determine her right to enrollment you will be duly notified.

Respectfully,

Chairman.

BIRTH AFFIDAVIT.

DEPARTMENT OF THE INTERIOR.
COMMISSION TO THE FIVE CIVILIZED TRIBES.

IN RE APPLICATION FOR ENROLLMENT, as a citizen of the   Choctaw   Nation, of
Clorine Curry   , born on the 9th   day of May   , 1904

Name of Father: B.P. Curry   a citizen of the   U.S.   Nation.
Name of Mother: Clara F Curry   a citizen of the   Choctaw   Nation.

Postoffice   New Castle I.T.

AFFIDAVIT OF MOTHER.

UNITED STATES OF AMERICA, Indian Territory, ⎫
    Southern   DISTRICT. ⎭

I, Clara F. Curry   , on oath state that I am 18 years of age and a citizen by
Blood   , of the   Choctaw   Nation; that I am the lawful wife of B.P. Curry   ,
who is a citizen, by   Blood   of the   U. S.   ~~Nation~~; that a   Female   child
was born to me on   9th   day of   May   , 1904, that said child has been named
Clorine Curry   , and is now living.

Clara F Curry

Witnesses To Mark:

Subscribed and sworn to before me this 5th day of Apr   , 1905.

J.H. Carlisle
Notary Public.

AFFIDAVIT OF ATTENDING PHYSICIAN OR MID-WIFE.

UNITED STATES OF AMERICA, Indian Territory, ⎫
    Southern   DISTRICT. ⎭

I,   N.J. Woodard   , a midwife   , on oath state that I attended on
Mrs. B.P. Curry   , wife of B.P. Curry   on the 9th   day of May , 1904; that
there was born to her on said date a   Female   child; that said child is now living and
is said to have been named Clorine Curry

N J Woodard
her mark x
By J.H. Carlisle

Witnesses To Mark:
  ⎰ J P Willey
  ⎱ A J Woodard

Subscribed and sworn to before me this 5th day of Apr   , 1905.

J.H. Carlisle
Notary Public.

Choc New Born 981
William J. Bohanan[sic] b. 1-21-05

BIRTH AFFIDAVIT.

DEPARTMENT OF THE INTERIOR.
COMMISSION TO THE FIVE CIVILIZED TRIBES.

IN RE APPLICATION FOR ENROLLMENT, as a citizen of the   Choctaw   Nation, of
William J. Bohanon   , born on the 21 day of January   , 1905

Name of Father: Emiziah Bohanon   a citizen of the   Choctaw   Nation.
Name of Mother: Sarah Bohanon nee Potts   a citizen of the   Choctaw   Nation.

Postoffice   Talihina I.T.

AFFIDAVIT OF MOTHER.

UNITED STATES OF AMERICA, Indian Territory, ⎫
  Central   DISTRICT. ⎬

I,   Sarah Bohanon nee Potts   , on oath state that I am 23   years of age and
a citizen by   blood   , of the   Choctaw   Nation; that I am the lawful wife of
Emiziah Bohanon   , who is a citizen, by   blood   of the   Choctaw
Nation; that a   male   child was born to me on   21 day of January   , 1905;
that said child has been named   William J. Bohanon   , and was living March 4, 1905.

her
Sarah x Bohanon
Witnesses To Mark: mark
  ⎰ Chas. T. Difendafer
  ⎱ OL Johnson

Subscribed and sworn to before me this 10 day of   April   , 1905

OL Johnson
Notary Public.

61

AFFIDAVIT OF ATTENDING PHYSICIAN OR MID-WIFE.

UNITED STATES OF AMERICA, Indian Territory,
Central   DISTRICT.

I, Emaline Bohanon , a midwife , on oath state that I attended on Mrs. Sarah Bohanon , wife of Emiziah Bohanon on the 21 day of January, 1905; that there was born to her on said date a male child; that said child was living March 4, 1905, and is said to have been named William J Bohanon

her
Emaline x Bohanon
mark

Witnesses To Mark:
  Chas. T. Difendafer
  OL Johnson

Subscribed and sworn to before me this 10 day of April , 1905

OL Johnson
Notary Public.

Choc New Born 982
  Bill Wooley Bell   b. 5-21-04

NEW BORN AFFIDAVIT

No ....

CHOCTAW ENROLLING COMMISSION

IN THE MATTER OF THE APPLICATION FOR ENROLLMENT as a citizen of the Choctaw Nation, of   Bill Wooley Bell   born on the 21 day of May 190 4

Name of father   U G Bell   a citizen of United States Nation,
final enrollment No...........
Name of mother   Eliza Bell   a citizen of Choctaw Nation,
final enrollment No. 13627

Foster I T   Postoffice.

Applications for Enrollment of Choctaw Newborn
Act of 1905 Volume XIV

AFFIDAVIT OF MOTHER

UNITED STATES OF AMERICA ⎫
    INDIAN TERRITORY   ⎬
DISTRICT   Southern ⎭

    I   Eliza Bell   , on oath state that I am   30   years of age and a citizen by   Blood   of the   Choctaw   Nation, and as such have been placed upon the final roll of the Choctaw   Nation, by the Honorable Secretary of the Interior my final enrollment number being 13627   ; that I am the lawful wife of   U G Bell   , who is a citizen of the   Choctaw   Nation, and as such has been placed upon the final roll of said Nation by the Honorable Secretary of the Interior, his final enrollment number being ....and that a   Male   child was born to me on the   21   day of May   190 4; that said child has been named   Bill Wooley Bill   , and is now living.

WITNESSETH: Eliza Bell
   Must be two witnesses ⎰ Thomas Gibson
   who are citizens   ⎱

    Subscribed and sworn to before me this, the   15 day of   March   , 190 5

                              W W Howerton
                                    Notary Public.
My Commission Expires: Feb 15 1906

Affidavit of Attending Physician or Midwife

UNITED STATES OF AMERICA, ⎫
    INDIAN TERRITORY,   ⎬
Central   DISTRICT ⎭

    I,   Susan Cartright[sic]   a   Midwife on oath state that I attended on Mrs. Eliza Bell   wife of U G Bell on the 21   day of May , 190 4, that there was born to her on said date a   Male   child, that said child is now living, and is said to have been named Bill Wooley Bell

                              Susie Cartright   M. D.

    Subscribed and sworn to before me this the   20" day of March   1905

                          J H Elliott
                              Notary Public.

WITNESSETH:
   Must be two witnesses ⎰ W L Wooley
   who are citizens and ⎬
   know the child.   ⎱ Sam Wooley

We hereby certify that we are well acquainted with   Susie Cartwright
a   midwife   and know   her   to be reputable and of good standing in the community.

Must be two citizen⎰ W L Wooley
witnesses.   ⎱ Sam Wooley

Choc New Born 983
> Catherine Camp   b. 9-6-04
> Alleyne Camp   b. 12-31-02

> No. 2   Dismissed 6-28-05

DEPARTMENT OF THE INTERIOR,
COMMISSION TO THE FIVE CIVILIZED TRIBES.

Record in the matter of the application for enrollment as a citizen by blood of the Choctaw Nation of-

ALLEYNE CAMP   7-NB-983.

BIRTH AFFIDAVIT.   #125

DEPARTMENT OF THE INTERIOR.
COMMISSION TO THE FIVE CIVILIZED TRIBES.

IN RE APPLICATION FOR ENROLLMENT, as a citizen of the   Choctaw   Nation, of
Alleyne Camp   , born on the   31   day of   Dec , 1902

Name of Father: Joseph A Camp   a citizen of the   Choctaw   Nation.
Name of Mother: Allie Camp   a citizen of the   Choctaw   Nation.

Postoffice   Paoli I.T.

Applications for Enrollment of Choctaw Newborn
Act of 1905   Volume XIV

AFFIDAVIT OF MOTHER.

UNITED STATES OF AMERICA, Indian Territory, ⎤
Southern   **DISTRICT.** ⎦

I,   Allie Camp   , on oath state that I am   34   years of age and a citizen by intermarriage   , of the   Choctaw   Nation; that I am the lawful wife of   Joseph A. Camp   , who is a citizen, by   Blood   of the   Choctaw   Nation; that a Female   child was born to me on   the 31st day of   December   , 1902, that said child has been named   Alleyne Camp   , and is now ~~living~~. *Dead*

Allie Camp

Witnesses To Mark:

⎧
⎨
⎩

Subscribed and sworn to before me this 22nd day of   February   , 1905.

A.S. Kelley
My commission expires Mch 12th 1908   Notary Public.

————————

UNITED STATES OF AMERICA,
   The Indian Territory,
Southern Judicial District.

J. B. MAPLES, being first duly sworn, on his oath states that he is a regular practicing physician of Paoli, Indian Territory in the southern District of the Indian Territory, duly licensed to practice medicine and surgery under the laws of the United States in force in the said Indian Territory; that he is acquainted with Jos. A. Camp and Allie Camp, wife of the said Jos. A. Camp; that he was the attending physical[sic] upon the said Allie Camp on December 31, 1902; that at said time a female child was born to the said Allie Camp; that it is ~~still living~~ now dead and ~~has been~~ was named Alleyne.

J.B. Maples MD

SUBSCRIBED AND SWORN to before me this 21   *day of Dec. 1904.*

A S Kelley
Notary Public.
My Comission[sic] Expires Mch 12-1908

————————

W.F.
7-NB-983.

DEPARTMENT OF THE INTERIOR,
COMMISSION TO THE FIVE CIVILIZED TRIBES.

In the matter of the application for the enrollment of Alleyne Camp as a citizen by blood of the Choctaw Nation.

--oOo--

It appears from the record herein that on April 25, 1905, there was filed with this Commission application for the enrollment of Alleyne Camp as a citizen by blood of the Choctaw Nation.

It further appears from the record herein and the records of the Commission that the applicant was born December 31, 1902; that she is a daughter of Joe A. Camp a recognized and enrolled citizen by blood of the Choctaw Nation, whose name appears opposite number 247 upon the final roll of citizens by blood of the Choctaw Nation, approved by the Secretary of the Interior December 12, 1902, and Allie Camp a recognized and enrolled citizen by intermarriage of the Choctaw Nation; and that the applicant died prior to March 4, 1905.

The Act of Congress approved March 3, 1905 (Public No. 212) among other things provides:

"That the Commission to the Five Civilized Tribes is authorized for sixty days after the date of the approval of this act to receive and consider applications for enrollment of children born subsequent to September twenty-fifth, nineteen hundred and two, and prior to March fourth, nineteen hundred and five, and who were living on said latter date, to citizens by blood of the Choctaw and Chickasaw tribes of Indians whose enrollment has been approved by the Secretary of the Interior prior to the date of the approval of this act; and to enroll and make allotments to such children."

It is, therefore, hereby ordered that the application for the enrollment of Alleyne Camp as a citizen by blood of the Choctaw Nation be dismissed in accordance with the order of the Commission of March 31, 1905.

COMMISSION TO THE FIVE CIVILIZED TRIBES.

Tams Bixby
Chairman.

Muskogee, Indian Territory.
JUN 28 1905

7-NB-983.

Muskogee, Indian Territory, June 28, 1905.

Joseph A. Camp,
    Paoli, Indian Territory.   **COPY**

Dear Sir:

    Inclosed herewith you will find a copy of the order of this Commission dated June 28, 1905, dismissing the application for the enrollment of Alleyne Camp as a citizen by blood of the Choctaw Nation.

                      Respectfully,

                         SIGNED   *Tams Bixby*
Registered.   Chairman.
Incl. 7-NB-983.

7-NB-983.

Muskogee, Indian Territory, June 28, 1905.

Mansfield, McMurray & Cornish,
    Attorneys for Choctaw and Chickasaw Nations,   **COPY**
        South McAlester, Indian Territory.

Gentlemen:

    Inclosed herewith you will find a copy of the order of this Commission, dated June 28, 1905, dismissing the application for the enrollment of Alleyne Camp as a citizen by blood of the Choctaw Nation.

                      Respectfully,

                         SIGNED   *Tams Bixby*
                                   Chairman.
Incl. 7-NB-983.

Applications for Enrollment of Choctaw Newborn
Act of 1905   Volume XIV

UNITED STATES OF AMERICA,
   The Indian Territory,
Southern Judicial District.

   J. B. MAPLES, being first duly sworn, on his oath states that he is a regular practicing physician of Paoli, Indian Territory in the southern District of the Indian Territory, duly licensed to practice medicine and surgery under the laws of the United States in force in the said Indian Territory; that he is acquainted with Jos. A. Camp and Allie Camp, wife of the said Jos. A. Camp; that he was the attending physician upon the said Allie Camp on September 6th, 1904; that at said time a female child was born to the said Allie Camp that it is still living and has been named Catherine.

J.B. Maples MD

SUBSCRIBED AND SWORN to before me this 21   *day of Dec. 1904.*

A S Kelley
N o t a r y   P u b l i c.
My Comission[sic] Expires Mch 12-1908

BIRTH AFFIDAVIT.   *#124*

DEPARTMENT OF THE INTERIOR.
COMMISSION TO THE FIVE CIVILIZED TRIBES.

IN RE APPLICATION FOR ENROLLMENT, as a citizen of the   Choctaw   Nation, of
Catherine Camp   , born on the 6th day of   Sept , 1904

Name of Father: Joseph A Camp   a citizen of the   Choctaw   Nation.
Name of Mother: Allie Camp   a citizen of the   Choctaw   Nation.

Postoffice   Paoli I.T.

AFFIDAVIT OF MOTHER.

UNITED STATES OF AMERICA, Indian Territory, ⎫
   Southern   **DISTRICT.** ⎬

   I,   Allie Camp   , on oath state that I am   34   years of age and a citizen by Intermarriage   , of the   Choctaw   Nation; that I am the lawful wife of   Joseph A. Camp   , who is a citizen, by   Blood   of the   Choctaw   Nation; that a Female   child was born to me on   the 6th day of   Sept   , 1904, that said child has been named   Catherine Camp   , and is now living.

Allie Camp

Witnesses To Mark:

{

Subscribed and sworn to before me this 22nd day of   Feb   , 1905.

A.S. Kelley
My commission expires Mch 12th 1908   Notary Public.

———————

BIRTH AFFIDAVIT.

DEPARTMENT OF THE INTERIOR.
COMMISSION TO THE FIVE CIVILIZED TRIBES.

———————

IN RE APPLICATION FOR ENROLLMENT, as a citizen of the   Choctaw   Nation, of
Catherine Camp   , born on the 6th day of   Sept , 1904

Name of Father: Joseph A Camp   a citizen of the   Choctaw   Nation.
Name of Mother: Allie Camp   a citizen of the   Choctaw   Nation.

Postoffice   Paoli I.T.

———————

AFFIDAVIT OF MOTHER.

UNITED STATES OF AMERICA, Indian Territory, ⎫
   Southern   DISTRICT. ⎰

   I,   Allie Camp   , on oath state that I am   33   years of age and a citizen by
marriage   , of the   Choctaw   Nation; that I am the lawful wife of   Joseph A
Camp   , who is a citizen, by blood   of the   Choctaw   Nation; that a
female   child was born to me on   6th day of   September   , 1904; that said child
has been named   Catherine Camp   , and was living March 4, 1905.

Allie Camp
Witnesses To Mark:

{

Subscribed and sworn to before me this   11th day of   April   , 1905

JE Williams
Notary Public.

———————

Applications for Enrollment of Choctaw Newborn
Act of 1905 Volume XIV

UNITED STATES OF AMERICA, Indian Territory, ⎱
   Southern   DISTRICT. ⎰

I, Lottie Wallace   , a Midwife   , on oath state that I attended on Mrs. Allie Camp , wife of Joseph A Camp   on the 6th day of September , 1904; that there was born to her on said date a   female   child; that said child was living March 4, 1905, and is said to have been named Catherine A̶l̶l̶i̶e̶ Camp

Lottie Wallace

Witnesses To Mark:

{

Subscribed and sworn to before me this 11th day of April   , 1905

JE Williams
Notary Public.

Choc New Born 984
   Willie May McCarty b. 6-7-04

DEPARTMENT OF THE INTERIOR.
COMMISSION TO THE FIVE CIVILIZED TRIBES.

IN RE APPLICATION FOR ENROLLMENT, as a citizen of the   Choctaw   Nation, of Willie May McCarty   , born on the 7" day of June , 1904

Name of Father: Robert L McCarty   a citizen of the Choctaw   Nation.
Name of Mother: Lizzie Y McCarty   a citizen of the   Do   Nation.

Postoffice   Scipio I.T.

UNITED STATES OF AMERICA, Indian Territory, ⎱
   Central   DISTRICT. ⎰

I, Lizzie Y McCarty   , on oath state that I am 24 years of age and a citizen by   Intermarriage   , of the Choctaw Nation; that I am the lawful wife of Robert L McCarty   , who is a citizen, by blood   of the   Choctaw

Nation; that a   female   child was born to me on   7   day of   June   , 1904; that said child has been named   Willie May McCarty   , and was living March 4, 1905.

Lizzie Y McCarty

Witnesses To Mark:

{

Subscribed and sworn to before me this   12th   day of   April   , 1905

AE Becker
Notary Public.

AFFIDAVIT OF ATTENDING PHYSICIAN OR MID-WIFE.

UNITED STATES OF AMERICA, Indian Territory,
Central   DISTRICT.

I,   Rachael A Sutton   , a   midwife   , on oath state that I attended on Mrs. Lizzie Y McCarty   , wife of   Robert L McCarty   on the 7" day of June, 1904; that there was born to her on said date a   female   child; that said child was living March 4, 1905, and is said to have been named Willie May McCarty

Rachael A Sutton

Witnesses To Mark:

{

Subscribed and sworn to before me this   12th   day of   April   , 1905

AE Becker
Notary Public.

Choc New Born 985
    Elizabeth Cole b. 4-18-03

7-NB-985.

Muskogee, Indian Territory, June 2, 1905.

Campbell Cole,
Jackson, Indian Territory.

Dear Sir:

There is enclosed you herewith for execution application for the enrollment of your infant child, Elizabeth Cole, born April 18, 1903.

In the application filed in this office on April 25, 1905, the affidavit of the attending physician is executed by William Robinson, while in the application filed April 18, 1905, this affidavit is executed by William Roberson. Although these names are apparently of the same person, they are spelled differently, and appear to have been signed in different handwriting. It will, therefore, be necessary that you have the enclosed affidavit of the attending physician or midwife executed by the person who was actually in attendance, signing the affidavit in his correct name.

You will also please secure the affidavit of another person to the fact that the person executing the above affidavit is the person who was in attendance upon your wife at the time of birth of the applicant.

In having the affidavit executed care should be exercised to see that all names are written in full, as they appear in the body of the affidavit. Signatures by mark must be attested by two witnesses. Each affidavit must be executed before a Notary Public and the notarial seal and signature of the officer must be attached to each separate affidavit.

Respectfully,

VR 1-12.   [sic]

7-NB-985

Muskogee, Indian Territory, July 11, 1905.

Campbell Cole,
Jackson, Indian Territory.

Dear Sir:

Receipt is hereby acknowledged of the affidavits of Mary Cole and William Robinson to the birth of Elizabeth Cole, daughter of Campbell and Mary Cole, April 18, 1903, and the same have been filed with the records of this office in the matter of the enrollment of said child.

Respectfully,

Commissioner.

7-NB-985

Muskogee, Indian Territory, August 4, 1905.

Campbell Cole,
    Jackson, Indian Territory.

Dear Sir:

Your attention is called to a communication addressed to you by the Commission to the Five Civilized Tribes, under date of June 2, 1905, in which you were requested to furnish the affidavit of some person to the fact that William Robinson attended upon your wife at the time of the birth of your infant child, Elizabeth Cole.

The affidavit requested has not been forwarded to this office, and you are again requested to give this matter your prompt attention, as no further action can be taken relative to the enrollment of your said child until the evidence desired is supplied.

Respectfully,

Commissioner.

7-NB-985

Muskogee, Indian Territory, September 13, 1905.

Campbell Cole,
    Bennington, Indian Territory.

Dear Sir:

Replying to your letter of September 5th, you are advised that the name of your minor child, Elizabeth Cole, was included upon a schedule of new-born citizens of the Choctaw Nation which was transmitted by the Commissioner to the Secretary of the Interior on August 26, 1905.

When the enrollment of your child has been approved by the Secretary of the Interior, you will be notified thereof.

Respectfully,

Acting Commissioner.

NEW-BORN AFFIDAVIT.

Number................

Choctaw Enrolling Commission.

IN THE MATTER OF THE APPLICATION FOR ENROLLMENT, as a citizen of the
Choctaw   Nation, of   Elizabeth Cole

born on the 18th   day of   April   190 3

Name of father   Campbell Cole   a citizen of   Choctaw
Nation final enrollment No 9697
Name of mother   Mary Cole   a citizen of   Choctaw
Nation final enrollment No 9698

Postoffice   Jackson, I.T.

AFFIDAVIT OF MOTHER.

UNITED STATES OF AMERICA, ⎱
    INDIAN TERRITORY,   ⎬
Central   DISTRICT ⎰

I   Mary Cole   on oath state that I am 20 years of
age and a citizen by   blood   of the   Choctaw   Nation, and as such have been
placed upon the final roll of the   Choctaw   Nation, by the Honorable Secretary of the
Interior my final enrollment number being 9698 ; that I am the lawful wife of   Campbell
Cole   , who is a citizen of the   Choctaw   Nation, and as such has been placed
upon the final roll of said Nation by the Honorable Secretary of the Interior, his final
enrollment number being 9697   and that a   female   child was born to me on the   18th
day of   April   190 3 ; that said child has been named   Elizabeth Cole   , and is
now living.   her
                              Mary Cole x
WITNESSETH: mark
   Must be two ⎱ William Robinson
   Witnesses who ⎰
   are Citizens.   Anna Homer

Subscribed and sworn to before me this   16th   day of   Jan   190 5

W A Shoney
Notary Public.
My commission expires Jan 10, 1909

74

AFFIDAVIT OF ATTENDING PHYSICIAN OR MIDWIFE

UNITED STATES OF AMERICA
INDIAN TERRITORY
Central   DISTRICT

I,   William Robinson   a   attendant
on oath state that I attended on Mrs.   Mary Cole   wife of   Campbell Cole
on the 18th day of April , 190 3, that there was born to her on said date a   female   child,
that said child is now living, and is said to have been named   Elizabeth Cole

William Robinson   M.D.

Subscribed and sworn to before me this, the   16   day of   Jan   190 5

W.A. Shoney
Notary Public.

WITNESSETH:
Must be two witnesses   ⎰ William Robinson
who are citizens and   ⎱
know the child.   ⎰ Anna Homer

We hereby certify that we are well acquainted with   William Robinson
a   attendant   and know   him   to be reputable and of good standing in the
community.

C M Byington

(Name Illegible)

BIRTH AFFIDAVIT.

DEPARTMENT OF THE INTERIOR.
COMMISSION TO THE FIVE CIVILIZED TRIBES.

IN RE APPLICATION FOR ENROLLMENT, as a citizen of the   Choctaw   Nation, of
Elizabeth Cole   , born on the 18th   day of April , 1903

Name of Father: Campbell Cole   a citizen of the   Choctaw   Nation.
Name of Mother: Mary Cole   a citizen of the   Choctaw   Nation.

Postoffice   Jackson I.T.

Applications for Enrollment of Choctaw Newborn
Act of 1905   Volume XIV

AFFIDAVIT OF MOTHER.

UNITED STATES OF AMERICA, Indian Territory, ⎱
  Cent   DISTRICT. ⎰

I,   Mary Cole   , on oath state that I am about 25   years of age and a citizen by   blood   , of the   Choctaw   Nation; that I am the lawful wife of   Campbell Cole   , who is a citizen, by blood   of the   Choctaw   Nation; that a Female   child was born to me on 18th   day of   April   , 1903; that said child has been named   Elizabeth Cole   , and was living March 4, 1905.

Mary Cole

Witnesses To Mark:
⎰

Subscribed and sworn to before me this 12th   day of   April   , 1905

B.W. Williams
Notary Public.

AFFIDAVIT OF ATTENDING PHYSICIAN OR MID-WIFE.

UNITED STATES OF AMERICA, Indian Territory, ⎱
  Cent   DISTRICT. ⎰

I,   William Robinson   , a   attendant   , on oath state that I attended on Mrs.   Mary Cole   , wife of   Campbell Cole   on the   18th day of   April   , 1903; that there was born to her on said date a .... child; that said child was living March 4, 1905, and is said to have been named Elizabeth Cole

William Roberson[sic]

Witnesses To Mark:
⎰

Subscribed and sworn to before me this 12th   day of   April   , 1905

B.W. Williams
Notary Public.

Applications for Enrollment of Choctaw Newborn
Act of 1905   Volume XIV

DEPARTMENT OF THE INTERIOR.
COMMISSION TO THE FIVE CIVILIZED TRIBES.

IN RE APPLICATION FOR ENROLLMENT, as a citizen of the   Choctaw   Nation, of
Elizabeth Cole   , born on the 18th day of April , 1903

Name of Father: Campbell Cole   Roll 9697   a citizen of the   Choctaw   Nation.
Name of Mother: Mary Cole   Roll 9698   a citizen of the   Choctaw   Nation.

Postoffice   Jackson I.T.

AFFIDAVIT OF MOTHER.

UNITED STATES OF AMERICA, Indian Territory,⎫
      Central   DISTRICT. ⎰

I,   Mary Cole   , on oath state that I am 20   years of age and a citizen by
blood   , of the   Choctaw   Nation; that I am the lawful wife of   Campbell Cole   ,
who is a citizen, by blood   of the   Choctaw   Nation; that a   female   child
was born to me on   18th day of   April   , 1903; that said child has been named
Elizabeth Cole   , and was living March 4, 1905.

                                           her
                                    Mary x Cole
Witnesses To Mark: mark
⎰ Sam Durant
⎱ J L Durant

Subscribed and sworn to before me this 6th day of   July   , 1905

                                    B.W. Williams
                                        Notary Public.

AFFIDAVIT OF ATTENDING PHYSICIAN OR MID-WIFE.

UNITED STATES OF AMERICA, Indian Territory,⎫
      Central   DISTRICT. ⎰

I,   William Robinson   , a   attendant   , on oath state that I attended on
Mrs.   Mary Cole   , wife of   Campbell Cole   on the   18th day of April   ,
1903; that there was born to her on said date a   female   child; that said child was living
March 4, 1905, and is said to have been named Elizabeth Cole

                                    William Robinson
                                    Identy[sic] *Ross Frazier*

77

Witnesses To Mark:

{

Subscribed and sworn to before me this 6th day of   July   , 1905

B.W. Williams
Notary Public.

Choc New Born 986
Ozious James W. Tucker   b. 11-13-04

BIRTH AFFIDAVIT.

DEPARTMENT OF THE INTERIOR.
COMMISSION TO THE FIVE CIVILIZED TRIBES.

IN RE APPLICATION FOR ENROLLMENT, as a citizen of the   Chocktaw[sic]   Nation,
of   Ozious James W. Tucker   , born on the   13   day of   Nov   , 1904

Name of Father: William Tucker   a citizen of the   Chocktaw   Nation.
Name of Mother: Janie Tucker   a citizen of the   Choctaw   Nation.

Postoffice   Simon Chickasaw Nation I.T.

AFFIDAVIT OF MOTHER.

UNITED STATES OF AMERICA, Indian Territory, }
     Southern   DISTRICT. }

I,   Janie Tucker   , on oath state that I am   Thirty five   years of age and a
citizen by   Intermarriage   , of the   Choctaw   Nation; that I am the lawful wife
of   William Tucker   , who is a citizen, by   Blood   of the   Chocktaw
Nation; that a   male   child was born to me on 13   day of   November   , 1904;
that said child has been named   Ozious James W Tucker   , and was living March 4,
1905.

Janie Tucker

Witnesses To Mark:
{ Ozious James P Rector
{ Eliza Ellen Rector

78

Subscribed and sworn to before me this 10   day of   April   , 1905

T.J. Briscoe
Notary Public.
Dist 26, Sou Dist.

AFFIDAVIT OF ATTENDING PHYSICIAN OR MID-WIFE.

UNITED STATES OF AMERICA, Indian Territory, ⎫
Southern   DISTRICT. ⎭

I,   J.N. D^{e}Frece   , a   Physician   , on oath state that I attended on Mrs.   Janie Tucker   , wife of   William Tucker   on the 13 day of   Nov   , 1904; that there was born to her on said date a   male   child; that said child was living March 4, 1905, and is said to have been named Ozious James W Tucker

J.N. DeFrece M.D.

Witnesses To Mark:
⎧ M L Mitchell
⎩ Ozious James P Rector

Subscribed and sworn to before me this 11   day of   April   , 1905

T.J. Briscoe
Notary Public.

7-263

Muskogee, Indian Territory, April 17, 1905.

William Tucker,
Simon, Indian Territory.

Dear Sir:

Receipt is hereby acknowledged of the affidavits of Janie Tucker and J. N. DeFrece to the birth of Ozious James W. Tucker, son of William and Janie Tucker, November 13, 1904, and the same have been filed with our records as an application for the enrollment of said child.

Respectfully,

Chairman.

79

<u>Choc New Born 987</u>
Edgar G. Crabtree   b. 11-9-03

_____

7-3347

Muskogee, Indian Territory April 17, 1905.

David C. Crabtree,
Blackrock, Indian Territory.

Dear Sir:

Receipt is hereby acknowledged of the affidavits of Georgia A. Crabtree and W.C. Threlkeld to the birth of Edgar G. Crabtree, son of David C. and Georgia A. Crabtree, November 9, 1903, and the same have been filed with our records as an application for the enrollment of said child.

Respectfully,

Chairman.

_____

NEW-BORN AFFIDAVIT.

Number...............

...Choctaw Enrolling Commission...

_____

IN THE MATTER OF THE APPLICATION FOR ENROLLMENT, as a citizen of the Choctaw   Nation, of   Edgar G Crabtree

born on the 9 day of ____November____ 190 3

Name of father   David C. Crabtree   a citizen of   Choctaw
Nation final enrollment No. 188
Name of mother   Georgia C Crabtree   a citizen of   Choctaw
Nation final enrollment No. 9609

Postoffice   Black Rock

80

AFFIDAVIT OF MOTHER.

UNITED STATES OF AMERICA
INDIAN TERRITORY
Central   DISTRICT

I   Georgia A Crabtree   , on oath state that I am 30   years of age and a citizen by   blood   of the   Choctaw   Nation, and as such have been placed upon the final roll of the   Choctaw   Nation, by the Honorable Secretary of the Interior my final enrollment number being   9609   ; that I am the lawful wife of   David C Crabtree   , who is a citizen of the   Choctaw   Nation, and as such has been placed upon the final roll of said Nation by the Honorable Secretary of the Interior, his final enrollment number being   188   and that a   Male   child was born to me on the 9   day of   November   190 3; that said child has been named   Edgar G Crabtree   , and is now living.

Georgia A Crabtree

Witnesseth.

Must be two Witnesses who are Citizens.   W.W. Barnett

S.A. Barnett

Subscribed and sworn to before me this   11   day of   Feb   190 5

J.L . Cart

Notary Public.

My commission expires: June 27-1908

AFFIDAVIT OF ATTENDING PHYSICIAN OR MIDWIFE

UNITED STATES OF AMERICA
INDIAN TERRITORY
Central   DISTRICT

I,   W.C. Threlkeld   a   physician on oath state that I attended on Mrs. Georgia A Crabtree   wife of   David C Crabtree on the   9   day of   November   , 190 3 , that there was born to her on said date a   male child, that said child is now living, and is said to have been named   Edgar G Crabtree

W.C. Threlkeld   M.D.

Subscribed and sworn to before me this, the   14   day of February   190 5

WITNESSETH: J.L. Cart   Notary Public.

Must be two witnesses who are citizens   W.W. Barnett

AM Cummings

Applications for Enrollment of Choctaw Newborn
Act of 1905 Volume XIV

We hereby certify that we are well acquainted with   W C Threlkeld
a   Physician   and know   him   to be reputable and of good standing in the community.

W W Barnett

_____

A M Cummings

_____

_____

BIRTH AFFIDAVIT.

DEPARTMENT OF THE INTERIOR.
COMMISSION TO THE FIVE CIVILIZED TRIBES.

_____

IN RE APPLICATION FOR ENROLLMENT, as a citizen of the   Choctaw   Nation, of
Edgar G. Crabtree   , born on the 9 day of   November   , 1903

Name of Father: David C. Crabtree   a citizen of the   Choctaw   Nation.
Name of Mother: Georgia A Crabtree   a citizen of the   Choctaw   Nation.

Postoffice   Blackrock I.T.

_____

AFFIDAVIT OF MOTHER.

UNITED STATES OF AMERICA, Indian Territory, ⎫
    Central   **DISTRICT.** ⎭

I,   Georgia A Crabtree   , on oath state that I am   31   years of age and a
citizen by   blood   , of the   Choctaw   Nation; that I am the lawful wife of
David C Crabtree   , who is a citizen, by   marriage   of the   Choctaw
Nation; that a   male   child was born to me on 9   day of   November   , 1903;
that said child has been named   Edgar G Crabtree   , and was living March 4, 1905.

Georgia A Crabtree

Witnesses To Mark:

⎰
⎱

Subscribed and sworn to before me this 8 day of   April   , 1905

My Commission expires   J.L. Cart
June 27-1908   Notary Public.

_____

82

Applications for Enrollment of Choctaw Newborn
Act of 1905   Volume XIV

AFFIDAVIT OF ATTENDING PHYSICIAN OR MID-WIFE.

UNITED STATES OF AMERICA, Indian Territory, ⎫
   Central   DISTRICT. ⎭

I, W. C. Threlkeld   , a physician   , on oath state that I attended on
Mrs. Georgia A Crabtree   , wife of   David C Crabtree   on the 9 day of
November   , 1903; that there was born to her on said date a   male   child; that said
child was living March 4, 1905, and is said to have been named Edgar G Crabtree

                           W.C. Threlkeld M.D.

Witnesses To Mark:

{

Subscribed and sworn to before me this 10 day of   April   , 1905

My Commission expires   J.L. Cart
June 27-1908   Notary Public.

Choc New Born 988
    Roy Hiberd   b. 12-15-03

_____

                           7-3390

Muskogee, Indian Territory, April 17, 1905.

Willie P. Hibbard[sic],
    Blue, Indian Territory.

Dear Sir:

Receipt is hereby acknowledged of the affidavits of Laura Hiberd and Ruthie
Kyle to the birth of Roy Hiberd, son of Willie and Laura Hiberd, December 15, 1903, and
the same have been filed with our records as an application for the enrollment of said
child.

                   Respectfully,

                         Chairman.

_____

BIRTH AFFIDAVIT.

DEPARTMENT OF THE INTERIOR.
COMMISSION TO THE FIVE CIVILIZED TRIBES.

IN RE APPLICATION FOR ENROLLMENT, as a citizen of the   Choctaw   Nation, of
Roy Hiberd   , born on the   15   day of December , 1903

Name of Father: Willie P Hiberd   a citizen of the   Choctaw   Nation.
Name of Mother: Laura Hiberd   a citizen of the   Choctaw   Nation.

Postoffice   Blue Ind Ter

AFFIDAVIT OF MOTHER.

UNITED STATES OF AMERICA, Indian Territory,
Central   DISTRICT.

I,   Laura Hiberd   , on oath state that I am   30   years of age and a citizen by
Intermarriage   , of the   Choctaw   Nation; that I am the lawful wife of   Willie P
Hiberd   , who is a citizen, by Blood   of the   Choctaw   Nation; that a
male   child was born to me on   15   day of December   , 1903; that said child
has been named   Roy   , and was living March 4, 1905.

Laura Hiberd

Witnesses To Mark:

Subscribed and sworn to before me this   12 day of   April   , 1905

JM Routh
Notary Public.

AFFIDAVIT OF ATTENDING PHYSICIAN OR MID-WIFE.

UNITED STATES OF AMERICA, Indian Territory,
Central   DISTRICT.

I,   Ruthie Kyle   , a midwife   , on oath state that I attended on
Mrs. Laura Hiberd   , wife of   Willie P Hiberd   on the 15 day of   December,
1903; that there was born to her on said date a   male   child; that said child was living
March 4, 1905, and is said to have been named Roy

her
Ruthie x Kyle
mark

Applications for Enrollment of Choctaw Newborn
Act of 1905   Volume XIV

Witnesses To Mark:
{ T D Russell
{ Andrea Russell

Subscribed and sworn to before me this 12 day of   April   , 1905

JM Routh
Notary Public.

Choc New Born 989
>   Margie C Reese   b. 5-4-03
>   Orville Reese   b. 11-3-04

BIRTH AFFIDAVIT.

DEPARTMENT OF THE INTERIOR.
COMMISSION TO THE FIVE CIVILIZED TRIBES.

IN RE APPLICATION FOR ENROLLMENT, as a citizen of the   Choctaw   Nation, of
Orville Reese   , born on the 3rd   day of November   , 1904

Name of Father: John Reese, a non-citizen   a citizen of the ....Nation.
Name of Mother: Mollie Reese   a citizen of the   Choctaw   Nation.

Postoffice   Durant, Indian Territory.

AFFIDAVIT OF MOTHER.

UNITED STATES OF AMERICA, Indian Territory, ⎫
     Central   DISTRICT.⎭

I,   Mollie Reese   , on oath state that I am   27   years of age and a citizen by
blood   , of the   Choctaw   Nation; that I am the lawful wife of   John Reese, who is
not a citizen   , who is a citizen, by .... of the ....Nation;
that a   Male   child was born to me on   3rd day of   November   , 1904; that
said child has been named   Orville Reese   , and was living March 4, 1905.

Mollie Reese

Witnesses To Mark:
{

Subscribed and sworn to before me this   12th day of   April   , 1905

A.H. Ferguson
Notary Public.

———————

AFFIDAVIT OF ATTENDING PHYSICIAN OR MID-WIFE.

UNITED STATES OF AMERICA, Indian Territory, ⎫
Central   **DISTRICT.** ⎬

I,   Jas. L. Shuler   , a   Physician   , on oath state that I attended on
Mrs.   Mollie Reese , wife of   John Reese   on the   3rd day of   November   ,
1904; that there was born to her on said date a   male   child; that said child was living
March 4, 1905, and is said to have been named   Orville Reese

Jas. L. Shuler
Witnesses To Mark:

{

Subscribed and sworn to before me this   12th day of   April   , 1905

A.H. Ferguson
Notary Public.

———————

BIRTH AFFIDAVIT.

DEPARTMENT OF THE INTERIOR.
COMMISSION TO THE FIVE CIVILIZED TRIBES.

———————

IN RE APPLICATION FOR ENROLLMENT, as a citizen of the   Choctaw   Nation, of
Orville Reese   , born on the 3rd day of   November   , 1904

Name of Father: John Reese   a citizen of the   non citizen   Nation.
Name of Mother: Mollie Reese   Roll 9725   a citizen of the   Choctaw   Nation.

Postoffice   Durant, I.T.

———————

AFFIDAVIT OF MOTHER.

UNITED STATES OF AMERICA, Indian Territory, ⎫
....DISTRICT. ⎬

I,   Mollie Reese   , on oath state that I am   27   years of age and a citizen by
blood   , of the   Choctaw   Nation; that I am the lawful wife of   John Reese, who is
not a citizen   , who is a citizen, ~~by~~ ——— of the   United States   Nation; that a

86

male   child was born to me on   3rd day of   November   , 1904; that said child
has been named   Orville Reese   , and was living March 4, 1905.

Mollie Reese

Witnesses To Mark:

{

Subscribed and sworn to before me this 6th day of   November   , 1905

D.A. Richardson
Notary Public.

AFFIDAVIT OF ATTENDING PHYSICIAN OR MID-WIFE.

UNITED STATES OF AMERICA, Indian Territory, }
  Central   **DISTRICT.** }

I,   Jas. L. Shuler   , a   Physician   , on oath state that I attended on
Mrs.   Mollie Reese , wife of   John Reese   on the 3rd day of   Nov   , 1904;
that there was born to her on said date a   male   child; that said child was living
March 4, 1905, and is said to have been named   Orville Reese

Jas. L. Shuler

Witnesses To Mark:

{

Subscribed and sworn to before me this 6th day of   June[sic]   , 1905

D.A. Richardson
Notary Public.

7-3408

Muskogee, Indian Territory, April 17, 1905.

Furgeson & Richardson,
        Attorneys at Law,
                Durant, Indian Territory.

Gentlemen:

Receipt is hereby acknowledged of your letter of April 12, 1905, enclosing
affidavits of Mollie Reese and Jas. L. Shuler to the birth of Orville Reese, son of John
and Mollie Reese, November 3, 1904; also affidavits of Mollie Reese and G. M. Rushing

to the birth of Margie C. Reese, daughter of John and Mollie Reese, May 4, 1903, and the same have been filed with our records as applications for the enrollment of said children.

Respectfully,

Chairman.

_____

NEW-BORN AFFIDAVIT.

Number..................

Choctaw Enrolling Commission.

IN THE MATTER OF THE APPLICATION FOR ENROLLMENT, as a citizen of the Choctaw   Nation, of   Margie C. Reese

born on the 4th day of   May   190 3

Name of father   John Reese   a citizen of   white
Nation final enrollment   ———
Name of mother   Mollie Reese   a citizen of   Choctaw
Nation final enrollment No   9725

Postoffice   Durant I.T.

AFFIDAVIT OF MOTHER.

UNITED STATES OF AMERICA, ⎱
   INDIAN TERRITORY, ⎰
................................DISTRICT ⎰

I   Mollie Reese   on oath state that I
am   27 years of age and a citizen by   blood   of the   Choctaw   Nation, and as
such have been placed upon the final roll of the   Choctaw   Nation, by the Honorable
Secretary of the Interior my final enrollment number being   9725   ; that I am the lawful
wife of   John Reese   , who is a citizen of the   white   Nation, and as such
has been placed upon the final roll of said Nation by the Honorable Secretary of the Interior,
his final enrollment number being —— and that a   female   child was born to me on the 4th
day of   May   190 3 ; that said child has been named   Margie C Rose   , and is
now living.

Mollie Reese

WITNESSETH:
  Must be two ⎱   Alex Robinson
  Witnesses who ⎰
  are Citizens.   Thos J Sexton

88

Subscribed and sworn to before me this   14th   day of   January   190 5

W A Shoney

Notary Public.

My commission expires   Jan 10, 1909

AFFIDAVIT OF ATTENDING PHYSICIAN OR MIDWIFE

UNITED STATES OF AMERICA
INDIAN TERRITORY
  Central   DISTRICT

I,   G. M. Rushing   a   physician
on oath state that I attended on Mrs.   Mollie Reese   wife of   John Reese
on the 4th   day of   May , 190 3, that there was born to her on said date a   female   child,
that said child is now living, and is said to have been named   Margie C Reese

G.M. Rushing   M.D.

Subscribed and sworn to before me this, the   14th   day of   Jan   190 5

W A Shoney

Notary Public.

WITNESSETH:

Must be two witnesses { J.J. Gardner
who are citizens and
know the child.   *(Name Illegible)*

We hereby certify that we are well acquainted with   G M Rushing
a   physician   and know   him   to be reputable and of good standing in the
community.

Thos J Sexton

{

J.J. Gardner

BIRTH AFFIDAVIT.

DEPARTMENT OF THE INTERIOR.
COMMISSION TO THE FIVE CIVILIZED TRIBES.

IN RE APPLICATION FOR ENROLLMENT, as a citizen of the   Choctaw   Nation, of
Margie C. Reese   , born on the   4th day of   May   , 1903

Name of Father: John Reese, a non-citizen   a citizen of the .... Nation.
Name of Mother: Mollie Reese   a citizen of the   Choctaw   Nation.

Applications for Enrollment of Choctaw Newborn
Act of 1905   Volume XIV

Postoffice   Durant, Indian Territory.

AFFIDAVIT OF MOTHER.

UNITED STATES OF AMERICA, Indian Territory, ⎱
Central   **DISTRICT.** ⎰

I, Mollie Reese   , on oath state that I am   27   years of age and a citizen by blood   , of the   Choctaw   Nation; that I am the lawful wife of   John Reese, who is not a citizen   , who is a citizen, by .... of the .... Nation; that a Female   child was born to me on   4th   day of   May   , 1903; that said child has been named   Margie C. Reese   , and was living March 4, 1905.

Mollie Reese

Witnesses To Mark:
{

Subscribed and sworn to before me this 12th   day of   April   , 1905

A.H. Ferguson
Notary Public.

AFFIDAVIT OF ATTENDING PHYSICIAN OR MID-WIFE.

UNITED STATES OF AMERICA, Indian Territory, ⎱
Central   **DISTRICT.** ⎰

I,   G. M. Rushing   , a   Physician   , on oath state that I attended on Mrs.   Mollie Reese   , wife of   John Reese   on the 4th day of   May   , 1903; that there was born to her on said date a   Female   child; that said child was living March 4, 1905, and is said to have been named   Margie C. Reese

G.M. Rushing

Witnesses To Mark:
{

Subscribed and sworn to before me this 12th   day of   April   , 1905

A.H. Ferguson
Notary Public.

90

7-NB989.

Muskogee, Indian Territory, June 2, 1905.

John Reese,
    Durant, Indian Territory.

Dear Sir:

There is enclosed you herewith for execution application for the enrollment of your infant child, Orville Reese.

In the affidavits of January 14, 1905, heretofore filed in this office, the date of the applicant's birth is given as November 4, 1904, while in the affidavits of April 12, 1905, it is given as November 3, 1904. In the enclosed application the date of birth is left blank. Please insert the correct date and when the affidavits are properly executed return them to this office.

In having these affidavits executed care should be exercised to see that all names are written in full, as they appear in the body of the affidavit, and in the event that either of the persons signing the affidavits are unable to write, signatures by mark must be attested by two witnesses. Each affidavit must be executed before a Notary Public and the notarial seal and signature of the officer must be attached to each separate affidavit.

Respectfully,

VR 2-11.   [sic]

7-NB-989

Muskogee, Indian Territory, June 10, 1905.

John Reese,
    Durant, Indian Territory.

Dear Sir:

Receipt is hereby acknowledged of your letter of June 6, transmitting the affidavits of Mollie Reese and Jas. L. Shuler to the birth of Orville Reese, son of John and Mollie Reese, November 3, 1904, and the same have been filed with our records in the matter of the enrollment of said child.

Respectfully,

Chairman.

91

NEW-BORN AFFIDAVIT.

Number...............

Choctaw Enrolling Commission.

IN THE MATTER OF THE APPLICATION FOR ENROLLMENT, as a citizen of the
Choctaw   Nation, of   Orver[sic] Reese

born on the 4th   day of   November   190 4

Name of father   John Reese   a citizen of   white
Nation final enrollment No ——
Name of mother   Mollie Reese   a citizen of   Choctaw
Nation final enrollment No   9725

Postoffice   Durant I.T.

AFFIDAVIT OF MOTHER.

UNITED STATES OF AMERICA, ⎫
   INDIAN TERRITORY, ⎬
  Central   DISTRICT ⎭

    I   Mollie Reese   on oath state that I
am 27 years of age and a citizen by   blood   of the   Choctaw   Nation, and as
such have been placed upon the final roll of the   Choctaw   Nation, by the Honorable
Secretary of the Interior my final enrollment number being   9725   ; that I am the lawful
wife of   John Reese   , who is a citizen of the   white   Nation, and as such
has been placed upon the final roll of said Nation by the Honorable Secretary of the Interior,
his final enrollment number being ——and that a   male   child was born to me on the 4th
day of   November   190 4 ; that said child has been named   Orver Reese   , and is
now living.

Mollie Reese

WITNESSETH:

  Must be two ⎫ Alex Robinson
  Witnesses who ⎬
  are Citizens. ⎭ Thos J. Sexton

Subscribed and sworn to before me this   14th   day of   January   190 5

W.A. Shoney
Notary Public.

My commission expires   Jan 10, 1909

AFFIDAVIT OF ATTENDING PHYSICIAN OR MIDWIFE

UNITED STATES OF AMERICA
INDIAN TERRITORY
Central   DISTRICT

I,   J.L. Shuler   a   physician
on oath state that I attended on Mrs.   Mollie Reese   wife of   John Reese
on the   4th day of   November , 190 4, that there was born to her on said date a   male
child, that said child is now living, and is said to have been named   Orver[sic] Reese

J.L. Shuler   M.D.

Subscribed and sworn to before me this, the   14   day of   Jan   190 5

W A Shoney
Notary Public.

WITNESSETH:

Must be two witnesses   { J.J. Gardner
who are citizens and
know the child.   (Name Illegible)

We hereby certify that we are well acquainted with   Dr JL Shuler
a   physician   and know   him   to be reputable and of good standing in the
community.

Thos J Sexton

J.J. Gardner

Choc New Born 990
Lorena Cobb   b. 12-23-04

7-708

Muskogee, Indian Territory, April 17, 1905.

Sampson Cobb,
Bethel, Indian Territory.

Dear Sir:

Receipt is hereby acknowledged of the affidavits of Sophie Cobb and Sampson
Cobb to the birth of Luema[sic] Cobb, daughter of Sampson and Sophie Cobb, December

28, 1904, and the same have been filed with our records as an application for the enrollment of said child.

Respectfully,

Chairman.

7--NB--990

Muskogee, Indian Territory, June 3, 1905.

Sampson Cobb,
Bethel, Indian Territory.

Dear Sir:

Referring to the application for the enrollment of your infant child, Luema[sic] Cobb, it is noted that you attended upon your wife at the time of the birth of the applicant.

In this event it will be necessary that the affidavits of two persons, who are disinterested and not related to the applicant, who have actual knowledge of the facts that the child was born, the date of her birth; that she was living on March 4, 1905, and that Sophie Cobb is her mother be filed in this office. For this purpose there are enclosed you herewith blank affidavits.

It also appears from the affidavits heretofore filed with the Commission that this child was born on December 28[sic], but the year of birth is not given. For the purpose of securing the correct date of the birth of this applicant there is enclosed herewith affidavit to be executed by the mother. In the enclosed affidavits the date of birth has been left blank and you are requested to insert correct date and when affidavits have been properly executed return to this office.

In having the affidavits executed care should be exercised to see that all names are written in full, as they appear in the body of the affidavits and in the event that either of the persons signing same are unable to write, signatures by mark must be attested by two witnesses. Each affidavit must be executed before a Notary Public and the notarial seal and signature of the officer must be attached to each separate affidavit.

This matter should receive your immediate attention as no further action can be taken relative to the enrollment of said child until the Commission has been furnished these affidavits.

Respectfully,

Commissioner in Charge.

FVK-27

Choctaw N B 990

Muskogee, Indian Territory, June 28, 1905.

Sampson Cobb,
      Bethel, Indian Territory.

Dear Sir:

Receipt is hereby acknowledged of the affidavit of Sophie Cobb and joint affidavit of David Dyer, Jr. and Sarah Stephens to the birth of Louena Cobb, daughter of Sampson and Sophie Cobb, and the same have been filed with our records in the matter of the enrollment of said child.

The name of the child appears as Louena Cobb in the affidavits above referred to while in your affidavit and the affidavit of Sophie Cobb, executed April 3, 1905, the name appears as Luema Cobb. You are therefore requested to state which is the correct name of this child, and whether you desire to have her enrolled as Louena or Luema Cobb. Please give this matter your immediate attention, forwarding your reply in the inclosed envelope.

      Respectfully,

            Chairman.

7-NB-990

Muskogee, Indian Territory, July 25, 1905.

Sampson Cobb,
      Noah, Indian Territory.

Dear Sir:

Receipt is hereby acknowledged of your letter of July 14, 1905, in which you state that the correct name of your child is Lorena Cobb.

This information has been made a part of the record in the matter of the application for the enrollment of your child Lorena Cobb as a citizen by blood of the Choctaw Nation.

      Respectfully,

            Commissioner.

(The letter below typed as given.)

7/15   05

Comisner at Muskogee, I T

Dear sir your of June 28 at hend contents noted

My Daughters name

is Louena

your truley

Sampson cobb
Noah I T

(The letter below typed as given.)

7/16/05

Comisner at Muskogee, I.T.

Dear sir our of June 28 at hand contents noted

my daughter name is Lorena

yours truly

Sampson Cobb

Noah, I.T.

BIRTH AFFIDAVIT.

DEPARTMENT OF THE INTERIOR.
COMMISSION TO THE FIVE CIVILIZED TRIBES.

IN RE APPLICATION FOR ENROLLMENT, as a citizen of the   Choctaw   Nation, of
Luema Cobb   , born on the   28[sic]   day of   December   , 1904

Name of Father: Sampson Cobb   a citizen of the   Choctaw   Nation.
Name of Mother: Sophie Cobb   a citizen of the   Choctaw   Nation.

Postoffice   Bethel Ind Teritary[sic]

Applications for Enrollment of Choctaw Newborn
Act of 1905   Volume XIV

AFFIDAVIT OF MOTHER.

UNITED STATES OF AMERICA, Indian Territory, ⎱
.... DISTRICT. ⎰

I,   Sophie Cobb   , on oath state that I am   about 30   years of age and a citizen by   blood   , of the   Choctaw   Nation; that I am the lawful wife of Sampson Cobb   , who is a citizen, by Blood   of the   Choctaw   Nation; that a   Female   child was born to me on   28   day of   December   , 1904; that said child has been named   Luema Cobb   , and was living March 4, 1905.

Witnesses To Mark:
⎰ Paul Stephens Noah IT
⎱ *(Name Illegible)*

Sophie x Cobb
her mark

Subscribed and sworn to before me this 3   day of   April   , 1905

J H Matthews
Notary Public.

AFFIDAVIT OF ATTENDING PHYSICIAN OR MID-WIFE.

UNITED STATES OF AMERICA, Indian Territory, ⎱
.... DISTRICT. ⎰

I,   Sampson Cobb   , a ...., on oath state that I attended on Mrs.   Sophie Cobb   , wife of   Sampson Cobb   on the   28   day of   December, 1904; that there was born to her on said date a   Female   child; that said child was living March 4, 1905, and is said to have been named   Luema Cobb

Witnesses To Mark:
⎰ Paul Stephens Noah IT
⎱ Lymon Starnes Noah I.T.

Sampson x Cobb
his mark

Subscribed and sworn to before me this 3   day of   April   , 1905

J H Matthews
Notary Public.

Applications for Enrollment of Choctaw Newborn
Act of 1905   Volume XIV

DEPARTMENT OF THE INTERIOR.
COMMISSION TO THE FIVE CIVILIZED TRIBES.

IN RE APPLICATION FOR ENROLLMENT, as a citizen of the   Choctaw   Nation, of
Louena Cobb   , born on the   23   day of   December   , 1904

Name of Father: Sampson Cobb Roll 1716   a citizen of the   Choctaw   Nation.
Name of Mother: Sophie Cobb Roll 1717   a citizen of the   Choctaw   Nation.

Postoffice   Bethel I.T.

AFFIDAVIT OF MOTHER.

UNITED STATES OF AMERICA, Indian Territory, }
Central   DISTRICT. ⌡

I,   Sophie Cobb   , on oath state that I am   about 30   years of age and a
citizen by   blood   , of the   Choctaw   Nation; that I am the lawful wife of
Sampson Cobb   , who is a citizen, by blood   of the   Choctaw   Nation;
that a   female   child was born to me on   23   day of   December   , 1904; that
said child has been named   Louena Cobb   , and was living March 4, 1905.

Sophie x Cobb
Witnesses To Mark: her mark
⌠ David Dyer Jr Hochatown I.T.
⌡ R S Allen Mena Ark

Subscribed and sworn to before me this 23   day of   June   , 1905

J H Matthews
Notary Public.

AFFIDAVIT OF ATTENDING PHYSICIAN OR MID-WIFE.

UNITED STATES OF AMERICA, Indian Territory, }
Central   DISTRICT. ⌡

am acquainted with
I,................................., a ...., on oath state that I ~~attended on~~
Mrs.   Sophie Cobb   , wife of   Sampson Cobb   *and that on or about* the 23   day
of   December, 1904; that there was born to her on said date a   female   child; that
said child was living March 4, 1905, and is said to have been named   Louena Cobb *and*
that I am not related to the parents of said child

98

David Dyer Jr Hochatown IT
her
Witnesses To Mark: Sarah x Stephens Noah I.T.
  ⎰ David Dyer Jr   mark
  ⎱ JH Matthews

Subscribed and sworn to before me this 23   day of   June   , 1905

J H Matthews
Notary Public.

Choc New Born 991
     Andy C. Beal   b. 5-13-04

_____

7-3560

Muskogee, Indian Territory, April 17, 1905.

Andy P. Beal,
    Utica, Indian Territory.

Dear Sir:

    Receipt is hereby acknowledged of the affidavits of F. B. Beal and A. J. Wells to the birth of Andy C. Beal, son of Andy P. Beal and F. B. Beal, May 13, 1904, and the same have been filed with our records as an application for the enrollment of said child.

Respectfully,

Chairman.

_____

7--NB--991

Muskogee, Indian Territory, June 2, 1905.

Andrew P. Beal,
    Utica, Indian Territory.

Dear Sir:

There is enclosed you herewith for execution affidavit in support of the application for the enrollment of your infant child, Andy C. Beal.

In the affidavit of the mother of this applicant executed April 10, 1905, it is shown that the applicant was born May 13, 1904, while in the affidavit of attending physician dated April 10, 1905, the date of the birth of this child is not given. In the enclosed affidavit the date of birth has been left blank. Please insert the correct date of birth and when the affidavit has been properly executed return to this office.

In having the affidavit executed care should be exercised to see that all names are written in full, as they appear in the body of the affidavit and in the event that the person signing the same is unable to write, signature by mark must be attested by two witnesses. The affidavit must be executed before a Notary Public and the notarial seal and signature of the officer must be attached thereto.

This matter should receive your immediate attention as no further action can be taken relative to the enrollment of said child until the Commission has been furnished this affidavit.

Respectfully,

Commissioner in Charge.

Enc-FVK-17

---

7 NB 991

Muskogee, Indian Territory, June 20, 1905.

Andrew P. Beal,
    Utica, Indian Territory.

Dear Sir:

Receipt is hereby acknowledged of the affidavits of F. B. Beal and A. J. Wells to the birth of Andy C. Beal, son of Andrew P. and F. B. Beal, May 13, 1904, and the same have been filed with our records in the matter of the enrollment of said child.

Respectfully,

Chairman.

NEW-BORN AFFIDAVIT.

Number...............

Choctaw Enrolling Commission.

IN THE MATTER OF THE APPLICATION FOR ENROLLMENT, as a citizen of the Choctaw   Nation, of   Andy Claude Beal

born on the   13th   day of   May   190 4

Name of father   Andrew P. Beal   a citizen of   Choctaw
Nation final enrollment No   10095
Name of mother   Fernandy B. Beal   a citizen of   white
Nation final enrollment No ——

Postoffice   Utica I.T.

AFFIDAVIT OF MOTHER.

UNITED STATES OF AMERICA, ⎫
   INDIAN TERRITORY,   ⎬
   Central   DISTRICT   ⎭

   I   Fernandy B. Beal   on oath state that I
am 39 years of age and a citizen by   white   of the ——— Nation, and as such have
been placed upon the final roll of the   ———   Nation, by the Honorable Secretary of the
Interior my final enrollment number being — ; that I am the lawful wife of   Andrew P Beal,
who is a citizen of the   Choctaw   Nation, and as such has been placed upon the final
roll of said Nation by the Honorable Secretary of the Interior, his final enrollment number
being 10095   and that a   male   child was born to me on the   13th   day of   May
190 4 ; that said child has been named   Andy Claude Beal   , and is now living.

WITNESSETH: F. B. Beal
   Must be two ⎫ Pinkney Beal
   Witnesses who ⎬
   are Citizens. ⎭ Reuben Beal

        Subscribed and sworn to before me this   14th   day of   Jan   190 5

                                W A Shoney
                                      Notary Public.
My commission expires ....

101

Affidavit of Attending Physician or Midwife

UNITED STATES OF AMERICA, ⎫
   INDIAN TERRITORY, ⎬
Central   DISTRICT ⎭

I, A. J. Wells   a   Physician
on oath state that I attended on Mrs. F. B. Beal   wife of   Andrew P. Beal
on the 13th day of May , 190 4, that there was born to her on said date a male child,
that said child is now living, and is said to have been named Andy Claude Beal

A.J. Wells   M. D.

Subscribed and sworn to before me this the 16 day of January   1905

P.L. Cain
Notary Public.

WITNESSETH:
Must be two witnesses ⎰ Thomas T Beal
who are citizens and ⎱
know the child.   Pinkney Beal

    We hereby certify that we are well acquainted with   A.J. Wells
a   physician   and know him   to be reputable and of good standing in the
community.

Must be two citizen ⎰ Thomas T Beal
witnesses.   ⎱ Pinkney Beal

BIRTH AFFIDAVIT.

DEPARTMENT OF THE INTERIOR.
COMMISSION TO THE FIVE CIVILIZED TRIBES.

IN RE APPLICATION FOR ENROLLMENT, as a citizen of the   Choctaw   Nation, of
Andy C. Beal   , born on the 13th day of May , 1904

Name of Father: Andy P. Beal   a citizen of the Choctaw Nation.
Name of Mother: F. B. Beal   a citizen of the   —— Nation.

Postoffice   Utica I.T.

Applications for Enrollment of Choctaw Newborn
Act of 1905   Volume XIV

AFFIDAVIT OF MOTHER.

UNITED STATES OF AMERICA, Indian Territory, ⎱
   Central   DISTRICT. ⎰

I,   F. B. Beal   , on oath state that I am 39   years of age and a citizen by ——— , of the   ———Nation; that I am the lawful wife of   Andy P. Beal   , who is a citizen, by Blood   of the   Choctaw   Nation; that a   Male   child was born to me on 13th day of May   , 1904; that said child has been named Andy C. Beal   , and was living March 4, 1905.

F. B. Beal

Witnesses To Mark:
{

Subscribed and sworn to before me this 10th day of April   , 1905

W.J. O'Donby
Notary Public.

AFFIDAVIT OF ATTENDING PHYSICIAN OR MID-WIFE.

UNITED STATES OF AMERICA, Indian Territory, ⎱
   Central   DISTRICT. ⎰

I,   A.J. Wells   , a Physician   , on oath state that I attended on Mrs. F. B. Beal   , wife of Andy P Beal on the 13th day of May , 1.......; that there was born to her on said date a Male child; that said child was living March 4, 1905, and is said to have been named Andy C. Beal

A.J. Wells M.D.

Witnesses To Mark:
{

Subscribed and sworn to before me this 10th day of April   , 1905

W.J. O'Donby
Notary Public.

103

BIRTH AFFIDAVIT.

DEPARTMENT OF THE INTERIOR.
COMMISSION TO THE FIVE CIVILIZED TRIBES.

_____

IN RE APPLICATION FOR ENROLLMENT, as a citizen of the   Choctaw   Nation, of
Andy C. Beal   , born on the 13ᵗʰ   day of   May , 1904

Name of Father: Andrew P. Beal   R 10095   a citizen of the   Choctaw   Nation.
Name of Mother: F. B. Beal   a citizen of the   non citizen Nation.

Postoffice   Utica I.T.

_____

AFFIDAVIT OF ATTENDING PHYSICIAN OR MID-WIFE.

UNITED STATES OF AMERICA, Indian Territory, ⎫
....DISTRICT. ⎭

I,   A.J. Wells   , a   Physician   , on oath state that I attended on
Mrs.   F. B. Beal   , wife of   Andrew P Beal   on the 13ᵗʰ   day of   May   ,
1......; that there was born to her on said date a   Male   child; that said child was living
March 4, 1905, and is said to have been named Andy C. Beal

A.J. Wells M.D.

Witnesses To Mark:

{

Subscribed and sworn to before me this 15ᵗʰ   day of   June   , 1905

W.J. O'Donby
Notary Public.

_____

BIRTH AFFIDAVIT.

DEPARTMENT OF THE INTERIOR.
COMMISSION TO THE FIVE CIVILIZED TRIBES.

_____

IN RE APPLICATION FOR ENROLLMENT, as a citizen of the   Choctaw   Nation, of
Andy C. Beal   , born on the 13ᵗʰ   day of   May , 1904

Name of Father: Andrew P. Beal   a citizen of the   Choctaw   Nation.
Name of Mother: F. B. Beal   a citizen of the   non citizen Nation.

Postoffice ....

_____

104

Applications for Enrollment of Choctaw Newborn
Act of 1905   Volume XIV

AFFIDAVIT OF MOTHER.

UNITED STATES OF AMERICA, Indian Territory,
Central   DISTRICT.

I,   F. B. Beal   , on oath state that I am 39   years of age and a citizen by non citizen , of the .... Nation; that I am the lawful wife of   Andrew P. Beal   , who is a citizen, by Blood   of the   Choctaw   Nation; that a Male   child was born to me on 13th day of   May   , 1904; that said child has been named   Andy C. Beal   , and was living March 4, 1905.

F. B. Beal

Witnesses To Mark:

Subscribed and sworn to before me this 15th day of   June   , 1905

W.J. O'Donby
Notary Public.

AFFIDAVIT OF ATTENDING PHYSICIAN OR MID-WIFE.

UNITED STATES OF AMERICA, Indian Territory,
Central   DISTRICT.

I,   A.J. Wells   , a   Physician   , on oath state that I attended on Mrs.   F. B. Beal   , wife of   Andrew P Beal   on the 13th day of   May   , 1.......; that there was born to her on said date a   Male   child; that said child was living March 4, 1905, and is said to have been named   Andy C. Beal

A.J. Wells M.D.

Witnesses To Mark:

Subscribed and sworn to before me this 15th day of   June   , 1905

W.J. O'Donby
Notary Public.

Applications for Enrollment of Choctaw Newborn
Act of 1905   Volume XIV

Choc New Born 992
  Leroy Burney   b, 9-13-03

7-2196

Muskogee, Indian Territory, April 17, 1905.

Alfred Burney,
  Allison, Indian Territory.

Dear Sir:

Receipt is hereby acknowledged of the affidavits of Sarah Burney and L. D. Jones to the birth of Leroy Burney, son of Alfred and Sarah Burney, September 13, 1903, and the same have been filed with our records as an application for the enrollment of said child.

Respectfully,

Chairman.

BIRTH AFFIDAVIT.
DEPARTMENT OF THE INTERIOR.
COMMISSION TO THE FIVE CIVILIZED TRIBES.

IN RE APPLICATION FOR ENROLLMENT, as a citizen of the   Choctaw   Nation, of
Leroy Burney   , born on the 13th day of   September   , 1903

Name of Father: Alfred Burney   a citizen of the   Choctaw   Nation.
Name of Mother: Sarah Burney   a citizen of the   Choctaw   Nation.

Postoffice   Alison[sic] IT

AFFIDAVIT OF MOTHER.

UNITED STATES OF AMERICA, Indian Territory, ⎱
  Central   **DISTRICT.** ⎰

I,   Sarah Burney   , on oath state that I am   21   years of age and a citizen by blood   , of the   Choctaw   Nation; that I am the lawful wife of   Alfred Burney   , who is a citizen, by blood   of the   Choctaw   Nation; that a   male   child was born to me on   13th day of   September   , 1903; that said child has been named Leroy Burney   , and was living March 4, 1905.

Sarah Burney

Witnesses To Mark:

{

Subscribed and sworn to before me this 12th   day of   April   , 1905

B.F. Moreman
My commission expires   Notary Public.
on Nov. 11th 1907.

AFFIDAVIT OF ATTENDING PHYSICIAN OR MID-WIFE.

UNITED STATES OF AMERICA, Indian Territory, ⎫
   Central   **DISTRICT.** ⎰

   I,   L D Jones   , a Physician   , on oath state that I attended on
Mrs.   Sarah Burney   , wife of   Alfred Burney   on the   13th day of
September   , 1903; that there was born to her on said date a   male   child; that said
child was living March 4, 1905, and is said to have been named Leroy

L D Jones M.D.

Witnesses To Mark:

{

Subscribed and sworn to before me this 1st   day of   April   , 1905

My commission expires Jan. 4, 1908
Commission from U.S. Court, So. McAlester I.T.   CA Welch
MY OFFICE TALIHINA, I.T.   Notary Public.

Choc New Born 993
        Mabel Puckett
              born Dec 30, 1903

Affidavit of Attending Physician or Midwife

UNITED STATES OF AMERICA, ⎤
   INDIAN TERRITORY,   ⎬
   Central   DISTRICT   ⎦

   I,   A. J. Wells   a   Physician
on oath state that I attended on Mrs. Liddy Puckett   wife of William Puckett
on the   30th day of   December , 190 3, that there was born to her on said date a   Female
child, that said child is now living, and is said to have been named Mable[sic] Puckett

107

A.J. Wells   M. D.

Subscribed and sworn to before me this the   22   day of   Feb   1905

W.J. O'Donby
Notary Public.

WITNESSETH:

Must be two witnesses
who are citizens and
know the child.
{ Sidney G Hogan

  Abner W Willis

We hereby certify that we are well acquainted with   A. J. Wells
a   Physician   and know   him   to be reputable and of good standing in the community.

Must be two citizen{ Sidney G Hogan
witnesses.   Abner W Willis

BIRTH AFFIDAVIT.

DEPARTMENT OF THE INTERIOR.
COMMISSION TO THE FIVE CIVILIZED TRIBES.

IN RE APPLICATION FOR ENROLLMENT, as a citizen of the   Choctaw   Nation, of
Mabel Puckett   , born on the   30   day of   December   , 1903

Name of Father: William Puckett   a citizen of the   Choctaw   Nation.
Name of Mother: Liddy Puckett   a citizen of the   Choctaw   Nation.

Postoffice   Blue Ind Ter

AFFIDAVIT OF MOTHER.

UNITED STATES OF AMERICA, Indian Territory, ⎤
    Central   DISTRICT. ⎦

I, Liddy Puckett   , on oath state that I am   21   years of age and a citizen by
Intermarriage   , of the   Choctaw   Nation; that I am the lawful wife of   William
Puckett   , who is a citizen, by Blood   of the   Choctaw   Nation; that a
Female   child was born to me on   30   day of   December   , 1903; that said child
has been named   Mabel   , and was living March 4, 1905.

Liddy Puckett

Witnesses To Mark:
{

108

Subscribed and sworn to before me this   12   day of   April   , 1905

J M Routh
Notary Public.

AFFIDAVIT OF ATTENDING PHYSICIAN OR MID-WIFE.

UNITED STATES OF AMERICA, Indian Territory, ⎫
   Central   DISTRICT. ⎭

I,   Martha Hendrix   , a   midwife   , on oath state that I attended on Mrs.   Liddy Puckett   , wife of   William Puckett   on the   30   day of December, 1903; that there was born to her on said date a   Female   child; that said child was living March 4, 1905, and is said to have been named   Mabel

Martha Hendrix

Witnesses To Mark:
   {

Subscribed and sworn to before me this   12   day of   April   , 1905

J M Routh
Notary Public.

NEW BORN AFFIDAVIT

No ....

CHOCTAW ENROLLING COMMISSION

IN THE MATTER OF THE APPLICATION FOR ENROLLMENT as a citizen of the Choctaw Nation, of   Mable Puckett   born on the   30th   day of   December   190 3

Name of father   William Puckett   a citizen of   Choctaw   Nation, final enrollment No.   10942

Name of mother   Liddy Puckett   a citizen of   InterMarriage   Nation, final enrollment No.   1007

Blue I.T.   Postoffice.

AFFIDAVIT OF MOTHER

UNITED STATES OF AMERICA   ⎫
    INDIAN TERRITORY   ⎬
DISTRICT   Central   ⎭

    I   Liddy Puckett   , on oath state that I am   21   years of age and a citizen by   marriage   of the   Choctaw   Nation, and as such have been placed upon the final roll of the   Choctaw   Nation, by the Honorable Secretary of the Interior my final enrollment number being   1007   ; that I am the lawful wife of   William Puckett   , who is a citizen of the   Choctaw   Nation, and as such has been placed upon the final roll of said Nation by the Honorable Secretary of the Interior, his final enrollment number being   10942   and that a   Female   child was born to me on the   30th   day of December   190 3; that said child has been named   Mable Puckett   , and is now living.

WITNESSETH: Liddy Puckett

    Must be two witnesses ⎰   Sidney G Hogan
    who are citizens   ⎱   Abner W Willis

    Subscribed and sworn to before me this, the   22nd   day of   Feb   , 190 5

                          W J ODonby
                               Notary Public.
My Commission Expires: Dec 17th 1905

                                     7-3884

           Muskogee, Indian Territory, April 17, 1905.

William Puckett,
         Blue, Indian Territory.

Dear Sir:

       Receipt is hereby acknowledged of the affidavits of Liddy Puckett and Martha Hendrix to the birth of Mabel Puckett, daughter of William and Liddy Puckett, December 30, 1903, and the same have been filed with our records as an application for the enrollment of said child.

                       Respectfully,

                            Chairman.

Choc New Born 994
Ruth Shields Downing   b.   9-27-04

NEW BORN AFFIDAVIT

No ....

CHOCTAW ENROLLING COMMISSION

IN THE MATTER OF THE APPLICATION FOR ENROLLMENT as a citizen of the Choctaw
Nation, of   Ruth Shields Downing   born on the 27 day
of   September   190 4

Name of father   Sam Downing   a citizen of   Choctaw   Nation,
final enrollment No. 14068
Name of mother   Maud Downing   a citizen of   Choctaw   Nation,
final enrollment No. 527

Atoka I.T.   Postoffice.

AFFIDAVIT OF MOTHER

UNITED STATES OF AMERICA ⎫
   INDIAN TERRITORY ⎬
DISTRICT   Central ⎭

  I   Maud Downing   , on oath state that I am   32   years of age and a
citizen by   marriage   of the   Choctaw   Nation, and as such have been placed
upon the final roll of the   Choctaw   Nation, by the Honorable Secretary of the Interior my
final enrollment number being   527   ; that I am the lawful wife of   Sam Downing   ,
who is a citizen of the   Choctaw   Nation, and as such has been placed upon the final
roll of said Nation by the Honorable Secretary of the Interior, his final enrollment number
being   14068   and that a   Female   child was born to me on the   27th   day of
September   190 4; that said child has been named   Ruth Shields Downing   , and is now
living.

                              Maud Downing

WITNESSETH:
Must be two witnesses ⎰ W.F. Rogers
  who are citizens   ⎱ J H McGahey

Subscribed and sworn to before me this, the 21st day of February   , 190 5

A.E. Folsom
Notary Public.

My Commission Expires:
Jan 9-1909

Affidavit of Attending Physician or Midwife

UNITED STATES OF AMERICA, ⎫
    INDIAN TERRITORY,   ⎬
Central   DISTRICT   ⎭

I,   J.S. Fulton   a   Practicing Physician
on oath state that I attended on Mrs. Maud Downing   wife of Sam Downing
on the   27th   day of   September , 190 4, that there was born to her on said date a
Female   child, that said child is now living, and is said to have been named   Ruth Shields
Downing

J.S. Fulton   M. D.

Subscribed and sworn to before me this the   21st   day of   February   1905

A.E. Folsom
Notary Public.

WITNESSETH:

Must be two witnesses ⎧ W.F. Rogers
who are citizens and ⎨
know the child.   ⎩ J H McGahey

We hereby certify that we are well acquainted with   Dr J.S. Fulton
a   Practicing Physician   and know   him   to be reputable and of good standing in
the community.

Must be two citizen⎧ W.F. Rogers
witnesses.   ⎩ J.H. McGahey

112

BIRTH AFFIDAVIT.

DEPARTMENT OF THE INTERIOR.
COMMISSION TO THE FIVE CIVILIZED TRIBES.

IN RE APPLICATION FOR ENROLLMENT, as a citizen of the   Choctaw   Nation, of
Ruth Shields Downing   , born on the 27th day of   September , 1904

Name of Father: Sam Downing   a citizen of the   Choctaw   Nation.
Name of Mother: Maud Downing   a citizen of the   Choctaw   Nation.

Postoffice   Atoka, I T

AFFIDAVIT OF MOTHER.

UNITED STATES OF AMERICA, Indian Territory, ⎫
    Central   **DISTRICT.** ⎭

    I,   Maud Downing   , on oath state that I am   32   years of age and a citizen
by   intermarriage   , of the   Choctaw   Nation; that I am the lawful wife of Sam
Downing   , who is a citizen, by blood   of the   Choctaw   Nation; that a
female   child was born to me on 27th day of   September   , 1904; that said
child has been named   Ruth Shields Downing   , and was living March 4, 1905.

Maud Downing

Witnesses To Mark:

{

Subscribed and sworn to before me this 31st day of   March   , 1905

W.H. Angell
Notary Public.

AFFIDAVIT OF ATTENDING PHYSICIAN OR MID-WIFE.

UNITED STATES OF AMERICA, Indian Territory, ⎫
    Central   **DISTRICT.** ⎭

    I,   J. S. Fulton   , a physician   , on oath state that I attended on
Mrs.   Maud Downing   , wife of   Sam Downing   on the 27th day of
September   , 1904; that there was born to her on said date a   female   child; that
said child was living March 4, 1905, and is said to have been named Ruth Shields
Downing

J.S. Fulton

Witnesses To Mark:

{

Subscribed and sworn to before me this   13th   day of   April   , 1905

W.H. Angell
Notary Public.

Choc New Born 995
Sampson Stephen   b. 3-7-04

Choctaw 709.

Muskogee, Indian Territory, April 17, 1905.

Arion Stephen,
Noah, Indian Territory.

Dear Madam:

Receipt is hereby acknowledged of the affidavits of Arion Stephen and Margaret Frazier to the birth of Sampson Stephen, son of Arion Stephen, March 7, 1904, and the same have been filed with our records as an application for the enrollment of said child.

Respectfully,

Chairman.

BIRTH AFFIDAVIT.

DEPARTMENT OF THE INTERIOR.
COMMISSION TO THE FIVE CIVILIZED TRIBES.

IN RE APPLICATION FOR ENROLLMENT, as a citizen of the   Choctaw   Nation, of
Sampson Stephen   , born on the 7th   day of   March   , 1904

Name of Father: Not known   a citizen of the   ———   Nation.
Name of Mother: Arion Stephen   a citizen of the   Choctaw   Nation.

Postoffice   Noah, Ind. Ter.

114

AFFIDAVIT OF MOTHER.

UNITED STATES OF AMERICA, Indian Territory, ⎫
Central   DISTRICT. ⎭

I,   Arion Stephen   , on oath state that I am   16   years of age and a citizen by   blood   , of the   Choctaw   Nation; that I am the lawful wife of   ————, who is a citizen, by ——— of the ——— Nation; that a   male   child was born to me on   7th   day of   March   , 1904; that said child has been named   Sampson Stephen   , and was living March 4, 1905.

Witnesses To Mark:
⎰ *(Name Illegible)* Noah IT
⎱ *(Name Illegible)* Noah I.T.

Arion x Stephen
her mark

Subscribed and sworn to before me this   8 day of   April   , 1905

J H Matthews   Bethel I.T.
Notary Public.

AFFIDAVIT OF ATTENDING PHYSICIAN OR MID-WIFE.

UNITED STATES OF AMERICA, Indian Territory, ⎫
Central   DISTRICT. ⎭

I,   Margaret Frazier   Noah IT , a   mid-wife   , on oath state that I attended on ~~Mrs.~~   Arion Stephen   , wife of   ———   on the   7th   day of   March   , 1904; that there was born to her on said date a   male   child; that said child was living March 4, 1905, and is said to have been named Sampson Stephen

Witnesses To Mark:
⎰ *(Name Illegible)* Noah IT
⎱ *(Name Illegible)* Noah I.T.

Margaret x Frazier Noah I.T.
her mark

Subscribed and sworn to before me this   8 day of   April   , 1905

J H Matthews   Bethel I.T.
Notary Public.

Choc New Born 996
Jordan Wilson   b. 1-29-03

Choctaw 1344.

Muskogee, Indian Territory, April 17, 1905.

Nelson Wilson,
Goodwater, Indian Territory.

Dear Sir:

Receipt is hereby acknowledged of the affidavits of Maggie Wilson and Elatema Wilson to the birth of Jordan Wilson, son of Nelson and Maggie Wilson, January 29, 1903, and the same have been filed with our records as an application for the enrollment of said child.

Respectfully,

Chairman.

NEW BORN AFFIDAVIT

No ....

CHOCTAW ENROLLING COMMISSION

IN THE MATTER OF THE APPLICATION FOR ENROLLMENT as a citizen of the Choctaw Nation, of   Jordan Wilson   born on the 29th day of   January   190 3

Name of father Nelson Wilson   a citizen of   Choctaw   Nation, final enrollment No. 3672

Name of mother   Maggie Wilson   a citizen of   Choctaw   Nation, final enrollment No.   702

Goodwater, I.T.   Postoffice.

Applications for Enrollment of Choctaw Newborn
Act of 1905   Volume XIV

AFFIDAVIT OF MOTHER

UNITED STATES OF AMERICA
   INDIAN TERRITORY
DISTRICT   Central

I   Maggie Wilson   , on oath state that I am 33   years of age and a citizen by Intermarriage   of the   Choctaw   Nation, and as such have been placed upon the final roll of the   Choctaw   Nation, by the Honorable Secretary of the Interior my final enrollment number being   702   ; that I am the lawful wife of   Nelson Wilson , who is a citizen of the   Choctaw   Nation, and as such has been placed upon the final roll of said Nation by the Honorable Secretary of the Interior, his final enrollment number being   3672   and that a   Male   child was born to me on the   29th day of   January   190 3; that said child has been named   Jordan Nelson[sic] , and is now living.

her
Maggie x Wilson
mark

WITNESSETH:

Must be two witnesses { Lonis Dyer
who are citizens   Arlington King

Subscribed and sworn to before me this, the 13th day of   March , 190 5

W.A. Shoney
Notary Public.

My Commission Expires: Jan 10, 1909

Affidavit of Attending Physician or Midwife

UNITED STATES OF AMERICA,
   INDIAN TERRITORY,
Central   DISTRICT

I,   Elatema Wilson   a   mid wife on oath state that I attended on Mrs. Maggie Wilson   wife of Nelson Wilson on the 29th   day of January , 190 3, that there was born to her on said date a   male child, that said child is now living, and is said to have been named   Jordan Nelson[sic]

Elatema Wilson   M. D.

Subscribed and sworn to before me this the 13th day of   March   1905

W.A. Shoney
Notary Public.

WITNESSETH:

Must be two witnesses { Lonis Dyer
who are citizens and
know the child.   Arlington King

117

Applications for Enrollment of Choctaw Newborn
Act of 1905   Volume XIV

We hereby certify that we are well acquainted with   Elatema Wilson
a   midwife   and know   her   to be reputable and of good standing in the community.

Must be two citizen⌠   Lonis Dyer
witnesses.   ⌡   Arlington King

BIRTH AFFIDAVIT.

DEPARTMENT OF THE INTERIOR.
COMMISSION TO THE FIVE CIVILIZED TRIBES.

IN RE APPLICATION FOR ENROLLMENT, as a citizen of the   Choctaw   Nation, of
Jordan Wilson   , born on the 29 day of Jan , 1903

Name of Father: Nelson Wilson   a citizen of the   Choctaw   Nation.
Name of Mother: Maggie Wilson   a citizen of the   Choctaw   Nation.

Postoffice   Goodwater I.T.

AFFIDAVIT OF MOTHER.

UNITED STATES OF AMERICA, Indian Territory, ⎞
     Central   DISTRICT. ⎠

I, Maggie Wilson   , on oath state that I am 33   years of age and a citizen
by   Intermarriage   , of the   Choctaw   Nation; that I am the lawful wife of
Nelson Wilson   , who is a citizen, by Blood   of the   Choctaw   Nation;
that a   male   child was born to me on 29th day of   January   , 1903; that said
child has been named   Jordan Wilson   , and was living March 4, 1905.

her
Maggie x Wilson
Witnesses To Mark: mark
   ⌠ L.G. Battiest
   ⌡ Daniel Jefferson

Subscribed and sworn to before me this 10th day of April   , 1905

(Name Illegible)
Notary Public.

118

Applications for Enrollment of Choctaw Newborn
Act of 1905   Volume XIV

AFFIDAVIT OF ATTENDING PHYSICIAN OR MID-WIFE.

UNITED STATES OF AMERICA, Indian Territory, ⎫
  Central   DISTRICT. ⎭

I,   Elatema Wilson   , a   mid-wife   , on oath state that I attended on
Mrs.   Maggie Wilson   , wife of   Nelson Wilson   on the   29   day of   January ,
1903; that there was born to her on said date a   male   child; that said child was living
March 4, 1905, and is said to have been named   Jordan Wilson

                                                        her
                                        Elatema x Wilson
Witnesses To Mark: mark
  ⎧ L.G. Battiest
  ⎩ Daniel Jefferson

Subscribed and sworn to before me this 10ᵗʰ   day of   April   , 1905

                              (Name Illegible)
                              Notary Public.

Choc New Born 997
        Myrtle Sexton b. 3-1-03
        Pearl Sexton b. 2-16-05

                                            Choctaw 2350.

                    Muskogee, Indian Territory, April 17, 1905.

Henry Sexton,
        Summerfield, Indian Territory.

Dear Sir:

        Receipt is hereby acknowledged of the affidavits of Minnie Sexton and Emma
Halcomb to the birth of Myrtle Sexton; also the affidavits of Minnie Sexton and Dr. A. R.
Sisk to the birth of Pearl Sexton, daughters of Henry and Minnie Sexton, March 1, 1903
and February 16, 1905, respectively, and the same have been filed with our records as
applications for the enrollment of said children.

                        Respectfully,

                                        Chairman.

Applications for Enrollment of Choctaw Newborn
Act of 1905 Volume XIV

BIRTH AFFIDAVIT.

DEPARTMENT OF THE INTERIOR.
COMMISSION TO THE FIVE CIVILIZED TRIBES.

IN RE APPLICATION FOR ENROLLMENT, as a citizen of the   Choctaw   Nation, of
Myrtle Sexton   , born on the 1 day of March , 1903

Name of Father: Henry Sexton   a citizen of the   Choctaw   Nation.
Name of Mother: Minnie Sexton   a citizen of the   Choctaw   Nation.

Postoffice   Summerfield I.T.

AFFIDAVIT OF MOTHER.

UNITED STATES OF AMERICA, Indian Territory, }
     Central   DISTRICT. }

I,   Minnie Sexton   , on oath state that I am   22   years of age and a citizen
by   blood   , of the   Choctaw   Nation; that I am the lawful wife of   Henry
Sexton   , who is a citizen, by   blood   of the   Choctaw   Nation; that a
female   child was born to me on 1   day of   March   , 1903; that said child has
been named   Myrtle Sexton   , and was living March 4, 1905.

                                        her
                              Minnie x Sexton
Witnesses To Mark: mark
  { H.B. Mullens
  { S. Griffin

Subscribed and sworn to before me this 8   day of   April   , 1905

                              Robert E Lee
                              Notary Public.
My com expires Jan 11-1906

AFFIDAVIT OF ATTENDING PHYSICIAN OR MID-WIFE.

UNITED STATES OF AMERICA, Indian Territory, }
     Central   DISTRICT. }

I,   Emma Holcomb[sic]   , a nurse   , on oath state that I attended on
Mrs.   Minnie Sexton   , wife of   Henry Sexton   on the 1 day of   March   ,
1903; that there was born to her on said date a   female   child; that said child was
living March 4, 1905, and is said to have been named   Myrtle Sexton

120

Emma Halcomb

Witnesses To Mark:

{

Subscribed and sworn to before me this 8 day of   April   , 1905

Robert E Lee
Notary Public.

My com expires Jan 11-1906

Final enrollment No of Henry Sexton being No: 6803
Final enrollment No of Minnie Sexton being No: 15574

BIRTH AFFIDAVIT.

DEPARTMENT OF THE INTERIOR.
COMMISSION TO THE FIVE CIVILIZED TRIBES.

IN RE APPLICATION FOR ENROLLMENT, as a citizen of the   Choctaw   Nation, of
Pearl Sexton   , born on the 16 day of Feb , 1905

Name of Father: Henry Sexton   a citizen of the   Choctaw   Nation.
Name of Mother: Minny[sic] Sexton   a citizen of the   Choctaw   Nation.

Postoffice   Summerfield I.T.

AFFIDAVIT OF MOTHER.

UNITED STATES OF AMERICA, Indian Territory, }
Central   DISTRICT. }

I,   Minny Sexton   , on oath state that I am   22   years of age and a citizen
by   blood   , of the   Choctaw   Nation; that I am the lawful wife of   Henry
Sexton   , who is a citizen, by blood   of the   Choctaw   Nation; that a
female   child was born to me on 16   day of February   , 1905; that said child
has been named Pearl Sexton   , and was living March 4, 1905.

her
Minnie x Sexton
mark

Witnesses To Mark:
{ Oscar Davis
{ M.M. Owens

121

Subscribed and sworn to before me this 8   day of   April   , 1905

                                        Robert E Lee
                                        Notary Public.

My com expires Jan 11-1906

AFFIDAVIT OF ATTENDING PHYSICIAN OR MID-WIFE.

UNITED STATES OF AMERICA, Indian Territory, ⎱
Central   **DISTRICT.** ⎰

I,   A R Sisk   , a physician   , on oath state that I attended on
Mrs.   Minny Sexton   , wife of   Henry Sexton   on the 16   day of   February   ,
1905; that there was born to her on said date a   female   child; that said child was
living March 4, 1905, and is said to have been named Pearl Sexton

                                        Dr. A. R. Sisk
Witnesses To Mark:

    {

    Subscribed and sworn to before me this 8   day of   April   , 1905

                                        Robert E Lee
                                        Notary Public.

My com expires Jan 11-1906

Final enrollment No of Henry Sexton being No: 6803
Final enrollment No of Minnie Sexton being No: 15574

Choc New Born 998
    Thomas Gravitt   b. 1-2-03

Choctaw 3417.

Muskogee, Indian Territory, April 17, 1905.

John Gravitt,
      Caddo, Indian Territory.

Dear Sir:

      Receipt is hereby acknowledged of the affidavits of Maggie Gravitt and W. R. Bowman to the birth of Thomas Gravitt, son of John and Maggie Gravitt, January 2, 1903, and the same have been filed with our records as an application for the enrollment of said child.

                Respectfully,

                              Chairman.

7--NB--998

Muskogee, Indian Territory, June 2, 1905.

John Gravitt,
      Caddo, Indian Territory.

Dear Sir:

      There is enclosed you herewith for execution application for the enrollment of your infant child, Thomas Gravitt.

      In the affidavits executed February 7, 1905, the date of the applicant's birth is given as January 2, 1902, while in the affidavits under date of April 12, 1905, this date is given as January 2, 1903. In the enclosed application the date of birth has been left blank. Please insert the correct date of birth and when the affidavits are properly executed return same to this office.

      In having the enclosed affidavits executed care should be exercised to see that all names are written in full, as they appear in the body of the affidavits and in the event that either of the persons signing the affidavits are unable to write, signatures by mark must be attested by two witnesses. Each affidavit must be executed before a Notary Public and the notarial seal and signature of the officer must be attached to each separate affidavit.

      This matter should receive your immediate attention as no further action can be taken relative to the enrollment of said [sic] until the Commission has been furnished these affidavits.

123

Respectfully,

Commissioner in Charge.

Enc-FVK-18

_____

7-NB-998.

Muskogee, Indian Territory, June 10, 1905.

John Gravitt,
        Caddo, Indian Territory.

Dear Sir:

Receipt is hereby acknowledged of the affidavits of Maggie Gravitt and W. R. Bowman to the birth of Thomas Gravitt, son of John and Maggie Gravitt, January 2, 1902, and the same have been filed with our records in the matter of the enrollment of said child.

Respectfully,

Chairman.

_____

7 NB 998

Muskogee, Indian Territory, September 9, 1905.

C. H. Elting,
        Attorney at Law,
                Caddo, Indian Territory.

Dear Sir:

Replying to your letter of September 6, 1905, you are advised that on August 22, 1905, the Secretary of the Interior approved the enrollment of Thomas Gravitt as a citizen of the Choctaw Nation and the name of the child appears upon the final roll of new-born citizens by blood of the Choctaw Nation opposite number 1405.

The child is now entitled to an allotment and selection thereof should be made without delay at the land office for the nation in which the prospective allotment is located.

Respectfully,

Acting Commissioner.

_____

NEW BORN AFFIDAVIT

No ....

CHOCTAW ENROLLING COMMISSION

IN THE MATTER OF THE APPLICATION FOR ENROLLMENT as a citizen of the Choctaw
Nation, of   Thomas Gravitt   born on the 2" day
of   January   190 2

Name of father   John H Gravitt   a citizen of   ——   Nation,
final enrollment No. ——
Name of mother   Maggie Gravitt   a citizen of   Choctaw   Nation,
final enrollment No. 9748

Caddo I.T.   Postoffice.

AFFIDAVIT OF MOTHER

UNITED STATES OF AMERICA ⎫
     INDIAN TERRITORY   ⎬
DISTRICT   Central   ⎭

     I   Maggie Gravitt   , on oath state that I am   36   years of age and a
citizen by   blood   of the   Choctaw   Nation, and as such have been placed upon
the final roll of the   Choctaw   Nation, by the Honorable Secretary of the Interior my final
enrollment number being 9748   ; that I am the lawful wife of   John H Gravitt   , who
is a citizen of the   ——   Nation, and as such has been placed upon the final roll of said
Nation by the Honorable Secretary of the Interior, his final enrollment number being — and
that a   Male   child was born to me on the   2"   day of   January   190 2; that said child
has been named   Thomas Gravitt   , and is now living.

WITNESSETH: Maggie Gravitt
   Must be two witnesses ⎧ Chas Hill
   who are citizens   ⎩ Lena Jackson

     Subscribed and sworn to before me this, the 6th day of   February   , 190 5

                              A.E. Folsom
                                   Notary Public.
My Commission Expires:
   Jan 9-1909

Applications for Enrollment of Choctaw Newborn
Act of 1905   Volume XIV

Affidavit of Attending Physician or Midwife

UNITED STATES OF AMERICA, ⎫
    INDIAN TERRITORY, ⎬
  Central   DISTRICT ⎭

I,   W.R. Bowman   a   Practicing Physician
on oath state that I attended on Mrs.   Maggie Gravitt   wife of   John H Gravitt
on the 2"   day of   January , 190 2, that there was born to her on said date a   male   child,
that said child is now living, and is said to have been named   Thomas Gravitt

W.R. Bowman   M. D.

Subscribed and sworn to before me this the   6"   day of   February   1905

A.E. Folsom
Notary Public.

WITNESSETH:

Must be two witnesses ⎰ Chas Hill
who are citizens and ⎱
know the child.   Lena Jackson

We hereby certify that we are well acquainted with   W.R. Bowman
a   Physician   and know   him   to be reputable and of good standing in the
community.

Must be two citizen ⎰ Chas Hill
witnesses.   ⎱ Lena Jackson

BIRTH AFFIDAVIT.
DEPARTMENT OF THE INTERIOR.
COMMISSION TO THE FIVE CIVILIZED TRIBES.

IN RE APPLICATION FOR ENROLLMENT, as a citizen of the   Choctaw   Nation, of
Thomas Gravitt   , born on the 2nd day of   January , 1903
                 non
Name of Father: John Gravitt   a^citizen of the .... Nation.
Name of Mother: Maggie Gravitt   a citizen of the   Choctaw   Nation.

Postoffice   Caddo, I.T.

126

Applications for Enrollment of Choctaw Newborn
Act of 1905   Volume XIV

UNITED STATES OF AMERICA, Indian Territory, ⎱
   Central   DISTRICT. ⎰

I,   Maggie Gravitt   , on oath state that I am   36   years of age and a citizen by   Blood   , of the   Choctaw   Nation; that I am the lawful wife of   John Gravitt   , who is a citizen, by — of the ———— Nation; that a   male child was born to me on   2nd day of   January   , 1903; that said child has been named   Thomas Gravitt   , and was living March 4, 1905.

                                    Maggie Gravitt

Witnesses To Mark:

       Subscribed and sworn to before me this   12th day of   April   , 1905

                                 C.H. Elting
                                     Notary Public.

UNITED STATES OF AMERICA, Indian Territory, ⎱
   Central   DISTRICT. ⎰

I,   W.R. Bowman   , a   Physician   , on oath state that I attended on Mrs.   Maggie Gravitt   , wife of   John Gravitt   on the   2nd day of   January , 1903; that there was born to her on said date a   male   child; that said child was living March 4, 1905, and is said to have been named Thomas Gravitt

                                     WR Bowman

Witnesses To Mark:

       Subscribed and sworn to before me this   12th day of   April   , 1905

                                 C.H. Elting
                                     Notary Public.

Applications for Enrollment of Choctaw Newborn
Act of 1905   Volume XIV

BIRTH AFFIDAVIT.

DEPARTMENT OF THE INTERIOR.
COMMISSION TO THE FIVE CIVILIZED TRIBES.

_____

IN RE APPLICATION FOR ENROLLMENT, as a citizen of the   Choctaw   Nation, of
Thomas Gravitt   , born on the 2nd day of   January   , 1903

Name of Father: John Gravitt   a citizen of the non citizen   Nation.
Name of Mother: Maggie Gravitt   Roll 9748   a citizen of the   Choctaw   Nation.

Postoffice   Caddo, Ind Ter

_____

AFFIDAVIT OF MOTHER.

UNITED STATES OF AMERICA, Indian Territory, ⎱
    Central   DISTRICT. ⎰

I,   Maggie Gravitt   , on oath state that I am   36   years of age and a citizen
by   blood   , of the   Choctaw   Nation; that I am the lawful wife of   John
Gravitt   , who is a citizen, ~~by~~ ——— of the United States Nation; that a   male
child was born to me on   2nd day of   January   , 1903; that said child has been
named   Thomas Gravitt   , and was living March 4, 1905.

Maggie Gravitt
Witnesses To Mark:
⎰

Subscribed and sworn to before me this   6th day of   June   , 1905

C.H. Elting
Notary Public.

_____

AFFIDAVIT OF ATTENDING PHYSICIAN OR MID-WIFE.

UNITED STATES OF AMERICA, Indian Territory, ⎱
    Central   DISTRICT. ⎰

I,   W.R. Bowman   , a Physician   , on oath state that I attended on
Mrs.   Maggie Gravitt   , wife of   John Gravitt   on the 2nd day of   January ,
1903; that there was born to her on said date a   male   child; that said child was living
March 4, 1905, and is said to have been named Thomas Gravitt

WR Bowman MD
Witnesses To Mark:
⎰

Subscribed and sworn to before me this 6th day of   June   , 1905

C.H. Elting
Notary Public.

Choc New Born 999
    Ethan Alexander   b. 8-6-03

Choctaw 2061.

Muskogee, Indian Territory, April 17, 1905.

Henry Alexander,
    Talihina, Indian Territory.

Dear Sir:

Receipt is hereby acknowledged of the affidavits of Sarah Alexander and Hannah Frazier to the birth of Ethan Alexander, son of Henry and Sarah Alexander, August 6, 1903, and the same have been filed with our records as an application for the enrollment of said child.

Respectfully,

Chairman.

---

7 N.B. 999.

Muskogee, Indian Territory, May 29, 1905.

Sam T. Roberts,
    Talihina, Indian Territory.

Dear Sir:

Receipt is hereby acknowledged of your letter of May 24, asking if the birth affidavits for Ethan Alexander, son of Henry and Sarah Alexander, have been received.

In reply to your letter you are advised that the affidavits heretofore forwarded to the birth of Ethan Alexander, son of Henry and Sarah Alexander, have been filed with our records as an application for the enrollment of said child.

Applications for Enrollment of Choctaw Newborn
Act of 1905   Volume XIV

Respectfully,

Chairman.

DEPARTMENT OF THE INTERIOR.
COMMISSION TO THE FIVE CIVILIZED TRIBES.

IN RE APPLICATION FOR ENROLLMENT, as a citizen of the   Choctaw   Nation, of
Ethan Alexander   , born on the   6   day of   August   , 1903

Name of Father: Henry Alexander   a citizen of the   Choctaw   Nation.
Name of Mother: Sarah Alexander   a citizen of the   Choctaw   Nation.

Postoffice   Talihina I.T.

AFFIDAVIT OF MOTHER.

UNITED STATES OF AMERICA, Indian Territory, ⎫
    Central   **DISTRICT.** ⎭

I,   Sarah Alexander   , on oath state that I am   about 31   years of age and a
citizen by   Blood   , of the   Choctaw   Nation; that I am the lawful wife of
Henry Alexander   , who is a citizen, by   Blood   of the   Choctaw   Nation;
that a   male   child was born to me on   6   day of   August   , 1903, that said
child has been named   Ethan Alexander   , and is now living.

Sarah Alexander

Witnesses To Mark:
⎰
⎱

Subscribed and sworn to before me this 8 day of   April   , 1905.

Sam T. Roberts Jr
Notary Public.

E.P. Pitchlynn Interpreter

AFFIDAVIT OF ATTENDING PHYSICIAN OR MID-WIFE.

UNITED STATES OF AMERICA, Indian Territory, ⎫
    Central   **DISTRICT.** ⎭

I,   Hannah Frazier   , a   midwife   , on oath state that I attended on
Mrs. Sarah Alexander   , wife of   Henry Alexander   on the 6   day of August ,

1903; that there was born to her on said date a   male   child; that said child is now living and is said to have been named Ethan Alexander

Witnesses To Mark:

    { E P Pitchlynn
    { Willard Z Everett

her
Hannah x Frazier
mark

Subscribed and sworn to before me this 12 day of April   , 1905.

Sam T. Roberts Jr
Notary Public.

Choc New Born 1000
    Jacob McKinney b. 2-12-05

BIRTH AFFIDAVIT.

DEPARTMENT OF THE INTERIOR.
COMMISSION TO THE FIVE CIVILIZED TRIBES.

IN RE APPLICATION FOR ENROLLMENT, as a citizen of the   Choctaw   Nation, of
Jacob McKinney   , born on the 12 day of February   , 1905

Name of Father: Samuel McKinney   a citizen of the   Choctaw   Nation.
Name of Mother: Lucy McKinney   a citizen of the   Choctaw   Nation.

Postoffice   Cerro Gordo Arkansas

AFFIDAVIT OF MOTHER.

UNITED STATES OF AMERICA, Indian Territory, }
    Central   DISTRICT. }

I,   Lucy McKinney   , on oath state that I am   23   years of age and a citizen by   Blood   , of the   Choctaw   Nation; that I am the lawful wife of   Samuel McKinney   , who is a citizen, by Blood   of the   Choctaw   Nation; that a male   child was born to me on 12th day of   February   , 1905; that said child has been named   Jacob McKinney   , and was living March 4, 1905.

her
Lucy x McKinney
mark

131

Witnesses To Mark:
{ Nelson Kemp
{ Daniel Jefferson

Subscribed and sworn to before me this 10th day of April , 1905

(Name Illegible)
Notary Public.

AFFIDAVIT OF ATTENDING PHYSICIAN OR MID-WIFE.

UNITED STATES OF AMERICA, Indian Territory, }
   Central   **DISTRICT.** }

I, Sallie Billy , a mid-wife , on oath state that I attended on Mrs. Lucy McKinney , wife of Samuel McKinney on the 12th day of February , 1905; that there was born to her on said date a male child; that said child was living March 4, 1905, and is said to have been named Jacob McKinney

her
Sallie x Billy
Witnesses To Mark: mark
{ Nelson Kemp
{ Daniel Jefferson

Subscribed and sworn to before me this 10th day of April , 1905

(Name Illegible)
Notary Public.

Choc New Born 1001
   John Ripley
   (Born October 29, 1903)

BIRTH AFFIDAVIT.
DEPARTMENT OF THE INTERIOR.
COMMISSION TO THE FIVE CIVILIZED TRIBES.

IN RE APPLICATION FOR ENROLLMENT, as a citizen of the Choctaw Nation, of John Ripley , born on the 29 day of October , 1903

Name of Father: Dixson[sic] Ripley   a citizen of the Choctaw Nation.
Name of Mother: Lena Ripley (nee Amos)   a citizen of the Choctaw Nation.

Applications for Enrollment of Choctaw Newborn
Act of 1905   Volume XIV

Postoffice   Hughes I.T.

AFFIDAVIT OF MOTHER.

UNITED STATES OF AMERICA, Indian Territory, ⎫
   Central   DISTRICT. ⎭

    I,   Lena Ripley (nee Amos)   , on oath state that I am 22 years of age and a citizen by   blood   , of the   Choctaw   Nation; that I am the lawful wife of Dixson Ripley   , who is a citizen, by blood of the   Choctaw   Nation; that a   male   child was born to me on 29 day of October   , 1903; that said child has been named [sic] Ripley   , and was living March 4, 1905.

her
Lena x Ripley (nee Amos)
mark

Witnesses To Mark:
⎰ Ned W. Sockey
⎱ Edward Hickey

    Subscribed and sworn to before me this 8 day of April   , 1905

Robert E Lee

My Com expires Jan. 11-1906.   Notary Public.

AFFIDAVIT OF ATTENDING PHYSICIAN OR MID-WIFE.

UNITED STATES OF AMERICA, Indian Territory, ⎫
   Central   DISTRICT. ⎭

    I,   M D Brown   , a Midwife   , on oath state that I attended on Mrs. Lena Ripley (nee Amos)   , wife of Dixson Ripley   on the 29 day of October   , 1903; that there was born to her on said date a   male   child; that said child was living March 4, 1905, and is said to have been named John Ripley

Witnesses To Mark:

⎧
⎩

    Subscribed and sworn to before me this 8 day of April   , 1905

Robert E Lee

My Com expires Jan. 11-1906.   Notary Public.

Final enrollment of Dixson Ripley being No. 8609
Finnal[sic] enrollment of Lena Ripley (nee Amos) being No 8646

Applications for Enrollment of Choctaw Newborn
Act of 1905   Volume XIV

DEPARTMENT OF THE INTERIOR.
COMMISSION TO THE FIVE CIVILIZED TRIBES.

IN RE APPLICATION FOR ENROLLMENT, as a citizen of the   Choctaw   Nation, of
John Ripley   , born on the 29   day of   October   , 1903

Name of Father: Dixon Ripley   a citizen of the   Choctaw   Nation.
Name of Mother: Lena Ripley (Amos)   a citizen of the   Choctaw   Nation.

Postoffice   Hughes Ind. Ter.

AFFIDAVIT OF MOTHER.

UNITED STATES OF AMERICA, Indian Territory, ⎤
        Central   DISTRICT. ⎦

I,   Lena Ripley (Amos)   , on oath state that I am   22   years of age and a
citizen by   blood   , of the   Choctaw   Nation; that I am the lawful wife of
Dixon Ripley   , who is a citizen, by blood   of the   Choctaw   Nation;
that a   male   child was born to me on 29   day of   October   , 1903; that said
child has been named   John Ripley   , and was living March 4, 1905.

her

Lena x Ripley nee Amos

Witnesses To Mark: mark
⎰ E. Lee
⎱ Dixon Ripley

Subscribed and sworn to before me this 14 day of   July   , 1905

Robert E Lee

My Com expires Jan. 11-1906.   Notary Public.

AFFIDAVIT OF ATTENDING PHYSICIAN OR MID-WIFE.

UNITED STATES OF AMERICA, Indian Territory, ⎤
        Central   DISTRICT. ⎦

I,   Marium D. Brown   , a Midwife   , on oath state that I attended on
Mrs.   Lena Ripley (Amos)   , wife of   Dixon Ripley   on the   29 day of
October   , 1903; that there was born to her on said date a   male   child; that said
child was living March 4, 1905, and is said to have been named John Ripley

Marium D Brown

134

Applications for Enrollment of Choctaw Newborn
Act of 1905   Volume XIV

Witnesses To Mark:
  { E. Lee
   Dixon Ripley

Subscribed and sworn to before me this 14 day of   July   , 1905

My Com expires Jan. 11-1906.

                   Robert E Lee
                         Notary Public.

7-NB-1001

Muskogee, Indian Territory, July 21, 1905.

Dixon Ripley,
    Hughes, Indian Territory.

Dear Sir:

Receipt is hereby acknowledged of the affidavits of Lena Ripley, nee Amos, Indian Territory and Marium D. Brown, to the birth of John Ripley, son of Dixon and Lena Ripley, October 29, 1903, and the same have been filed with the record in this case.

Respectfully,

Commissioner.

7-NB-1001.

Muskogee, Indian Territory, June 1, 1905.

Dixson[sic] Ripley,
    Hughes, Indian Territory.

Dear Sir:

There is enclosed you herewith for execution application for the enrollment of your infant child, born October 29, 1903.

In the affidavits heretofore filed in this office the mother failed to give the christian-name[sic] of the applicant, and the affidavit purported to be executed by M. D. Brown, midwife, was not signed. It will, therefore, be necessary that you have both of the enclosed affidavits executed, inserting the applicant's name in the blank left for that purpose.

Applications for Enrollment of Choctaw Newborn
Act of 1905   Volume XIV

In having these affidavits executed care should be exercised to see that all names are written in full, as they appear in the body of the affidavit, and in the event that either of the persons signing the affidavit are unable to write, signatures by mark must be attested by two witnesses. Each affidavit must be executed before a Notary Public and the notarial seal and signature of the officer must be attached to each separate affidavit.

Respectfully,

VR 1-2.   Chairman.

Choc New Born 1002
> Ida May Wilson
> (Born March 9, 1903)
> Annie Dovie Wilson
> (Born Feb. 14, 1905)

BIRTH AFFIDAVIT.

DEPARTMENT OF THE INTERIOR.
COMMISSION TO THE FIVE CIVILIZED TRIBES.

IN RE APPLICATION FOR ENROLLMENT, as a citizen of the   Choctaw   Nation, of
Ida May Wilson   , born on the 9th   day of   March   , 1903

Name of Father: Willie Wilson   a citizen of the   Choctaw   Nation.
Name of Mother: Ollie M. Wilson   a citizen of the   Choctaw   Nation.

Postoffice   Goodwater, Ind. Ter.

AFFIDAVIT OF MOTHER.

UNITED STATES OF AMERICA, Indian Territory, ⎫
          Central   DISTRICT. ⎭

I,   Ollie M. Wilson   , on oath state that I am   21   years of age and a citizen by   marriage   , of the   Choctaw   Nation; that I am the lawful wife of   Willie Wilson   , who is a citizen, by   blood   of the   Choctaw   Nation; that a female   child was born to me on 9th   day of   March   , 1903; that said child has been named   Ida May Wilson   , and was living March 4, 1905.

Ollie M Wilson

Witnesses To Mark:
⎧
⎩

136

Subscribed and sworn to before me this   13th day of   April   , 1905

Wirt Franklin
Notary Public.

AFFIDAVIT OF ATTENDING PHYSICIAN OR MID-WIFE.

UNITED STATES OF AMERICA, Indian Territory, ⎱
Central   DISTRICT. ⎰

I,   Annie Phillips   , a mid-wife   , on oath state that I attended on Mrs. Ollie M. Wilson   , wife of   Willie Wilson   on the 9th day of March , 1903; that there was born to her on said date a   female   child; that said child was living March 4, 1905, and is said to have been named Ida May Wilson

Annie Phillips

Witnesses To Mark:
⎰

Subscribed and sworn to before me this   13th day of   April   , 1905

Wirt Franklin
Notary Public.

BIRTH AFFIDAVIT.
DEPARTMENT OF THE INTERIOR.
COMMISSION TO THE FIVE CIVILIZED TRIBES.

IN RE APPLICATION FOR ENROLLMENT, as a citizen of the   Choctaw   Nation, of Annie Dovie Wilson   , born on the 14th day of February , 1905

Name of Father: Willie Wilson   a citizen of the   Choctaw   Nation.
Name of Mother: Ollie M. Wilson   a citizen of the   Choctaw   Nation.

Postoffice   Goodwater, I.T.

AFFIDAVIT OF MOTHER.

UNITED STATES OF AMERICA, Indian Territory, ⎱
Central   DISTRICT. ⎰

I,   Ollie M. Wilson   , on oath state that I am   21   years of age and a citizen by   marriage   , of the   Choctaw   Nation; that I am the lawful wife of   Willie Wilson   , who is a citizen, by blood   of the   Choctaw   Nation; that a

137

female   child was born to me on 14th   day of   February   , 1905; that said child
has been named   Annie Dovie Wilson   , and was living March 4, 1905.

Ollie M Wilson

Witnesses To Mark:

{

Subscribed and sworn to before me this   13th day of   April   , 1905

Wirt Franklin
Notary Public.

_____

AFFIDAVIT OF ATTENDING PHYSICIAN OR MID-WIFE.

UNITED STATES OF AMERICA, Indian Territory, }
  Central   DISTRICT. }

I,   Annie Phillips   , a mid-wife   , on oath state that I attended on
Mrs.   Ollie M. Wilson   , wife of   Willie Wilson   on the   14th   day of
February   , 1905; that there was born to her on said date a   female   child; that said
child was living March 4, 1905, and is said to have been named Annie Dovie Wilson

Annie Phillips

Witnesses To Mark:

{

Subscribed and sworn to before me this   13th day of   April   , 1905

Wirt Franklin
Notary Public.

_____

7-NB-1002

Muskogee, Indian Territory, May 23, 1906/

Willie Wilson,
      Bennington, Indian Territory.

Dear Sir:

Receipt is hereby acknowledged of your letter of May 15, 1906, in which you
ask if you should appear before the Commissioner to the Five Civilized Tribes again in
the matter of the enrollment of your minor child.

138

In reply to your letter you are advised that you do not state the name of the child referred to in your letter and it is therefore impracticable to give you any definite information upon the subject.

It appears, however, that your children Ida May and Annie Dovie Wilson have been enrolled as new born citizens of the Choctaw Nation under the act of Congress approved March 3, 1905, and their enrollment as such approved by the Secretary of the Interior. If you have a child born since the enrollment of these children for whom you desire to make application under the act of Congress approved April 26, 1906, you should forward evidence to his birth upon the inclosed blank or appear at one of the appointments of the enrolling party in the field for the purpose of make application for the enrollment of said child.

Respectfully,

Acting Commissioner.

Choc New Born 1003
>Lucile Garrett Cook
>(Born July 28, 1904)

BIRTH AFFIDAVIT.

DEPARTMENT OF THE INTERIOR.
COMMISSION TO THE FIVE CIVILIZED TRIBES.

IN RE APPLICATION FOR ENROLLMENT, as a citizen of the   Choctaw   Nation, of Lucie[sic] Garrett Cook   , born on the 28   day of   July , 1904

United States

Name of Father: Chas H Cook   a citizen of the   ~~Choctaw~~   Nation.
Name of Mother: Lucie Garland P. Cook   a citizen of the   Choctaw   Nation.

Postoffice   Ardmore I.T.

AFFIDAVIT OF MOTHER.

UNITED STATES OF AMERICA, Indian Territory, ⎫
....DISTRICT. ⎰

I,   Lucie Garland Cook   , on oath state that I am 22 years of age and a citizen by   blood   , of the   ~~Chickas~~ Choctaw   Nation; that I am the lawful wife of Chas H Cook   , who is a citizen, ~~by   intermarriage   of the   Choctaw   Nation;~~

139

of the United States that a   female   child was born to me on   28   day of   July   ,
1904, that said child has been named   Lucie Garrit[sic] Cook   , and is now living.

Lucie Garland Cook

Witnesses To Mark:

{

Subscribed and sworn to before me this   10   day of   April   , 1905.

(Name Illegible)
Notary Public.

AFFIDAVIT OF ATTENDING PHYSICIAN OR MID-WIFE.

UNITED STATES OF AMERICA, Indian Territory,
....DISTRICT. }

I,   T. S. Booth   , a   M. D.   , on oath state that I attended on
Mrs.   Lucie G Cook   , wife of   Chas H Cook   on the   28   day of July , 1904;
that there was born to her on said date a   Female   child; that said child is now living
and is said to have been named   Lucie Garrett Cook

T S Booth M.D.

Witnesses To Mark:

{

Subscribed and sworn to before me this   10   day of   April   , 1905.

(Name Illegible)
Notary Public.

7-2939

Muskogee, Indian Territory, April 17, 1905.

Dixson[sic] Ripley,
          Hughes, Indian Territory.

Dear Sir:

Receipt is hereby acknowledged of the affidavits of Lena Ripley and M. D.
Brown to the birth of John Ripley, son of Dixson and Lena Ripley October 28, 1903, and
the same have been filed with our records as an application for the enrollment of said
child.

Respectfully,

Chairman.

140

Choc New Born 1004
    Frank Hall
    (Born Oct. 7, 1904)

DEPARTMENT OF THE INTERIOR,
COMMISSIONER TO THE FIVE CIVILIZED TRIBES FIVE CIVILIZED TRIBES.

Idabel, Indian Territory, April 27, 1906.

1004.
    In the matter of the death of Frank Hall, Choctaw New Born, Card Number

1906.
    Testimony taken three miles south of Garvin, Indian Territoey[sic], April 17,

WILLIAM ED Forbes[sic], being duly sworn, testified as follows:

BY THE COMMISSIONER:

Q What is your name? A William Ed Forbes.
Q What is your age? A 35.
Q What is your post office address? A Garvin, I.T.
Q Are you a citizen by blood of the Choctaw Nation? A Yes.
Q Were you acquainted with Nicholas Hall?
A Yes.
Q Was he a citizen by blood of the Choctaw Nation?
A Yes, sir
Q Do you know the name of Nicholas and Sinie Hall's youngest child?
A Yes.
Q What is it? A Frank Hall.
Q When was Frank Hall born?
A I could not tell you exactly when; I saw him a few days before Christmas 1904, and he had the appearance of being one or two months old then.
Q Do you know this child Frank Hall to have been living March 4, 1905? A Yes, sir.
Q You may state what circumstance causes you to know Frank Hall to have been living March 4, 1905.
A They lived about a mile from here, and I had them over here working for me picking up brush and such as that, and I was down there too. I went and told these parties they had better go to Idabel on the 12th and make application for the enrollment of the child, and they told me they did not have the money to pay the expenses, and I told them if they would work for me when they came back I would let them have the money, and they said

they would, and so I let them have the money and they went to Idabel to have the baby enrolled.

Q At the time that application was made for the enrollment of Frank Hall, was Nicholas Hall, the father, living?

A No, sir, he was dead.

Q You furnished Sinie Hall with the money to make the trip from here to Idabel for the purpose of enrolling the child?

A Yes, sir.

Q And the child was living at the time she made application?

A Yes, sir.

Q Is the child now living?

A No, he is dead.

Q When did he die?

A He died about the 1st day of June 1905.

Q Did you assist in the burial of the child?

A Yes, sir, I furnished the burial outfit and buried the child at Water Hole Church.

Q Where did the child die?

A At old Lady Louina Jackson's place.

Q About how far from you?

A About one mile from my place.

Q The records of the Commission to the Five Civilized Tribes show that on April 13, 1905, Sinie Hall appeared to make application for the enrollment of her son, Frank Hall: Who accompanied Sinie Hall when said application was made?

A Louina Jackson.

Q Did you pay Louina's expenses too?

A The whole business.

Witness Excused.

W.P. Covington, being first duly sworn, state that the above and foregoing is a full, true and correct transcript of his stenographic notes taken in said case on said date.

W.P. Covington

Subscribed and sworn to before me, this 28 day of   April   1906.

Lacey P Bobo
Notary Public.

NEW-BORN AFFIDAVIT.

Number..............

...Choctaw Enrolling Commission...

————

IN THE MATTER OF THE APPLICATION FOR ENROLLMENT, as a citizen of the Choctaw Nation, of   Frank Hall

born on the 12th[sic] day of   October   190 4

Name of father Nicholas Hall	a citizen of Choctaw
Nation final enrollment No. 13512	
Name of mother Siney[sic] Hall	a citizen of Choctaw
Nation final enrollment No. 13513	

Postoffice   Garvin I.T.

AFFIDAVIT OF MOTHER.

UNITED STATES OF AMERICA
INDIAN TERRITORY
 Central   DISTRICT

        I   Soney[sic] Hall   , on oath state that I am
 24   years of age and a citizen by blood of the   Choctaw   Nation,
and as such have been placed upon the final roll of the   Choctaw Nation, by the Honorable
Secretary of the Interior my final enrollment number being   13513 ; that I am the lawful
wife of   Nicholas Hall   , who is a citizen of the   Choctaw   Nation, and as such
has been placed upon the final roll of said Nation by the Honorable Secretary of the Interior,
his final enrollment number being   13512   and that a   male   child was born to me on
the   12th[sic]   day of   October   190 4; that said child has been named   Frank Hall
, and is now living.   her
                                        Siney x Hall
Witnesseth.   mark

  Must be two } Lyman Baker
  Witnesses who }
  are Citizens.   John Willis

        Subscribed and sworn to before me this   22   day of   Feb   190 5

                                W A Shoney
                                        Notary Public.
My commission expires: Jan 10, 1909

————

143

AFFIDAVIT OF ATTENDING PHYSICIAN OR MIDWIFE

UNITED STATES OF AMERICA
INDIAN TERRITORY
Central   DISTRICT

I,   Sammie Willis   a   midwife
on oath state that I attended on Mrs.   Siney Hall   wife of   Nicholas Hall
on the   12th[sic]   day of   October   , 190 4, that there was born to her on said date a   male
child, that said child is now living, and is said to have been named   Frank Hall

Sammie Hall[sic]   ~~M.D.~~

WITNESSETH:

Must be two witnesses
who are citizens and
know the child.

{ Lyman Baker

  John Willis

Subscribed and sworn to before me this, the   22   day of
Feb   190 5

W A Shoney   Notary Public.

We hereby certify that we are well acquainted with   Sammie Hall
a   midwife   and know   her   to be reputable and of good standing in the
community.

{ Lyman Baker

  John Willis

BIRTH AFFIDAVIT.

DEPARTMENT OF THE INTERIOR.
COMMISSION TO THE FIVE CIVILIZED TRIBES.

IN RE APPLICATION FOR ENROLLMENT, as a citizen of the   Choctaw   Nation, of
Frank Hall   , born on the   7th   day of   October   , 1904

Name of Father: Nicholas Hall   a citizen of the   Choctaw   Nation.
Name of Mother: Siney Hall   a citizen of the   Choctaw   Nation.

Postoffice   Garvin, Ind. Ter.

AFFIDAVIT OF MOTHER.

Child present.

W. F.

UNITED STATES OF AMERICA, Indian Territory, }
Central   DISTRICT.

I,   Siney Hall   , on oath state that I am   26   years of age and a citizen by blood   , of the   Choctaw   Nation; that I ~~am~~ *was* the lawful wife of   Nicholas Hall, deceased   , who ~~is~~ *was* a citizen, by   blood   of the   Choctaw   Nation; that a male   child was born to me on   7th day of   October   , 1904; that said child has been named   Frank Hall   , and was living March 4, 1905. *and that no one but my said husband was present when said child was born*   her

Siney x Hall
mark

Witnesses To Mark:
{ Robert Anderson
{ Vester W Rose

Subscribed and sworn to before me this 13th day of   April   , 1905

Wirt Franklin
Notary Public.

AFFIDAVIT OF ATTENDING PHYSICIAN OR MID-WIFE.

UNITED STATES OF AMERICA, Indian Territory, }
Central   DISTRICT.

am acquainted with

I,   Louina Jackson   , ~~a~~ .... , on oath state that I ~~attended on~~ Mrs.   Siney Hall   , wife of   Nicholas Hall, deceased; *that* on the 7th day of October   , 1904; that there was born to her on said date a   male   child; that said child was living March 4, 1905, and is said to have been named Frank Hall   her

Louina x Jackson
mark

Witnesses To Mark:
{ Robert Anderson
{ Vester W Rose

Subscribed and sworn to before me this 13th day of   April   , 1905

Wirt Franklin
Notary Public.

7-NB-1004

Muskogee, Indian Territory, June 1, 1905.

Siney Hall,
Garvin, Indian Territory.

Dear Madam:

Referring to the application for the enrollment of your infant child, Frank Hall, born October 7, 1904, it is noted from the affidavits heretofore filed in this office that your husband was the only one in attendance upon you at the time of borth[sic] of the applicant.

The affidavit of Louina Jackson to the applicant's birth and to the fact that he was living on March 4, 1905, has been filed in this office. It will, therefore, be necessary that you secure the affidavit of another person, who is disinterested and not related to the applicant, who has actual knowledge of the facts that the child was born, the date of his birth; that he was living on March 4, 1905, and that you are his mother.

In having this affidavit executed care should be exercised to see that all the names are written in full, as they appear in the body of the affidavit, and in the event that either of the persons signing the affidavit are unable to write, signatures by mark must be attested by two witnesses.   The affidavit must be executed before a Notary Public and the notarial seal and signature of the officer must be attached thereto.

Respectfully,

VR 1-3

Chairman.

_____

D. T.

REFER IN REPLY TO THE FOLLOWING:	**DEPARTMENT OF THE INTERIOR,**
7-NB-1004	**COMMISSIONER TO THE FIVE CIVILIZED TRIBES.**

Muskogee, Indian Territory, July 28, 1905.

Siney Hall,
Garvin, Indian Territory.

Dear Madam:

Your attention is called to a communication addressed to you by the Commission to the Five Civilized Tribes, under date of June 1, 1905, requesting additional evidence in the matter of the enrollment of your infant child, Frank Hall, born October 7, 1904.

146

In said letter you were advised that if your husband was the only one in attendance upon you at the time of the birth of the applicant it would be necessary to supply the affidavits of two witnesses who are disinterested and not related to the applicant, and who have actual knowledge of the facts, that the child was born, the date of his birth, that he was living March 4, 1905, and that you are his mother; you were also advised that the affidavit of Louvina[sic] Jackson to these facts had been filed and it would therefore be necessary for you to furnish the affidavit on one other person. No reply to this letter has been received.

The matter should receive your immediate attention as no further action can be taken relative to the enrollment of said child until the evidence heretofore requested has been supplied.

Respectfully,

Tams Bixby

Commissioner.

_____

(The above letter given again without letterhead.)

_____

(The letter of June 1, given again.)

Choc New Born 1005
     Ivy Wilmoth
     (Born Aug. 25, 1903)

_____

NEW-BORN AFFIDAVIT.

Number............

...Choctaw Enrolling Commission...

_____

IN THE MATTER OF THE APPLICATION FOR ENROLLMENT, as a citizen of the Choctaw   Nation, of   Ivy Wilmoth

born on the 25 day of ____August____ 190 3

Name of father   John W. Wilmoth   a citizen of   Choctaw
Nation final enrollment No............
Name of mother   Annie Watkins *now Wilmoth*   a citizen of   Choctaw
Nation final enrollment No............

Postoffice   Idabel I.T.

AFFIDAVIT OF MOTHER.

UNITED STATES OF AMERICA
INDIAN TERRITORY
Central   DISTRICT

I   Annie Watkins *now Wilmoth*   , on oath state that I am
20   years of age and a citizen by   blood   of the   Choctaw   Nation,
and as such have been placed upon the final roll of the   Choctaw   Nation, by the Honorable
Secretary of the Interior my final enrollment number being ....; that I am the lawful wife of
John W. Wilmoth   , who is a citizen of the   Choctaw   Nation, and as such has
been placed upon the final roll of said Nation by the Honorable Secretary of the Interior, his
final enrollment number being .... and that a   female   child was born to me on the
25   day of   August   190 3; that said child has been named   Ivy Wilmoth   , and is
now living.

her

Annie Wilmoth   x

Witnesseth.   mark

Must be two ⎫   S.E. Morris
Witnesses who ⎬
are Citizens. ⎭   W R Kirby

Subscribed and sworn to before me this   21   day of   Jan   190 5

W.A. Shoney

Notary Public.

My commission expires: Jan 10, 1909

AFFIDAVIT OF ATTENDING PHYSICIAN OR MIDWIFE

UNITED STATES OF AMERICA
INDIAN TERRITORY
Central   DISTRICT

I,   Laura Smith   a   midwife
on oath state that I attended on Mrs.   Annie Watkins   now Wilmoth   wife of   John W.
Wilmoth   on the   25th   day of   August   , 190 3 , that there was born to her on said date a
female   child, that said child is now living, and is said to have been named   Ivy Wilmoth

her

Laura Smith   x

mark

Subscribed and sworn to before me this, the   21   day of
Jan   190 5

WITNESSETH: .... Notary Public.
Must be two witnesses ⎰   S.E. Morris
who are citizens ⎱   W R Kirby

We hereby certify that we are well acquainted with   Laura Smith
a   midwife   and know   her   to be reputable and of good standing in the community.

S.E. Morris   _____

W R Kirby   _____

_____

BIRTH AFFIDAVIT.

DEPARTMENT OF THE INTERIOR.
COMMISSION TO THE FIVE CIVILIZED TRIBES.

_____

IN RE APPLICATION FOR ENROLLMENT, as a citizen of the   Choctaw   Nation, of
Ivy Wilmoth   , born on the 25th day of August , 1903

Name of Father: John W. Wilmoth   a citizen of the   Choctaw   Nation.
Name of Mother: Anna Wilmoth   a citizen of the   Choctaw   Nation.

Postoffice   Idabel, Ind. Ter.

_____

AFFIDAVIT OF MOTHER.

UNITED STATES OF AMERICA, Indian Territory, ⎫
        Central   **DISTRICT.** ⎰

I, Anna Wilmoth , on oath state that I am 19 years of age and a citizen
by   blood , of the   Choctaw   Nation; that I am the lawful wife of   John W.
Wilmoth , who is a citizen, by   marriage   of the   Choctaw   Nation; that a
female   child was born to me on   25th day of   August   , 1903; that said child
has been named   Ivy Wilmoth , and was living March 4, 1905.

                                                her
                                        Anna x Wilmoth
Witnesses To Mark: mark
⎰ Vester W Rose
⎱ Robert Anderson

Subscribed and sworn to before me this 12th day of   April   , 1905

                        Wirt Franklin
                                Notary Public.

_____

Applications for Enrollment of Choctaw Newborn
Act of 1905   Volume XIV

AFFIDAVIT OF ATTENDING PHYSICIAN OR MID-WIFE.

UNITED STATES OF AMERICA, Indian Territory, ⎫
Central   DISTRICT. ⎭

I,   Laura Smith   , a mid-wife   , on oath state that I attended on
Mrs.   Anna Wilmoth   , wife of   John W. Wilmoth   on the 25th   day of
August   , 1903; that there was born to her on said date a   female   child; that said
child was living March 4, 1905, and is said to have been named Ivy Wilmoth

                                         her
                                Laura x Smith
Witnesses To Mark: mark
 ⎧ Robert Anderson
 ⎩ Vester W Rose

        Subscribed and sworn to before me this 13th   day of   April   , 1905

                              Wirt Franklin
                                Notary Public.

Choc New Born 1006
    Judy Wilson
    (Born Sept. 12, 1903)

————————

BIRTH AFFIDAVIT.
DEPARTMENT OF THE INTERIOR.
COMMISSION TO THE FIVE CIVILIZED TRIBES.

————————

IN RE APPLICATION FOR ENROLLMENT, as a citizen of the   Choctaw   Nation, of
Judy Wilson   , born on the   12th day of September , 1903

Name of Father: John Wilson   a citizen of the   Choctaw   Nation.
Name of Mother: Jennie Wilson   a citizen of the   Choctaw   Nation.

                Postoffice   Eagletown, Ind Ter.

————————

AFFIDAVIT OF MOTHER.

UNITED STATES OF AMERICA, Indian Territory,⎱
  Central   DISTRICT. ⎰

I,   Jennie Wilson   , on oath state that I am   35   years of age and a citizen by   blood   , of the   Choctaw   Nation; that I ~~am~~ *was* the lawful wife of   John Wilson, deceased   , who ~~is~~ *was* a citizen, by   blood   of the   Choctaw   Nation; that a   female   child was born to me on   12th   day of   September   , 1903; that said child has been named   Judy Wilson   , and was living March 4, 1905. *and that no one but my said husband was present when said child was born*

her
Jennie x Wilson
mark

Witnesses To Mark:
⎰ Robert Anderson
⎱ Vester W Rose

Subscribed and sworn to before me this   13th   day of   April   , 1905

Wirt Franklin
Notary Public.

United States of America,   )
)
Indian Territory,   )   ss.
)
Central District.   )

I, Alfred Byington, on oath state that I am about fifty-four years of age and a citizen by blood of the Choctaw Nation; that my post office address is Eagletown, Indian Territory; that I am personally acquainted with Jennie Wilson, formerly the wife of John Wilson, deceased, and have known both of said parties all their lives; that during their married life I lived within one mile of where they lived, near Eagletown, Indian Territory, and I know of my own knowledge that on or about the 12th day of September, 1903, there was born to the said Jennie Wilson a female child; that said child is now living and has been named Judy Wilson.

his
Alfred x Byington
mark

Subscribed and sworn to before me this 13th day of April, 1905.

Wirt Franklin
Notary Public.

Witnesses to mark.
   Vester W Rose
   Robert Anderson

(The affidavit below typed as given.)

United States of America,
    Indian Territory,
Central District,

I   Edmund Homer   , on oath states that I am   34   years of age, that my post office address is Eagletown, I. T. that I was personally acquainted with   Jennie Wilson , and know that there was born to her on the   12th day of   September   1903, a   female child, which child was living on the fourth of march 1905, and said to have been named Judy Wilson.

Edmun Homer

Subscribed and sworn to before me this   20 day of   July   1905.

Jeff Gardner
Notary Public.

My commission expire 23 December 1905.

7-NB-1006

Muskogee, Indian Territory, July 28, 1905.

Jennie Wilson,
    Eagletown, Indian Territory.

Dear Madam:

    Receipt is hereby acknowledged of the affidavit of Edmon Homer to the birth of Judy Wilson, September 12, 1903, and the same has been filed with the records of this office in the matter of the enrollment of said child.

Respectfully,

Commissioner.

(The letter below given without letterhead.)

$W^m O.B.$

COMMISSIONERS:
TAMS BIXBY,
THOMAS B. NEEDLES,
C.R. BRECKINBRIDGE.

WM. O. BEALL
Secretary

DEPARTMENT OF THE INTERIOR,
COMMISSIONER TO THE FIVE CIVILIZED TRIBES.

REFER IN REPLY TO THE FOLLOWING:

7-NB-1006

ADDRESS ONLY THE
COMMISSION TO THE FIVE CIVILIZED TRIBES.

Muskogee, Indian Territory, June 1, 1905.

Jennie Wilson,
    Eagletown, Indian Territory.

Dear Madam:

Referring to the application for the enrollment of your infant child, Judy Wilson, born September 12, 1903, it is noted from the affidavits heretofore filed in this office that you were not attended by a physician or midwife at the time of the birth of the applicant.

In this event it will be necessary that the affidavits of two persons, who are disinterested and not related to the applicant, who have actual knowledge of the facts that the child was born, the date of her birth; that she was living on March 4, 1905, and that you are her mother be filed in this office.

The affidavit of Alfred Byington to these facts has been filed. It will, therefore, be necessary that you secure a simular[sic] affidavit of another person.

This matter should receive your immediate attention as no further action can be taken relative to the enrollment of your child until the Commission has been furnished this affidavit.

Respectfully,
T. B. Needles
Commissioner in Charge.

Choc New Born 1007
    Minnie Lee Phillips
    (Born May 8, 1904)

Applications for Enrollment of Choctaw Newborn
Act of 1905   Volume XIV

BIRTH AFFIDAVIT.

DEPARTMENT OF THE INTERIOR.
COMMISSION TO THE FIVE CIVILIZED TRIBES.

IN RE APPLICATION FOR ENROLLMENT, as a citizen of the   Choctaw   Nation, of
Minnie Lee Phillips   , born on the   8th   day of   May   , 1904

Name of Father: Tobe Phillips   a citizen of the   Choctaw   Nation.
Name of Mother: Annie Phillips   a citizen of the   Choctaw   Nation.

Postoffice   Norwood, Ind. Ter.

AFFIDAVIT OF MOTHER.

UNITED STATES OF AMERICA, Indian Territory, }
      Central   DISTRICT. }

I,   Annie Phillips   , on oath state that I am   22   years of age and a citizen
by   blood   , of the   Choctaw   Nation; that I am the lawful wife of   Tobe
Phillips   , who is a citizen, by   marriage   of the   Choctaw   Nation; that a
female   child was born to me on   8th   day of   May   , 1904; that said child has
been named   Minnie Lee Phillips   , and was living March 4, 1905.

Annie Phillips

Witnesses To Mark:
{

Subscribed and sworn to before me this   13th   day of   April   , 1905

Wirt Franklin
Notary Public.

AFFIDAVIT OF ATTENDING PHYSICIAN OR MID-WIFE.

UNITED STATES OF AMERICA, Indian Territory, }
      Central   DISTRICT. }

I,   Sarah Nichols   , a mid-wife   , on oath state that I attended on
Mrs. Annie Phillips   , wife of   Tobe Phillips   on the   8th   day of   May   ,
1904; that there was born to her on said date a   female   child; that said child was
living March 4, 1905, and is said to have been named Minnie Lee Phillips

Sarah Nichols

Witnesses To Mark:
{

154

Subscribed and sworn to before me this   13th day of   April   , 1905

Wirt Franklin
Notary Public.

Choc New Born 1008
      Henry Clay Wilson Barnett
      (Born Sept. 30, 1903)

BIRTH AFFIDAVIT.

DEPARTMENT OF THE INTERIOR.
COMMISSION TO THE FIVE CIVILIZED TRIBES.

IN RE APPLICATION FOR ENROLLMENT, as a citizen of the   Choctaw   Nation, of
Henry Clay Wilson Barnett   , born on the 30th day of September   , 1903

Name of Father: Alexander Barnett   a citizen of the   Choctaw   Nation.
Name of Mother: Susan Barnett   a citizen of the   Choctaw   Nation.

Postoffice   Garland, Ind. Terr.

AFFIDAVIT OF MOTHER.

UNITED STATES OF AMERICA, Indian Territory,
    Central   **DISTRICT.**

     I,   Susan Barnett   , on oath state that I am   forty   years of age and a citizen
by   blood   , of the   Choctaw   Nation; that I am the lawful wife of   Alexander
Barnett   , who is a citizen, by blood   of the   Choctaw   Nation; that a
male   child was born to me on 30th   day of   September   , 1903; that said child
has been named   Henry Clay Wilson Barnett   , and was living March 4, 1905.
                      this is
                  Susan x Barnett
Witnesses To Mark: my mark
    { Matthew Henry
    { Elum Bond

Subscribed and sworn to before me this 1st day of   April   , 1905

C.C. Jones
Notary Public.

Applications for Enrollment of Choctaw Newborn
Act of 1905   Volume XIV

AFFIDAVIT OF ATTENDING PHYSICIAN OR MID-WIFE.

UNITED STATES OF AMERICA, Indian Territory, ⎫
    Central   **DISTRICT.** ⎬

I,   Mary Jane Bond   , a mid-wife   , on oath state that I attended on Mrs.   Susan Barnett   , wife of   Alexander Barnett   on the 30th day of September   , 1903; that there was born to her on said date a   male   child; that said child was living March 4, 1905, and is said to have been named Henry Clay Wilson Barnett   this is

                                     Mary Jane x Bond

Witnesses To Mark: my mark
   ⎰ Matthew Henry
   ⎱ Elum Bond

    Subscribed and sworn to before me this 1ˢᵗ day of   April   , 1905

                                C.C. Jones
                                Notary Public.

                            7-2494

           Muskogee, Indian Territory, April 17, 1905.

A. O. Clark,
    Stigler, Indian Territory.

Dear Sir:

    Receipt is hereby acknowledged of your letter of April 4, 1905, enclosing affidavits of Susan Barnett and Mary Jane Bond to the birth of Henry Clay Wilson Barnett, son of Alexander and Susan Barnett, September 30, 1903, and the same have been filed with our records as an application for the enrollment of said child.

    Receipt is also acknowledged of the affidavits of Eliza Perry and R. F. Terrell to the birth of Bertha Perry, daughter of Daniel and Eliza Perry, November 17, 1904.

    It is stated in the affidavit of the mother that she is a citizen by blood of the Choctaw Nation. If this is correct you are requested to state the name under which she was enrolled, the names of her parents, and if she has selected an allotment of the lands of the Choctaw or Chickasaw Nations please give her roll number as it appears upon her allotment certificate.

                     Respectfully,

                              Chairman.

Substitute

7 NB 1008

Muskogee, Indian Territory, July 22, 1905.

Alex Barnett,
　　Garland, Indian Territory.

Dear Sir:

Receipt is hereby acknowledged of your letter of July 14, asking if an allotment can be selected for your child.

In reply to your letter you are advised that the name of your son, Henry Clay Wilson Barnett, has been placed upon a schedule of citizens by blood of the Choctaw Nation which has been forwarded to the Secretary of the Interior and you will be notified when his enrollment is approved. Until the approval of his enrollment, however, no selection of allotment can be made for said child.

Respectfully,

Commissioner.

_____

Blank 731.

_____
Choctaw Roll, Citizens By Blood.
_____
New Born.
_____
Act of Congress Approved March 3rd, 1905. (Public No. 212.)
_____

No.	Name	Age	Sex	Blood	Card No.
910	Barnett, Henry Clay Wilson	1	M	Full	1008

Choc New Born 1009
      Ranes M. Coley
      (Born Jan. 23, 1905)

BIRTH AFFIDAVIT.

DEPARTMENT OF THE INTERIOR.
COMMISSION TO THE FIVE CIVILIZED TRIBES.

IN RE APPLICATION FOR ENROLLMENT, as a citizen of the   Choctaw   Nation, of
Ranes M. Coley   , born on the 23   day of   Jan   , 1905

Name of Father: Johnson Coley No 8305   a citizen of the   Choctaw   Nation.
Name of Mother: Julia Coley No. 8442   a citizen of the   Choctaw   Nation.

Postoffice   Lodi Ind Ter

AFFIDAVIT OF MOTHER.

UNITED STATES OF AMERICA, Indian Territory, ⎱
     Central   **DISTRICT.** ⎰

     I,   Julia Coley   , on oath state that I am   21   years of age and a citizen by
Blood   , of the   Choctaw   Nation; that I am the lawful wife of   Johnson Coley   ,
who is a citizen, by Blood   of the   Choctaw   Nation; that a   male   child
was born to me on   23   day of   Jan   , 1905; that said child has been named   Ranes
M Coley   , and was living March 4, 1905.

                  Julia Coley
Witnesses To Mark:
    ⎰

     Subscribed and sworn to before me this   12   day of   April   , 1905

                  L N Hunt
                     Notary Public.
My com expires Jan 9 1908

Applications for Enrollment of Choctaw Newborn
Act of 1905   Volume XIV

AFFIDAVIT OF ATTENDING PHYSICIAN OR MID-WIFE.

UNITED STATES OF AMERICA, Indian Territory, ⎱
    Central   DISTRICT. ⎰

I,   Billy Dixon   , a Physician   , on oath state that I attended on
Mrs.   Julia Coley   , wife of   Johnson Coley   on the   23   day of   Jan   , 1905;
that there was born to her on said date a   male   child; that said child was living
March 4, 1905, and is said to have been named   Ranes M Coley

Billy Dixon

Witnesses To Mark:

{

Subscribed and sworn to before me this   12   day of   April   , 1905

L N Hunt
Notary Public.

My com expires Jan 9 1908

Choc New Born 1010
     Daniel Willis Sirmans
     (Born Feb. 28, 1903)
     Etanee Sirmans
     (Born Feb. 23, 1905)

BIRTH AFFIDAVIT.
DEPARTMENT OF THE INTERIOR.
COMMISSION TO THE FIVE CIVILIZED TRIBES.

IN RE APPLICATION FOR ENROLLMENT, as a citizen of the   Choctaw   Nation, of
Etanee Sirmans   , born on the   23   day of   Feb   , 1905

Name of Father: W^m O Sirmans   a citizen of the United States Nation.
Name of Mother: Elsie Sirmans   a citizen of the   Choctaw   Nation.

Postoffice   Brooken I T

AFFIDAVIT OF MOTHER.

UNITED STATES OF AMERICA, Indian Territory, ⎫
    Western   DISTRICT. ⎬

      I, Elsie Sirmans   , on oath state that I am 28   years of age and a citizen by Blood   , of the   Choctaw   Nation; that I am the lawful wife of   W^m O Sirmans , who is a citizen, by—— of the ——— Nation; that a   girl   child was born to me on 23 day of   Feb   , 1905; that said child has been named Etanee Sirmans   , and was living March 4, 1905.

Her
Elsie x Sirmans
mark

Witnesses To Mark:
   ⎧ J.L. Coffman
   ⎩ NC Coffman

      Subscribed and sworn to before me this 3 day of   April   , 1905

S P Davis
Notary Public.

AFFIDAVIT OF ATTENDING PHYSICIAN OR MID-WIFE.

UNITED STATES OF AMERICA, Indian Territory, ⎫
    Western   DISTRICT. ⎬

      I, Electa Jennings   , a midwife   , on oath state that I attended on Mrs. Elsie Sirmans   , wife of W^m O Sirmans   on the 23 day of Feb , 1905; that there was born to her on said date a   girl   child; that said child was living March 4, 1905, and is said to have been named Etanee Sirmans

Electa Jennings

Witnesses To Mark:
   ⎧
   ⎩

      Subscribed and sworn to before me this 3 day of   April   , 1905

S P Davis
Notary Public.

my commish expires Feb 9-07

Applications for Enrollment of Choctaw Newborn
Act of 1905 Volume XIV

BIRTH AFFIDAVIT.

DEPARTMENT OF THE INTERIOR.
COMMISSION TO THE FIVE CIVILIZED TRIBES.

IN RE APPLICATION FOR ENROLLMENT, as a citizen of the   Choctaw   Nation, of
Daniel Willis Sirmans   , born on the   28   day of   Feb   , 1903

Name of Father: W^m O Sirmans   a citizen of the United States Nation.
Name of Mother: Elsie Sirmans   a citizen of the   Choctaw   Nation.

Postoffice   Brooken I T

AFFIDAVIT OF MOTHER.

UNITED STATES OF AMERICA, Indian Territory, ⎫
   Western   DISTRICT. ⎭

I,   Elsie Sirmans   , on oath state that I am   28   years of age and a citizen by
Blood   , of the   Choctaw   Nation; that I am the lawful wife of   W^m O Sirmans   ,
who is a citizen, by——— of the   ———   Nation; that a   Boy   child was born to me
on   28   day of   Feb   , 1903; that said child has been named   Daniel Willis Sirmans   ,
and was living March 4, 1905.   Her
                                        Elsie x Sirmans
Witnesses To Mark: mark
  ⎧ J.L. Coffman
  ⎩ NC Coffman

Subscribed and sworn to before me this 3 day of   April   , 1905

S P Davis
Notary Public.

AFFIDAVIT OF ATTENDING PHYSICIAN OR MID-WIFE.

UNITED STATES OF AMERICA, Indian Territory, ⎫
   Western   DISTRICT. ⎭

I,   J D Clarkson   , a   Doctor   , on oath state that I attended on
Mrs.   Elsie Sirmans   , wife of   W^m O Sirmans   on the   28   day of   Feb   ,
1903; that there was born to her on said date a .... child; that said child was living
March 4, 1905, and is said to have been named Daniel Willis Sirmans

J C Clarkson MD

Witnesses To Mark:
  ⎧
  ⎩

161

Subscribed and sworn to before me this 11   day of   Apr   , 1905

S P Davis

Notary Public.

my commish expires Feb 9-07

NEW-BORN AFFIDAVIT.

Number............

...Choctaw Enrolling Commission...

IN THE MATTER OF THE APPLICATION FOR ENROLLMENT, as a citizen of the Choctaw   Nation, of   Daniel Willis Sirmans

born on the 28   day of ___February____190 3

Name of father   W. O. Sirmans   a citizen of   white
Nation final enrollment No. ——
Name of mother   Elsie Sirmans   a citizen of   Choctaw
Nation final enrollment No. 12400

Postoffice   Brooken, I.T.

AFFIDAVIT OF MOTHER.

UNITED STATES OF AMERICA
INDIAN TERRITORY
    Western   DISTRICT

        I   Elsie Sirmans   , on oath state that I am
    28   years of age and a citizen by   blood   of the   Choctaw   Nation, and
as such have been placed upon the final roll of the   Choctaw   Nation, by the Honorable
Secretary of the Interior my final enrollment number being   12400   ; that I am the lawful
wife of W.O. Sirmans   , who is a citizen of the   white   Nation, and as such has
been placed upon the final roll of said Nation by the Honorable Secretary of the Interior, his
final enrollment number being   ——   and that a   male   child was born to me on the 28th
day of   February   190 3; that said child has been named Daniel Willis Sirmans   ,
and is now living.

Elsie Sirmans

Witnesseth.

Must be two   }   T.J. Walls
Witnesses who }
are Citizens.   Jess Walls

Subscribed and sworn to before me this   5   day of   Jan   190 5

John M Linz

Notary Public.

My commission expires: Nov 27 1907

AFFIDAVIT OF ATTENDING PHYSICIAN OR MIDWIFE

UNITED STATES OF AMERICA
INDIAN TERRITORY
Western   DISTRICT

I,   J.D. Clarkston[sic]   a   practicing physician
on oath state that I attended on Mrs.   Elsie Sirmans   wife of   W O Sirmans
on the   28th   day of   February , 190 3 , that there was born to her on said date a   male
child, that said child is now living, and is said to have been named   Daniel Willis Sirmans

J D Clarkson   *m. D.*

Subscribed and sworn to before me this, the   20   day of
Jan   190 5

WITNESSETH: *My commission expires Feb 9.07*   S P Davis   Notary Public.

Must be two witnesses
who are citizens

{ T J Walls

Jess Walls

We hereby certify that we are well acquainted with   J D Clarkston[sic]
a   practicing physician   and know   him   to be reputable and of good standing in
the community.

T J Walls   _____

Jess Walls   _____

7-4466

Muskogee, Indian Territory, April 17, 1905.

W. O. Sirmans,
        Brooken, Indian Territory.

Dear Sir:

        Receipt is hereby acknowledged of the affidavits of Elsie Sirmans and
Electra[sic] Jennings to the birth of Etavee[sic] Sirmans daughter of William O. and Elsie

Sirmans, February 23, 1905; also affidavits of Elsie Sirmans and J. D. Clarkson to the birth of Daniel Willis Sirmans, son of William O. and Elsie Sirmans, February 28, 1903; and the same have been filed with our records as an application for the enrollment of said children.

Respectfully,

Chairman.

Choc New Born 1011
　　　Dorthula Thomas
　　　(Born Nov. 22, 1902)

BIRTH AFFIDAVIT.

Department of the Interior,
COMMISSION TO THE FIVE CIVILIZED TRIBES.

IN RE APPLICATION FOR ENROLLMENT, as a citizen of the   Choctaw   Nation, of   Dorthula Thomas   , born on the   22nd   day of   November   , 190 2

Name of Father: Andrew J Thomas   a citizen of the   Choctaw   Nation.
Name of Mother: Della Thomas   a citizen of the   Choctaw   Nation.

Post-Office: Silo I.T.

AFFIDAVIT OF MOTHER.

UNITED STATES OF AMERICA, ⎫
　　INDIAN TERRITORY,　　　 ⎬
　　Central　　　　District. ⎭

about 25

I,   Della Thomas   , on oath state that I am ~~acquaintance~~   years of age and a citizen by   Blood , of the   Choctaw   Nation; that I am the lawful wife of Andrew J Thomas   , who is a citizen, by Intermarriage   of the   Choctaw Nation; that a   Female   child was born to me on 22nd day of November , 190 2, that said child has been named Dorthula Thomas   , and is now living.

Della Thomas

WITNESSES TO MARK:
　⎧
　⎩

164

Applications for Enrollment of Choctaw Newborn
Act of 1905   Volume XIV

Subscribed and sworn to before me this 8th *day of*   April , *190* .

W.H. Ritchey
Notary Public.

AFFIDAVIT OF ATTENDING PHYSICIAN OR MID-WIFE.

UNITED STATES OF AMERICA, ⎫
INDIAN TERRITORY, ⎬
Southerland   District. ⎭

I,   Frank Jackman   , a   M. D.   , on oath state that I attended on Mrs. Della Thomas , wife of   Andrew J Thomas   on the 22 day of Nov , 190 2; that there was born to her on said date a   Female   child; that said child is now living and is said to have been named   Dorthula Thomas

Frank Jackman

WITNESSES TO MARK:

{

Subscribed and sworn to before me this 31   *day of*   march , *190* .

C M Inge
Notary Public.

7-362

Muskogee, Indian Territory, April 17, 1905.

Andy J. Thomas,
Silo, Indian Territory.

Dear Sir:

Receipt is hereby acknowledged of the affidavits of Della Thomas and Frank Jackman to the birth of Dorthular[sic] Thomas, daughter of Andrew J. and Della Thomas, November 22, 1902, and the same have been filed with the records as an application for the enrollment of said child.

Respectfully,

Chairman.

7-NB-1011

Muskogee, Indian Territory, July 21, 1905.

Andrew Thomas,
     Mead, Indian Territory.

Dear Sir:

     Receipt is hereby acknowledged of your letter of July 10, 1905, asking if the enrollment of Dorthular[sic] Thomas has been approved.

     In reply to your letter you are advised that the name of Dorthula Thomas has been placed upon a schedule of citizens by blood of the Choctaw Nation, prepared for forwarding to the Secretary of the Interior, and you will be notified when her enrollment is approved.

                   Respectfully,

                         Commissioner.

Choc New Born 1012
     Goldie Ruth Dobson
     (Born Oct. 15, 1903)

BIRTH AFFIDAVIT.

DEPARTMENT OF THE INTERIOR.
COMMISSION TO THE FIVE CIVILIZED TRIBES.

     IN RE APPLICATION FOR ENROLLMENT, as a citizen of the   Chocktaw[sic]   Nation, of   Goldie Ruth Dobson   , born on the 15th day of   Oct , 1903

Name of Father: William T. Dobson   a citizen of the   Chocktaw   Nation.
Name of Mother: Josie E Dobson   a citizen of the   Chocktaw   Nation.

               Postoffice   Robbers Roost I.T.

Applications for Enrollment of Choctaw Newborn
Act of 1905   Volume XIV

AFFIDAVIT OF MOTHER.

UNITED STATES OF AMERICA, Indian Territory, ⎱
    Central   DISTRICT. ⎰

    I,   Josie E Dobson   , on oath state that I am   22   years of age and a citizen by   intermarriage   , of the   Chocktaw   Nation; that I am the lawful wife of William T Dobson   , who is a citizen, by blood   of the   Chocktaw Nation; that a   female   child was born to me on 15th   day of   Oct   , 1903; that said child has been named   Goldie Ruth Dobson   , and was living March 4, 1905.

Josie E Dobson

Witnesses To Mark:
    ⎰ J W Brown
    ⎱ L F Brown

    Subscribed and sworn to before me this 12th day of   April   , 1905

C. T. Luttrell
Notary Public.
My commission expires March 22nd 1908

AFFIDAVIT OF ATTENDING PHYSICIAN OR MID-WIFE.

UNITED STATES OF AMERICA, Indian Territory, ⎱
    Western   DISTRICT. ⎰

    I,   J. C. Rumley   , a   Physician   , on oath state that I attended on Mrs. W[m] T. Dobson   , wife of   W[m] T. Dobson   on the 15" day of Oct   , 1903; that there was born to her on said date a   female   child; that said child was living March 4, 1905, and is said to have been named Goldie Ruth Dobson

J C Rumley, M.D.

Witnesses To Mark:

    ⎰
    ⎱

    Subscribed and sworn to before me this 7" day of   Feb   , 1905

A.L. Beckett
Notary Public.
My com. expires May 21" 1907

7-5340

Muskogee, Indian Territory, April 17, 1905.

William T. Dobson,
      Robbersroost, Indian Territory.

Dear Sir:

     Receipt is hereby acknowledged of the affidavits of Josie E. Dobson and J. C. Rumley to the birth of Goldie Ruth Dobson, daughter of William T. and Josie E. Dobson, October 15, 1903, and the same have been filed with our records as an application for the enrollment of said child.

                         Respectfully,

                               Chairman.

Choc New Born 1013
     Henry C. Folsom
     (Born Feb. 21, 1903)

BIRTH AFFIDAVIT.

DEPARTMENT OF THE INTERIOR.
COMMISSION TO THE FIVE CIVILIZED TRIBES.

IN RE APPLICATION FOR ENROLLMENT, as a citizen of the   Choctaw   Nation, of Henry C. Folsom   , born on the 21   day of   February , 1903

Name of Father: Loran S. W. Folsom   a citizen of the   Choctaw   Nation.
Name of Mother: Kattie Folsom   a citizen of the   Choctaw   Nation.

            Postoffice   Caddo, I.T.

AFFIDAVIT OF MOTHER.

UNITED STATES OF AMERICA, Indian Territory, }
    Central   **DISTRICT.** }

     I,   Kattie[sic] Folsom   , on oath state that I am   36   years of age and a citizen by   intermarriage   , of the   Choctaw   Nation; that I am the lawful wife of Loran S.W. Folsom   , who is a citizen, by Blood   of the   Choctaw

Nation; that a   male   child was born to me on 21   day of   February   , 1903; that said child has been named   Henry C. Folsom   , and was living March 4, 1905.

Katie Folsom

Witnesses To Mark:

{

Subscribed and sworn to before me this 6   day of   April   , 1905

J.T. Jackson
Notary Public.

AFFIDAVIT OF ATTENDING PHYSICIAN OR MID-WIFE.

UNITED STATES OF AMERICA, Indian Territory, ⎫
    Central   DISTRICT. ⎭

I,   Leroy Long   , a Physician   , on oath state that I attended on Mrs.   Katie Folsom   , wife of   Loran S. W. Folsom   on the   21   day of   February   , 1903; that there was born to her on said date a   male   child; that said child was living March 4, 1905, and is said to have been named Henry C Folsom

Leroy Long

Witnesses To Mark:

{

Subscribed and sworn to before me this 11th day of   April   , 1905

Brooks Fort
Notary Public.

Com ex 3/6/07

NEW BORN AFFIDAVIT

No ....

CHOCTAW ENROLLING COMMISSION

IN THE MATTER OF THE APPLICATION FOR ENROLLMENT as a citizen of the Choctaw
Nation, of   Henry C Folsom   born on the   21 day
of   February   190 3

Name of father   L.S.W. Folsom   a citizen of   Choctaw   Nation,
final enrollment No. 10246
Name of mother   Katie Folsom   a citizen of   Choctaw   Nation,
final enrollment No. 155

Caddo IT   Postoffice.

AFFIDAVIT OF MOTHER

UNITED STATES OF AMERICA ⎫
    INDIAN TERRITORY ⎬
DISTRICT   Central ⎭

    I   Katie Folsom   , on oath state that I am   36   years of age and a
citizen by   marriage   of the   Choctaw   Nation, and as such have been placed
upon the final roll of the   Choctaw   Nation, by the Honorable Secretary of the Interior my
final enrollment number being   155   ; that I am the lawful wife of L.S.W. Folsom   ,
who is a citizen of the   Choctaw   Nation, and as such has been placed upon the final
roll of said Nation by the Honorable Secretary of the Interior, his final enrollment number
being   10246   and that a   Male   child was born to me on the   21   day of   February
190 3; that said child has been named   Henry C Folsom   , and is now living.

WITNESSETH: Katie Folsom
  Must be two witnesses ⎰ Lena Jackson
  who are citizens   ⎱ J.T. Jackson

    Subscribed and sworn to before me this, the   15 day of   February   , 190 5

J.T. Jackson
Notary Public.

My Commission Expires: April 19st[sic] 1907

Affidavit of Attending Physician or Midwife

UNITED STATES OF AMERICA, ⎫
   INDIAN TERRITORY,   ⎬
 Central   DISTRICT ⎭

    I,   Le Roy Long   a   Practicing Physician
on oath state that I attended on Mrs. Katie Folsom   wife of L.S.W. Folsom
on the 21 day of February , 190 3, that there was born to her on said date a   male
child, that said child is now living, and is said to have been named Henry C Folsom

                       LeRoy Long   M. D.

    Subscribed and sworn to before me this the 16ᵗʰ day of Feby   1905

                    Brooks Fort
                          Notary Public.

WITNESSETH:
  Must be two witnesses ⎰ Lena Jackson
  who are citizens and   ⎱
  know the child.   J.T. Jackson

    We hereby certify that we are well acquainted with   Dʳ LeRoy Long
a   Physician   and know   him   to be reputable and of good standing in the
community.

                Must be two citizen⎰ Lena Jackson
                witnesses.   ⎱ J.T. Jackson

                         7-3626

          Muskogee, Indian Territory, April 17, 1905.

Loren[sic] S. W. Folsom,
       Caddo, Indian Territory.

Dear Sir
    Receipt is hereby acknowledged of the affidavits of Katie Folsom and Leroy
long to the birth of Henry C. Folsom, son of Loran S. W. and Katie Folsom, February 21,
1903, and the same have been filed with our records as an application for the enrollment
of said child.
                Respectfully,

                        Chairman.

Choc New Born 1014
>June Durant Buell
>(Born June 15, 1904)

BIRTH AFFIDAVIT.

DEPARTMENT OF THE INTERIOR.
COMMISSION TO THE FIVE CIVILIZED TRIBES.

IN RE APPLICATION FOR ENROLLMENT, as a citizen of the   Choctaw   Nation, of
June Durant Buell   , born on the 15   day of June   , 1904

Name of Father: Ward D. Buell   a citizen of the   U. S.   ~~Nation~~.
Name of Mother: Rosa Lee Buell   a citizen of the   Choctaw   Nation.

>Postoffice   Durant, Ind. Ter.

AFFIDAVIT OF MOTHER.

UNITED STATES OF AMERICA, Indian Territory, ⎫
>Central   **DISTRICT.** ⎭

I,   Rosa Lee Buell   , on oath state that I am   24   years of age and a citizen
by   blood   , of the   Choctaw   Nation; that I am the lawful wife of   Ward D.
Buell   , who is a citizen, by .... of the   U.S.   Nation; that a   female
child was born to me on   15   day of   June   , 1904; that said child has been named
June Durant Buell   , and was living March 4, 1905.

>Rosa Lee Buell
Witnesses To Mark:
>⎰ W.D. Gibbs
>⎱ G.M. Harney

Subscribed and sworn to before me this 11th day of   April   , 1905

>*(Name Illegible)*
>Notary Public.

AFFIDAVIT OF ATTENDING PHYSICIAN OR MID-WIFE.

State of Iowa

UNITED STATES OF AMERICA, ~~Indian Territory,~~ } ss
Southern Judicial ~~Polk County~~ DISTRICT. }

I, Hugh G. Welpton , a Physician , on oath state that I attended on Mrs. Rosa Lee Buell , wife of Ward D. Buell on the 15th day of June , 1904; that there was born to her on said date a female child; that said child was living March 4, 1905, and is said to have been named June Durant Buell

Hugh G Welpton M.D.

Witnesses To Mark:
{ Chas M West, M.D.
{ C A Webb

Subscribed and sworn to before me this 13 day of April , 1905

John J Halloran
Notary Public.

NEW-BORN AFFIDAVIT.

Number...............

Choctaw Enrolling Commission.

IN THE MATTER OF THE APPLICATION FOR ENROLLMENT, as a citizen of the Choctaw Nation, of June Durant Buell

born on the 15 day of June 190 4

Name of father   Ward D Buell   a citizen of   white
Nation final enrollment No ——
Name of mother   Rosa Lee Buell   a citizen of   Choctaw
Nation final enrollment No   9770

Postoffice   Durant I.T.

AFFIDAVIT OF MOTHER.

UNITED STATES OF AMERICA, }
   INDIAN TERRITORY, }
   Central   DISTRICT }

I   Rosa Lee Buell   on oath state that I am 25 years of age and a citizen by blood   of the Choctaw Nation, and as such have been placed upon the final roll of the   Choctaw   Nation, by the Honorable

173

Secretary of the Interior my final enrollment number being   9770   ; that I am the lawful wife of   Ward D Buell   , who is a citizen of the   white   Nation, and as such has been placed upon the final roll of said Nation by the Honorable Secretary of the Interior, his final enrollment number being —and that a   female   child was born to me on the 15   day of   June   190 4 ; that said child has been named   June Durant Buell , and is now living.

Mrs Rosa Lee Buell

WITNESSETH:

Must be two \
Witnesses who } E.E. Dyer \
are Citizens.

Cyrus Byington

Subscribed and sworn to before me this   16   day of   January   190 5

James Bower

Notary Public.

My commission expires Sept 23-1907

Affidavit of Attending Physician or Midwife.

UNITED STATES OF AMERICA \
INDIAN TERRITORY \
   Central   DISTRICT

I,   Ward D Buell   a   attendant on oath state that I attended on Mrs. Rosa Lee Buell my wife ~~wife of~~ .... on the 15   day of   June   , 190 4 , that there was born to her on said date a   female child, that said child is now living, and is said to have been named   June Durant Buell

Ward D Buell   ~~M.D.~~
Attendant

Subscribed and sworn to before me this, the 7 day of   Feby   190 5

(Name Illegible)

Notary Public.

WITNESSETH:

Must be two witnesses { Cyrus Byington \
who are citizens and \
know the child.   { E E Dyer

We hereby certify that we are well acquainted with   Ward D Buell a   Attendant   and know   him   to be reputable and of good standing in the community.

(Name Illegible)

Green Thompson

174

Choc New Born 1015
> Lois Aletha Parrish
> (Born April 19, 1904)

BIRTH AFFIDAVIT.

DEPARTMENT OF THE INTERIOR.
COMMISSION TO THE FIVE CIVILIZED TRIBES.

IN RE APPLICATION FOR ENROLLMENT, as a citizen of the   Choctaw   Nation, of
Lois Aletha Parrish   , born on the 19 day of   April , 1904

Name of Father: JB Parrish   a citizen of the   ————Nation.
Name of Mother: Lillie Josephine Parrish   a citizen of the Choctaw   Nation.

> Postoffice   Lone Elm, Ind. Ter.

AFFIDAVIT OF MOTHER.

UNITED STATES OF AMERICA, Indian Territory, ⎫
       Southern   DISTRICT. ⎰

I,   Lillie Josephine Parrish   , on oath state that I am   22   years of age and a
citizen by   blood   , of the   Choctaw   Nation; that I am the lawful wife of   J.
B. Parrish   , who is a *non* citizen, by —— of the   ——   Nation; that a
female   child was born to me on 19th   day of April   , 1904; that said child has
been named   Lois Aletha Parrish   , and was living March 4, 1905.

> Lillie Josephine Parrish

Witnesses To Mark:
⎰

Subscribed and sworn to before me this 10th   day of   April   , 1905

> Chas S Cannady
> Notary Public.

AFFIDAVIT OF ATTENDING PHYSICIAN OR MID-WIFE.

UNITED STATES OF AMERICA, Indian Territory, ⎫
       Southern   DISTRICT. ⎰

I,   Susan Arterberry[sic] , a   mid-wife   , on oath state that I attended on
Mrs.   Lillie Josephine Parrish   , wife of   J B Parrish   on the 19th   day of

April   , 1904; that there was born to her on said date a   female   child; that said child was living March 4, 1905, and is said to have been named Lois Aletha Parrish

Susan Arterbery

Witnesses To Mark:

{

Subscribed and sworn to before me this 10th   day of   April   , 1905

Chas S Cannady
Notary Public.

Choc New Born 1016
>Archie Mason Swarm
>(Born Feb. 17, 1903)
>Amanda Elizabeth Swarm
>(Born Dec. 23, 1904)

BIRTH AFFIDAVIT.

DEPARTMENT OF THE INTERIOR.
COMMISSION TO THE FIVE CIVILIZED TRIBES.

IN RE APPLICATION FOR ENROLLMENT, as a citizen of the   Choctaw   Nation, of Archie Mason Swarm   , born on the 17th   day of   February , 1903

Name of Father: Francis M. Swarm   a citizen of the United States ~~Nation~~.
Name of Mother: Inez Swarm   a citizen of the   Choctaw   Nation.

Postoffice   Garvin, Ind. Ter.

AFFIDAVIT OF MOTHER.

UNITED STATES OF AMERICA, Indian Territory, ⎤
     Central   **DISTRICT.** ⎦

     I,   Inez Swarm   , on oath state that I am   26   years of age and a citizen by blood   , of the   Choctaw   Nation; that I am the lawful wife of   Francis M Swarm , who is a citizen, ~~by~~ .... of the   United States ~~Nation~~; that a   male   child was born to me on   17th   day of   February   , 1903; that said child has been named Archie Mason Swarm   , and was living March 4, 1905.

Inez Swarm

Witnesses To Mark:

{

Subscribed and sworn to before me this 11th day of   April   , 1905

Wirt Franklin
Notary Public.

AFFIDAVIT OF ATTENDING PHYSICIAN OR MID-WIFE.

UNITED STATES OF AMERICA, Indian Territory, }
  Central   **DISTRICT.** }

I,   L. E. Bunn   , a mid-wife   , on oath state that I attended on
Mrs.   Inez Swarm   , wife of   Francis M Swarm   on the   17th   day of
February   , 1903; that there was born to her on said date a   male   child; that said
child was living March 4, 1905, and is said to have been named Archie Mason Swarm
                                                                                    her
                                                            L. E. x Bunn
Witnesses To Mark: mark
  { Vester W. Rose
  { Robert Anderson

Subscribed and sworn to before me this 11th day of   April   , 1905

Wirt Franklin
Notary Public.

BIRTH AFFIDAVIT.

DEPARTMENT OF THE INTERIOR.
COMMISSION TO THE FIVE CIVILIZED TRIBES.

IN RE APPLICATION FOR ENROLLMENT, as a citizen of the   Choctaw   Nation, of
Amanda Elizabeth Swarm   , born on the 23rd   day of   December , 1904

Name of Father: Francis M. Swarm   a citizen of the United States ~~Nation~~.
Name of Mother: Inez Swarm   a citizen of the   Choctaw   Nation.

Postoffice   Garvin, Ind. Ter.

AFFIDAVIT OF MOTHER.

UNITED STATES OF AMERICA, Indian Territory,
Central   DISTRICT.

I, Inez Swarm, on oath state that I am 26 years of age and a citizen by blood, of the Choctaw Nation; that I am the lawful wife of Francis M Swarm, who is a citizen, ~~by~~ .... of the United States ~~Nation~~; that a female child was born to me on 23rd day of December, 1904; that said child has been named Amanda Elizabeth Swarm, and was living March 4, 1905.

Inez Swarm

Witnesses To Mark:
{

Subscribed and sworn to before me this 11th day of April, 1905

Wirt Franklin
Notary Public.

AFFIDAVIT OF ATTENDING PHYSICIAN OR MID-WIFE.

UNITED STATES OF AMERICA, Indian Territory,
Central   DISTRICT.

I, L. E. Bunn, a mid-wife, on oath state that I attended on Mrs. Inez Swarm, wife of Francis M Swarm on the 23rd day of December, 1904; that there was born to her on said date a female child; that said child was living March 4, 1905, and is said to have been named Amanda Elizabeth Swarm

her
L. E. x Bunn
mark

Witnesses To Mark:
{ Vester W. Rose
  Robert Anderson

Subscribed and sworn to before me this 11th day of April, 1905

Wirt Franklin
Notary Public.

<u>Choc New Born 1017</u>
   Nancy Iva Webster
   (Born November 20, 1903)

_____

BIRTH AFFIDAVIT.

DEPARTMENT OF THE INTERIOR.
COMMISSION TO THE FIVE CIVILIZED TRIBES.

_____

IN RE APPLICATION FOR ENROLLMENT, as a citizen of the   Choctaw   Nation, of
Nancy Iva Webster   , born on the 20th   day of   November   , 1903

Name of Father: Daniel Webster   a citizen of the   Choctaw   Nation.
Name of Mother: Nannie W. Webster   a citizen of the   Choctaw   Nation.

Postoffice   Idabel, Ind. Ter.

_____

AFFIDAVIT OF MOTHER.

UNITED STATES OF AMERICA, Indian Territory, ⎫
   Central   DISTRICT. ⎭

   I,   Nannie W. Webster   , on oath state that I am   33   years of age and a
citizen by   marriage   , of the   Choctaw   Nation; that I am the lawful wife of
Daniel Webster   , who is a citizen, by blood   of the   Choctaw   Nation;
that a   female   child was born to me on   20th   day of   November   , 1903; that
said child has been named   Nancy Iva Webster   , and was living March 4, 1905.

                                        her
                        Nannie W. x Webster
Witnesses To Mark: mark
   ⎰ Robert Anderson
   ⎱ Vester W. Rose

   Subscribed and sworn to before me this 12th day of   April   , 1905

                        Wirt Franklin
                           Notary Public.

_____

179

AFFIDAVIT OF ATTENDING PHYSICIAN OR MID-WIFE.

UNITED STATES OF AMERICA, Indian Territory, ⎫
  Central   DISTRICT. ⎭

I,   Fannie Robinson   , a mid-wife   , on oath state that I attended on
Mrs. Nannie W. Webster   , wife of   Daniel Webster   on the 20th day of
November   , 1903; that there was born to her on said date a   female   child; that
said child was living March 4, 1905, and is said to have been named Nancy Iva Webster

                                 her
                       Fannie x Robinson
Witnesses To Mark: mark
    ⎧ Robert Anderson
    ⎩ Vester W. Rose

Subscribed and sworn to before me this 12th day of   April   , 1905

                       Wirt Franklin
                         Notary Public.

NEW BORN AFFIDAVIT

No ....

CHOCTAW ENROLLING COMMISSION

IN THE MATTER OF THE APPLICATION FOR ENROLLMENT as a citizen of the Choctaw
Nation, of   Nancy Ivy Webster   born on the 20th day
of November   190 3

Name of father Daniel Webster   a citizen of Choctaw   Nation,
final enrollment No. 2890
Name of mother Nannie W Webster   a citizen of Choctaw   Nation,
final enrollment No. 561

                    Idabel, I.T.   Postoffice.

AFFIDAVIT OF MOTHER

UNITED STATES OF AMERICA ⎫
   INDIAN TERRITORY ⎬
DISTRICT   Central ⎭

    I   Nannie W. Webster   , on oath state that I am 33   years of age and a citizen by   Intermarriage   of the   Choctaw   Nation, and as such have been placed upon the final roll of the   Choctaw   Nation, by the Honorable Secretary of the Interior my final enrollment number being   561   ; that I am the lawful wife of   Daniel Webster   , who is a citizen of the   Choctaw   Nation, and as such has been placed upon the final roll of said Nation by the Honorable Secretary of the Interior, his final enrollment number being   2890   and that a   female   child was born to me on the   20th day of   November   190 3; that said child has been named   Nancy Ivy Webster   , and is now living.

her

Nannie W. Webster   x

mark

WITNESSETH:

   Must be two witnesses ⎰   L.M. Leflore
   who are citizens   ⎱   John R White

    Subscribed and sworn to before me this, the   14th   day of   Feb   , 190 5

W.A. Shoney

Notary Public.

My Commission Expires:
     Jan 10, 1909

Affidavit of Attending Physician or Midwife

UNITED STATES OF AMERICA, ⎫
   INDIAN TERRITORY, ⎬
Central   DISTRICT ⎭

    I,   E. C. Davis   a   midwife on oath state that I attended on Mrs. Nannie W. Webster   wife of Daniel Webster on the   20th   day of   Nov , 190 3, that there was born to her on said date a   female child, that said child is now living, and is said to have been named   Nancy Ivy Webster

her

E.C. Davis   x   ~~M. D.~~

mark

    Subscribed and sworn to before me this the   17   day of   Feb   1905

W.A. Shoney

Notary Public.

Applications for Enrollment of Choctaw Newborn
Act of 1905   Volume XIV

WITNESSETH:

Must be two witnesses
who are citizens and
know the child.

{ John R White

Q. Herndon

We hereby certify that we are well acquainted with   E. C. Davis
a   midwife   and know   her   to be reputable and of good standing in
the community.

Must be two citizen{ John R White
witnesses.   Q. Herndon

Choc New Born 1018
> Elizabeth M. Hopkins
> (Born Aug. 9, 1904)

BIRTH AFFIDAVIT.

DEPARTMENT OF THE INTERIOR.
COMMISSION TO THE FIVE CIVILIZED TRIBES.

IN RE APPLICATION FOR ENROLLMENT, as a citizen of the   Choctaw   Nation, of
Elizabeth M. Hopkins   , born on the   9th   day of   August   , 1904

Name of Father: Thomas W. Hopkins   a citizen of the   Choctaw   Nation.
Name of Mother: Nova W. Hopkins   a citizen of the   Choctaw   Nation.

Postoffice   Garvin, Ind. Ter.

AFFIDAVIT OF MOTHER.

UNITED STATES OF AMERICA, Indian Territory, }
Central   DISTRICT. }

I,   Nova W. Hopkins   , on oath state that I am   26   years of age and a
citizen by   blood   , of the   Choctaw   Nation; that I am the lawful wife of
Thomas W. Hopkins   , who is a citizen, by   marriage   of the   Choctaw
Nation; that a   female   child was born to me on   9th day of   August   , 1904;
that said child has been named   Elizabeth M. Hopkins   , and was living March 4,
1905.

Nova W Hopkins

182

Witnesses To Mark:

{

Subscribed and sworn to before me this 10th   day of   April   , 1905

Wirt Franklin
Notary Public.

AFFIDAVIT OF ATTENDING PHYSICIAN OR MID-WIFE.

UNITED STATES OF AMERICA, Indian Territory, ⎫
    Central   **DISTRICT.** ⎭

I,   Ben L Denison   , a   Physician   , on oath state that I attended on Mrs.   Nova W. Hopkins   , wife of   Thomas W. Hopkins   on the 9th   day of August   , 1904; that there was born to her on said date a   Female   child; that said child was living March 4, 1905, and is said to have been named   Elizabeth M. Hopkins

B. L. Denison

Witnesses To Mark:

{

Subscribed and sworn to before me this 10th   day of   April   , 1905

Wirt Franklin
Notary Public.

Choc New Born 1019
    Selton Jones
    (Born Jan. 13, 1903)

Applications for Enrollment of Choctaw Newborn
Act of 1905   Volume XIV

United States of America,	)
	)
Indian Territory,	) ss.
	)
Central District.	)

I, John Tonihka, on oath state that I am twenty-seven years of age and a citizen by blood of the Choctaw Nation; that my post office address is Eagletown, Indian Territory; that I am personally acquainted with Viney Jones, wife of Thomas Jones, and have known said parties nearly all my like; that since their marriage, about four years ago, I have lived within three miles of where they have lived, near Eagletown, Indian Territory, that on or about the 13th day of January, 1903, there was born to the said Viney Jones a male child; that aid child is now living and is said to have been named Selton Jones.

John Tonihka

Subscribed and sworn to before me this 11th day of April, 1905.

Wirt Franklin
Notary Public.

BIRTH AFFIDAVIT.

DEPARTMENT OF THE INTERIOR.

COMMISSION TO THE FIVE CIVILIZED TRIBES.

IN RE APPLICATION FOR ENROLLMENT, as a citizen of the   Choctaw   Nation, of Selton Jones   , born on the 13th   day of   January , 1903

Name of Father: Thomas Jones   a citizen of the   Choctaw   Nation.
Name of Mother: Viney Jones   a citizen of the   Choctaw   Nation.

Postoffice   Eagletown, Ind. Ter.

AFFIDAVIT OF MOTHER.

UNITED STATES OF AMERICA, Indian Territory, ⎫
    Central   DISTRICT. ⎭

I,   Viney Jones   , on oath state that I am   26   years of age and a citizen by blood   , of the   Choctaw   Nation; that I am the lawful wife of   Thomas Jones , who is a citizen, by blood   of the   Choctaw   Nation; that a   male   child was born to me on   13th   day of   January   , 1903; that said child has been named Selton Jones   , and was living March 4, 1905.   her

Viney x Jones
mark

184

Witnesses To Mark:
   { Robert Anderson
    Vester W. Rose

      Subscribed and sworn to before me this   11th day of   April   , 1905

                    Wirt Franklin
                    Notary Public.

AFFIDAVIT OF ATTENDING PHYSICIAN OR MID-WIFE.

UNITED STATES OF AMERICA, Indian Territory, }
  Central   **DISTRICT.** }

      I, Thomas Jones   , ~~a~~ ...., on oath state that I attended on
Mrs. Viney Jones   , ~~wife of~~ *my wife* on the 13th day of   January   ,
1903; that there was born to her on said date a   male   child; that said child was living
March 4, 1905, and ~~is said to have~~ *has* been named Selton Jones

                        Thomas Jones
Witnesses To Mark:
   {

      Subscribed and sworn to before me this   11th day of   April   , 1905

                    Wirt Franklin
                    Notary Public.

                      7--NB--1019

            Muskogee, Indian Territory, June 2, 1905.

Thomas Jones,
      Eagletown, Indian Territory.

Dear Sir:

      Referring to the application for the enrollment of your infant child, Selton
Jones, born January 13, 1903, it is noted from the affidavits heretofore filed in this office
that you were the only one in attendance upon your wife at the time of the birth of the
applicant.

      In this event it will be necessary that the affidavits of two persons, who are
disinterested and not related to the applicant, who have actual knowledge of the facts that

the child was born, the date of his birth; that he was living March 4, 1905, and that Viney Jones is his mother be filed in this office.

The affidavit of John Tonihka to these facts has been filed. It will, therefore, be necessary that you secure a simular[sic] affidavit from another person.

This matter should receive your immediate attention as no further action can be taken relative to the enrollment of said child until the Commission has been furnished this affidavit.

Respectfully,

[sic]

7-NB-1019

Muskogee, Indian Territory, July 25, 1905.

Thomas Jones,
    Eagletown, Indian Territory.

Dear Sir:

Receipt is hereby acknowledged of the affidavits of Edmon Homer and Foston Wilson to the birth of Selton Jones January 13, 1903, and the same have been filed with the records of this office in the matter of the enrollment of said child.

Respectfully,

Commissioner.

(The affidavit below typed as given.)

United States of America,
    Indian territory,
    Central District.

I   Edmond Homma on oath states that I am   34 years of age, that my post office address is   Eagletown I.T.   that I was personally acquainted with   Viney Jones and know that there was born to her on the   13th   day of   January   1903   a   male child, which child was living on March 4, 1905, and said to have been named   Selton Jones

Edmon Homer

Sworn to and subscribed before me this the   15th day of   July   1905.

Jeff Gardner
Notary Public.

My commission expire 23, december 1905.

(The affidavit below typed as given.)

United States of America,
   Indian territory,
   Central District.

     I   Foston Wilson   on oath states that I am   23   years of age, that my post office address is   Eagletown I.T.   that I was personally acquainted with   Viney Jones and know that there was born to her on the   13th   day of   January   1903   a   male child, which child was living on March 4, 1905, and said to have been named   Selton Jones

Foston Wilson

Sworn to and subscribed before me this the   15th day of   July   1905.

Jeff Gardner
Notary Public.

My commission expire 23, december 1905.

Thomas Jones, roll
No. 3288.

Viney Jones father's
name Wilson Dyer (Dead)
Mother's name Emeline Dyer
(Dead). Was formerly wife
of Cole Wilson.

Choc New Born 1020
　　Folsom Jacob
　　(Born Feb. 10, 1904)

———————

BIRTH AFFIDAVIT.

DEPARTMENT OF THE INTERIOR,
COMMISSION TO THE FIVE CIVILIZED TRIBES.

———————

In Re Application for Enrollment, as a citizen of the　Choctaw　Nation,
of　Folsom Jacob　, born on the　10th　day of　February　, 1904

Name of Father:　Eli Jacob　　　　　a citizen of the　Choctaw　Nation.
Name of Mother:　Malin[sic] Jacob　　　a citizen of the　Choctaw　Nation.

Post-office　　Glover Ind Ter

———————

AFFIDAVIT OF MOTHER.

———————

UNITED STATES OF AMERICA, ⎫
　INDIAN TERRITORY,　　　⎬
　Central　　　District. ⎭

　　I,　Malin Jacob　, on oath state that I am　27　years of age and a citizen by
Blood　, of the　Choctaw　Nation; that I am the lawful wife of　Eli Jacob　, who
is a citizen, by Blood of the　Choctaw　Nation; that a　male　child was born to
me on　10　day of　February　, 1904 , that said child has been named　Folsom
Jacob　, and is now living.　　　　　　　　　　her
　　　　　　　　　　　　　　　　　Malin　x　Jacob
WITNESSES TO MARK:　　　　　　　　　　mark
　⎧ Ephraim McKinney
　⎩ Gaines Colbert

　　Subscribed and sworn to before me this　12th　day of　April AD　, 1905.

　　　　　　　　　　Simon Taylor
　　　　　　　　　　NOTARY PUBLIC.

———————

AFFIDAVIT OF ATTENDING PHYSICIAN OR MID-WIFE.

UNITED STATES OF AMERICA,
   INDIAN TERRITORY,
   Central   District.

    I,   Celia James   , a   Midwife   , on oath state that I attended on Mrs. Malin Jacob , wife of Eli Jacob on the 10th day of February A.D. , 1904 ; that there was born to her on said date a   male   child; that said child is now living and is said to have been named   Folsom Jacob

her
Celia x James
mark

WITNESSES TO MARK:
   { Ephraim McKinney
   { Gaines Colbert

    Subscribed and sworn to before me this 12th day of   April AD , 1905.

Simon Taylor
NOTARY PUBLIC.

BIRTH AFFIDAVIT.

DEPARTMENT OF THE INTERIOR.
COMMISSION TO THE FIVE CIVILIZED TRIBES.

   IN RE APPLICATION FOR ENROLLMENT, as a citizen of the   Choctaw   Nation, of Folsom Jacob   , born on the   10th   day of   February , 1904

Name of Father: Eli Jacob   a citizen of the   Choctaw   Nation.
Name of Mother: Milin[sic] Jacob   a citizen of the   Choctaw   Nation.

Postoffice   Lukfata, Ind. Ter.

AFFIDAVIT OF MOTHER.

UNITED STATES OF AMERICA, Indian Territory,
   Central   **DISTRICT.**

    I,   Milin Jacob   , on oath state that I am   about 30   years of age and a citizen by   blood   , of the   Choctaw   Nation; that I am the lawful wife of   Eli Jacob   , who is a citizen, by blood   of the   Choctaw   Nation; that a male   child was born to me on   10th   day of   February   , 1904; that said child has been named   Folsom Jacob   , and was living March 4, 1905.

189

her

Milin x Jacob

mark

Witnesses To Mark:

⎰ Robert Anderson

⎱ Vester W. Rose

Subscribed and sworn to before me this 19th day of April , 1905

Wirt Franklin

Notary Public.

AFFIDAVIT OF ATTENDING PHYSICIAN OR MID-WIFE.

UNITED STATES OF AMERICA, Indian Territory, ⎤

Central   DISTRICT. ⎦

I, Sillie James , a mid-wife , on oath state that I attended on
Mrs. Milin Jacob , wife of Eli Jacob on the 10th day of February ,
1904; that there was born to her on said date a male child; that said child was living
March 4, 1905, and is said to have been named Folsom Jacob

her

Sillie x James

mark

Witnesses To Mark:

⎰ Robert Anderson

⎱ Vester W. Rose

Subscribed and sworn to before me this 19th day of April , 1905

Wirt Franklin

Notary Public.

Choc New Born 1021

Mary Ida William

(Born Jan. 17, 1905)

BIRTH AFFIDAVIT.

DEPARTMENT OF THE INTERIOR.
COMMISSION TO THE FIVE CIVILIZED TRIBES.

IN RE APPLICATION FOR ENROLLMENT, as a citizen of the　　　Choctaw　　　Nation, of
Mary Ida William　　　, born on the 17th　day of　January　, 1905

Name of Father: Moses William　　　　　a citizen of the　Choctaw　Nation.
Name of Mother: Sophie William　　　　　a citizen of the　Choctaw　Nation.

Postoffice　　Garvin, Ind. Ter

AFFIDAVIT OF MOTHER.

UNITED STATES OF AMERICA, Indian Territory, ⎱
　　Central　　　　　　　DISTRICT. ⎰

I,　Moses William　, on oath state that I am　22　years of age and a citizen
by　blood　, of the　Choctaw　Nation; that I am the lawful ~~wife~~ *husband* of
Sophie William　, who is a citizen, by　blood　of the　Choctaw　Nation;
that a　female　child was born to ~~me~~ *us* on　17th　day of　January　, 1905;
that said child has been named　Mary Ida William　, and was living March 4, 1905.
and that the mother of said child is now sick and unable to appear before the Commission

　　　　　　　　　　　　Moses William
Witnesses To Mark:
⎰

Subscribed and sworn to before me this 11th　day of　April　, 1905

　　　　　　　　　Wirt Franklin
　　　　　　　　　　Notary Public.

AFFIDAVIT OF ATTENDING PHYSICIAN OR MID-WIFE.

UNITED STATES OF AMERICA, Indian Territory, ⎱
　　Central　　　　　　　DISTRICT. ⎰

I,　Sampson William　, a ...., on oath state that I attended on
Mrs.　Sophie William　, wife of　Moses William　on the　17th　day of
January　, 1905; that there was born to her on said date a　female　child; that said
child was living March 4, 1905, and is said to have been named　Mary Ida William

his
Sampson x William
mark

Witnesses To Mark:
- Robert Anderson
- Vester W. Rose

Subscribed and sworn to before me this 11th   day of   April   , 1905

Wirt Franklin
Notary Public.

BIRTH AFFIDAVIT.

DEPARTMENT OF THE INTERIOR.
COMMISSION TO THE FIVE CIVILIZED TRIBES.

IN RE APPLICATION FOR ENROLLMENT, as a citizen of the   Choctaw   Nation, of
Mary Ida William   , born on the   17th   day of   January   , 1905

Name of Father: Moses William   a citizen of the   Choctaw   Nation.
Name of Mother: Sophie William   a citizen of the   Choctaw   Nation.

Postoffice   Garvin, Ind. Ter

AFFIDAVIT OF MOTHER.

UNITED STATES OF AMERICA, Indian Territory,
Central   **DISTRICT.**

I,   Sophie William   , on oath state that I am   27   years of age and a citizen
by   blood   , of the   Choctaw   Nation; that I am the lawful wife of   Moses
William   , who is a citizen, by   blood   of the   Choctaw   Nation; that a
female   child was born to me on   17th   day of   January   , 1905; that said child
has been named   Mary Ida William   , and was living March 4, 1905.

her
Sophie x William
mark

Witnesses To Mark:
- Ephraim McKinney
- Melvina Taylor

Subscribed and sworn to before me this   15th   day of   April   , 1905

Simon Taylor
Notary Public.

Applications for Enrollment of Choctaw Newborn
Act of 1905   Volume XIV

AFFIDAVIT OF ATTENDING PHYSICIAN OR MID-WIFE.

UNITED STATES OF AMERICA, Indian Territory, ⎫
  Central   DISTRICT. ⎭

I,   Patsey Tanitobbi   , a Midwife   , on oath state that I attended on
Mrs.   Sophie William   , wife of   Moses William   on the 17th   day of
January   , 1905; that there was born to her on said date a   Female   child; that said
child was living March 4, 1905, and is said to have been named Mary Ida William

                          her
                    Patsey x Tanitobbi
Witnesses To Mark: mark
  { Ephraim McKinney
  { Melvina Taylor

Subscribed and sworn to before me this   15th   day of   April   , 1905

                    Simon Taylor
                      Notary Public.

Choctaw 501.

Muskogee, Indian Territory, April 18, 1905.

Moses William,
      Garvin, Indian Territory.

Dear Sir:

     Receipt is hereby acknowledged of the affidavits of Sophie Williams[sic] and
Patsey Tanitobbi to the birth of Mary Ida William, daughter of Moses and Sophie
William, January 17, 1905, and the same have been filed with our records as an
application for the enrollment of said child.

                Respectfully,

                        Chairman.

Choc New Born 1022
     Everett Loyd Hammers
     (Born Feb. 6, 1905)

Applications for Enrollment of Choctaw Newborn
Act of 1905   Volume XIV

BIRTH AFFIDAVIT.

DEPARTMENT OF THE INTERIOR.
COMMISSION TO THE FIVE CIVILIZED TRIBES.

_____

IN RE APPLICATION FOR ENROLLMENT, as a citizen of the   Choctaw   Nation, of
Everett Loyd Hammers   , born on the 6th   day of   February   , 1905

Name of Father: Albert Hammers   a citizen of the United States ~~Nation~~.
Name of Mother: Lora B Hulsey-Hammers   a citizen of the   Choctaw   Nation.
by blood enrolled as Lora B Hulsey No 8725

Postoffice   Pauls Valley I.T.

_____

AFFIDAVIT OF MOTHER.

UNITED STATES OF AMERICA, Indian Territory, ⎫
    Southern   DISTRICT. ⎰

I,   Lora B Hulsey Hammers   , on oath state that I am   nineteen   years of
age and a citizen by   blood   , of the   Choctaw   Nation; that I am the lawful wife
of   Albert Hammers   , who is a citizen, ~~by~~ *of the United States, that my maiden name
was Lora B Hulsey enrolled as such Choctaw roll 8725* that a   male   child was born to
me on   the Sixth   day of   February   , 1905; that said child has been named
Everett Loyd Hammers   , and was living March 4, 1905.

Lora B Hulsey Hammers

Witnesses To Mark:
⎰

Subscribed and sworn to before me this 3[d] day of   April   , 1905

Claude Weaver
Notary Public.
*in and for the Southern District of
the Indian Territory.*

_____

AFFIDAVIT OF ATTENDING PHYSICIAN OR MID-WIFE.

UNITED STATES OF AMERICA, Indian Territory, ⎫
    Central   DISTRICT. ⎰

I,   E.L. Evins   , a Physician   , on oath state that I attended on
Mrs.   Lora B Hulsey Hammers   , wife of   Albert Hammers   on the Sixth   day
of   February   , 1905; that there was born to her on said date a   male   child; that

194

said child was living March 4, 1905, and is said to have been named   Everett Loyd Hammers

E.L. Evins M.D.

Witnesses To Mark:

{

Subscribed and sworn to before me this 4 day of   April   , 1905

W.P. MᶜGinnis
Notary Public.
In and for the Central District Ind. Ter.

Com expires Mar 17 1909

Choc New Born 1023
    Lekoda James
    (Born Dec. 30, 1904)

BIRTH AFFIDAVIT.

DEPARTMENT OF THE INTERIOR.
COMMISSION TO THE FIVE CIVILIZED TRIBES.

IN RE APPLICATION FOR ENROLLMENT, as a citizen of the   Choctaw   Nation, of Lekoda James   , born on the 30th day of Dec   , 1904

Name of Father: Acie W James   a citizen of the   Choctaw   Nation.
Name of Mother: Lela James   a citizen of the   Choctaw   Nation.

Postoffice   Albany Ind. T.

AFFIDAVIT OF MOTHER.

UNITED STATES OF AMERICA, Indian Territory, ⎱
....DISTRICT. ⎰

I,   Lela James   , on oath state that I am 27   years of age and a citizen by Marriage   , of the   Choctaw   Nation; that I am the lawful wife of   Acie W. James, who is a citizen, by Blood   of the   Choctaw   Nation; that a   Female child was born to me on 30th day of Dec   , 1904; that said child has been named Lekoda James   , and was living March 4, 1905.

Lela James

Witnesses To Mark:
  Andrew C Hondage
  Ollie Hutchirson[sic]

Subscribed and sworn to before me this 7th day of   April   , 1905

J.M. Reasor
Notary Public.

AFFIDAVIT OF ATTENDING PHYSICIAN OR MID-WIFE.

UNITED STATES OF AMERICA, Indian Territory,
  Central   **DISTRICT.**

I,   P.L. Cain   , a   Physician   , on oath state that I attended on
Mrs.   Lela James   , wife of   Acie W James   on the   30th day of   December ,
1904; that there was born to her on said date a   Female   child; that said child was
living March 4, 1905, and is said to have been named Lekoda James

P.L. Cain

Witnesses To Mark:
  Andrew C Hondage
  Ollie Hutchirson[sic]

Subscribed and sworn to before me this 24th day of   March   , 1905

J.M. Reasor
Notary Public.

7-NB-1023

Muskogee, Indian Territory, July 25, 1905.

Acie W. James,
        Albany, Indian Territory.

Dear Sir:

Receipt is hereby acknowledged of your letter of July 18, 1905, asking the status of the enrollment of your child, Lekoda James.

In reply to your letter you are advised that the name of your child Lekoda James has been placed upon a schedule of citizens by blood of the Choctaw Nation which has been forwarded the Secretary of the Interior, and you will be notified when her enrollment is approved.

196

Respectfully,

Commissioner.

Choc New Born 1024
    Kermit Dillard
    (Born June 30, 1903)

BIRTH AFFIDAVIT.
DEPARTMENT OF THE INTERIOR.
COMMISSION TO THE FIVE CIVILIZED TRIBES.

IN RE APPLICATION FOR ENROLLMENT, as a citizen of the   Chocktaw[sic]   Nation,
of Kermit Dillard   , born on the 30 day of June , 1903

Name of Father: Hamilton Dillard   a citizen of the   Chocktaw   Nation.
Name of Mother: Victoria Dillard   a citizen of the   Chocktaw   Nation.

Postoffice   Keller I.T.

AFFIDAVIT OF MOTHER.

UNITED STATES OF AMERICA, Indian Territory, ⎱
    Southern   **DISTRICT.** ⎰

    I,   Victora[sic] Dillard   , on oath state that I am 38   years of age and a
citizen by   Marriage   , of the   Chocktaw   Nation; that I am the lawful wife of
Hamilton Dillard   , who is a citizen, by Blood   of the   Chocktaw
Nation; that a   male   child was born to me on 30 day of June   , 1903; that
said child has been named Kermit Dillard   , and was living March 4, 1905.

                  Victoria Dillard

Witnesses To Mark:
    ⎰ J C Triplett
    ⎱ F.G. Robinson

    Subscribed and sworn to before me this 7 day of   April   , 1905

                J.D. Wiggins
                  Notary Public.

AFFIDAVIT OF ATTENDING PHYSICIAN OR MID-WIFE.

UNITED STATES OF AMERICA, Indian Territory, ⎫
  Southern   DISTRICT. ⎭

I,   A.B. Davis M.D.   , a   Physician   , on oath state that I attended on
Mrs.   Victoria Dillard   , wife of   Hamilton Dillard   on the 30 day of   June ,
1903; that there was born to her on said date a   Male   child; that said child was
living March 4, 1905, and is said to have been named Kermit Dillard

                              A.B. Davis
Witnesses To Mark:
  ⎧ J C Triplett
  ⎩ F.G. Robinson

      Subscribed and sworn to before me this 7 day of   April   , 1905

                         J.D. Wiggins
                              Notary Public.

Choc New Born 1025
     Peter Jay Hudson, Jr.
     (Born Feb. 6, 1903)

NEW-BORN AFFIDAVIT.

            Number...............

...Choctaw Enrolling Commission...

      IN THE MATTER OF THE APPLICATION FOR ENROLLMENT, as a citizen of the
Choctaw   Nation, of   Peter Jay Hudson

born on the 16th   day of ___February___ 190 3

Name of father   Peter J Hudson   a citizen of   Choctaw
Nation final enrollment No. 5483
Name of mother   Amanda J Hudson   a citizen of   Choctaw
Nation final enrollment No. 5484

                         Postoffice   Tushkahoma[sic] I.T.

AFFIDAVIT OF MOTHER.

UNITED STATES OF AMERICA
INDIAN TERRITORY
Central   DISTRICT

I   Amanda J Hudson   , on oath state that I am
30   years of age and a citizen by   Blood   of the   Choctaw   Nation,
and as such have been placed upon the final roll of the   Choctaw   Nation, by the Honorable
Secretary of the Interior my final enrollment number being   5484 ; that I am the lawful wife
of   Peter J Hudson   , who is a citizen of the   Choctaw   Nation, and as such has
been placed upon the final roll of said Nation by the Honorable Secretary of the Interior, his
final enrollment number being   5483   and that a   Male   child was born to me on the
16th day of   February   190 3; that said child has been named   Peter Jay Hudson   ,
and is now living.

Amanda J Hudson

Witnesseth.

Must be two   } E B McKinney
Witnesses who

are Citizens.   *(Name Illegible)*

Subscribed and sworn to before me this   31st day of   Jan   190 5

Peter W Hudson
Notary Public.

My commission expires:
My Commission Expires Feb. 24, 1906.

AFFIDAVIT OF ATTENDING PHYSICIAN OR MIDWIFE

UNITED STATES OF AMERICA
INDIAN TERRITORY
Central   DISTRICT

I,   Julia H Williams   a   midwife
on oath state that I attended on Mrs.   Amanda J Hudson   wife of Peter J Hudson
on the   16th day of   February , 190 3 , that there was born to her on said date a   male
child, that said child is now living, and is said to have been named   Peter Jay Hudson

Julia H Williams   *M.D.*
Subscribed and sworn to before me this, the   31   day of
January   190 5

WITNESSETH: Peter W Hudson   Notary Public.
Must be two witnesses { EB McKinney   My Commission Expires Feb. 24, 1906.
who are citizens

(Name Illegible)

We hereby certify that we are well acquainted with Julia H Williams
a Midwife and know her to be reputable and of good standing in the community.

E.B. McKinney

(Name Illegible)

_____

7 - 5483 - 5484

BIRTH AFFIDAVIT.

DEPARTMENT OF THE INTERIOR.
COMMISSION TO THE FIVE CIVILIZED TRIBES.

_____

IN RE APPLICATION FOR ENROLLMENT, as a citizen of the Choctaw Nation, of
Peter Jay Hudson Jr , born on the 16 day of February , 1903

Name of Father: Peter J Hudson   a citizen of the Choc Nation.
Name of Mother: Amana Hudson   a citizen of the Choc Nation.

Postoffice Tuskahoma I.T.

_____

AFFIDAVIT OF MOTHER.

UNITED STATES OF AMERICA, Indian Territory,
Central   **DISTRICT.**

    I, Amanda Hudson , on oath state that I am 30 years of age and a citizen by blood , of the Choc Nation; that I am the lawful wife of Peter J Hudson , who is a citizen, by blood of the Choctaw Nation; that a male child was born to me on 16 day of February , 1903; that said child has been named Peter Jay Hudson Jr , and was living March 4, 1905.

Amanda Hudson

Witnesses To Mark:

    Subscribed and sworn to before me this 12 day of April , 1905

OL Johnson
Notary Public.

_____

Applications for Enrollment of Choctaw Newborn
Act of 1905   Volume XIV

AFFIDAVIT OF ATTENDING PHYSICIAN OR MID-WIFE.

UNITED STATES OF AMERICA, Indian Territory, ⎱
   Central   DISTRICT. ⎰

    I, Julia Williams   , a midwife   , on oath state that I attended on
Mrs. Amanda Hudson   , wife of   Peter J Hudson   on the 16 day of
February   , 1903; that there was born to her on said date a   male   child; that said
child was living March 4, 1905, and is said to have been named Peter Jay Hudson Jr

her
Julia x Williams
mark

Witnesses To Mark:
  ⎰ *(Name Illegible)*
  ⎱ John McGill

    Subscribed and sworn to before me this 6 day of April   , 1905

My Commission Expires Feb. 24, 1906.   PW Hudson
                                   Notary Public.

Choc New Born 1026
    Sweeney John
    (Born Jan. 21, 1903)

BIRTH AFFIDAVIT.
DEPARTMENT OF THE INTERIOR.
COMMISSION TO THE FIVE CIVILIZED TRIBES.

    IN RE APPLICATION FOR ENROLLMENT, as a citizen of the   Choctaw   Nation, of
Sweeney John   , born on the 21st day of January , 1903

Name of Father: Albert John   a citizen of the Choctaw   Nation.
Name of Mother: Elizabeth John   a citizen of the Choctaw   Nation.

                   Postoffice   Lukfata, Ind. Ter.

AFFIDAVIT OF MOTHER.

Child present
W.J.

UNITED STATES OF AMERICA, Indian Territory, ⎫
Central   DISTRICT. ⎭

I,   Elizabeth John   , on oath state that I am   about 33   years of age and a citizen by   blood   , of the   Choctaw   Nation; that I am the lawful wife of Albert John   , who is a citizen, by blood   of the   Choctaw   Nation; that a   male   child was born to me on   21st day of   January   , 1903; that said child has been named   Sweeney John   , and was living March 4, 1905. *and that no physician or midwife attended me when said child was born.*

                                              her
                                    Elizabeth x John
Witnesses To Mark: mark
⎰ Robert Anderson
⎱ Vester W. Rose

Subscribed and sworn to before me this 13th day of   April   , 1905

                          Wirt Franklin
                          Notary Public.

AFFIDAVIT OF ATTENDING PHYSICIAN OR MID-WIFE.

UNITED STATES OF AMERICA, Indian Territory, ⎫
Central   DISTRICT. ⎭

I,   Albert John   , ~~a~~ ...., on oath state that I attended on Mrs.   Elizabeth John   , ~~wife of~~ *my wife*   on the 21st day of   January   , 1903; that there was born to her on said date a   male   child; that said child was living March 4, 1905, and ~~is said to have~~ *has* been named   Sweeney John; *and that no one else was present when said child was born.*

                          Albert John
Witnesses To Mark:
⎰

Subscribed and sworn to before me this 13th day of   April   , 1905

                          Wirt Franklin
                          Notary Public.

NEW-BORN AFFIDAVIT.

Number...............

Choctaw Enrolling Commission.

IN THE MATTER OF THE APPLICATION FOR ENROLLMENT, as a citizen of the Choctaw   Nation, of   Sweeney John

born on the   21ˢᵗ   day of   Jan   190 3

Name of father   Albert John   a citizen of   Choctaw
Nation final enrollment No   2635
Name of mother   Elizabeth John   a citizen of   Choctaw
Nation final enrollment No 2636

Postoffice   Lukfatah IT

AFFIDAVIT OF MOTHER.

UNITED STATES OF AMERICA, ⎫
    INDIAN TERRITORY,   ⎬
    Central   DISTRICT ⎭

I   Elizabeth John   on oath state that I
am   40   years of age and a citizen by   blood   of the   Choctaw   Nation, and as
such have been placed upon the final roll of the   Choctaw   Nation, by the Honorable
Secretary of the Interior my final enrollment number being   2636   ; that I am the lawful
wife of   Albert John   , who is a citizen of the   Choctaw   Nation, and as
such has been placed upon the final roll of said Nation by the Honorable Secretary of the
Interior, his final enrollment number being   2635   and that a   male   child was born to
me on the   21ˢᵗ   day of   Jan   190 3 ; that said child has been named   Sweeney John ,
and is now living.   her
                              Elizabeth John x
WITNESSETH: mark
    Must be two ⎫ Sina Hinson
    Witnesses who ⎬
    are Citizens. ⎭ Phillip Ish Conner

Subscribed and sworn to before me this   17   day of   Jan   190 5

W.A. Shoney
                                        Notary Public.
My commission expires   Jan 10, 1909

203

Affidavit of Attending Physician or Midwife

UNITED STATES OF AMERICA, ⎫
    INDIAN TERRITORY, ⎬
  Central   DISTRICT ⎭

I,   Albert John   a   attendant
on oath state that I attended on Mrs. Elizabeth John   wife of Albert John
on the 21ˢᵗ   day of Jan , 190 3, that there was born to her on said date a   male   child,
that said child is now living, and is said to have been named Sweeney John

Albert John   M. D.

Subscribed and sworn to before me this the   16   day of Jan   1905

W.A. Shoney
Notary Public.

WITNESSETH:

Must be two witnesses ⎰ Mrs Sina Hinson
who are citizens and ⎱
know the child.   Phillip Ish Conner

We hereby certify that we are well acquainted with   Albert John
a Attendant   and know   him   to be reputable and of good standing in the
community.

Must be two citizen⎰ Sina Hinson
witnesses.   ⎱ Phillip Ish Conner

(The affidavit below typed as given.)

Central District
Choctaw Nation

I David Hinson on his oath states that he is not related to Albert John or his Family in any
way, and has no intrust in this case and that on the 21 day of January A.D. 1903 there was
borned[sic] to Elizabeth John a male child and said child is now living, and has been
named Sweeney John
I am 34 years of age and my Post Office is Glover Ind Ter
Signed   David Hinson
    Subscribed and sworn to before me this 31 day of July A D 1905
J.L. Merry
Notary Public
My Commission expires My 8th 1908

204

United States of America,)
)
Indian Territory,   )   ss.
)
Central District.   )

    I, Sina Hickman, on oath state that I am twenty-six years of age and a citizen by blood of the Choctaw Nation; that my post office address is Lukfata, Indian Territory; that I am personally acquainted with Elizabeth John, wife of Albert John, and have known said parties for about ten years; that I live within one mile of where they live, near Lukfata, Indian Territory; that I am at their home quite often; that I know of my own knowledge that on or about the 21st day of January, 1903, there was born to the said Elizabeth John a male child; that said child is now living and has been named Sweeney John.

Sina Hickman

Subscribed and sworn to before me this 13th day of April, 1905.

Wirt Franklin
Notary Public.

W^mO.B.

| COMMISSIONERS:
TAMS BIXBY,
THOMAS B. NEEDLES,
C.R. BRECKINRIDGE.

WM. O. BEALL
Secretary | DEPARTMENT OF THE INTERIOR,
COMMISSIONER TO THE FIVE CIVILIZED TRIBES. | REFER IN REPLY TO THE FOLLOWING:

7--NB--1026 |

ADDRESS ONLY THE
COMMISSION TO THE FIVE CIVILIZED TRIBES.

Muskogee, Indian Territory, June 1, 1905.

Albert John,
    Lukfata, Indian Territory.

Dear Sir:

    Referring to the application for the enrollment of your infant child, Sweeney John, born January 21, 1903, it is noted from the affidavits heretofore filed in this office that you were the only one in attendance upon your wife at the time of the birth of the applicant.

    In this event it will be necessary that the affidavits of two persons, who are disinterested and not related to the applicant, who have actual knowledge of the facts that the child was born, the date of birth; that he was living on March 4, 1905, and that Elizabeth John is his mother be filed in this office.

205

The affidavit of Sina Hickman to these facts has been filed. It will, therefore, be necessary that you secure a similar affidavit of another person.

This matter should receive your immediate attention as no further action can be taken relative to the enrollment of said child until the Commission has been furnished this affidavit.

Respectfully,

T.B. Needles
Commissioner in Charge.

7-NB-1026

Muskogee, Indian Territory, July 28, 1905.

Albert John,
Lukfata, Indian Territory.

Dear Sir:

Your attention is called to a communication addressed to you by the Commission to the Five Civilized Tribes under date of June 1, 1905, relative to the enrollment of your infant child, Sweeney John, born January 21, 1903, in which you were requested to supply additional evidence of one witness, who is disinterested and not related to the applicant, and who has actual knowledge of the facts, that the child was born, the date of its birth, and that he was living March 4, 1905, also that Elizabeth John is his mother. No reply to this letter has been received.

The matter should receive your immediate attention as no further action can be taken relative to the enrollment of said child until the evidence requested is supplied.

Respectfully,

Commissioner.

7-NB-1026

Muskogee, Indian Territory, August 7, 1905.

Albert John,
Lukfata, Indian Territory.

Dear Sir:

Receipt is hereby acknowledged of the affidavit of David Hinson to the birth of Sweeney John son of Albert and Elizabeth John, January 21, 1903, and the same has been filed with the records of this office in the matter of the enrollment of said child.

Respectfully,

Commissioner.

Choc New Born 1027
William Harvey Stidham
(Born Dec. 23, 1904)

BIRTH AFFIDAVIT.
DEPARTMENT OF THE INTERIOR.
COMMISSION TO THE FIVE CIVILIZED TRIBES.

IN RE APPLICATION FOR ENROLLMENT, as a citizen of the   Choctaw   Nation, of
William Harvey Stidham   , born on the   23   day of   December   , 1904

Name of Father: Jessie Stidham   a citizen of the   Choctaw   Nation.
Name of Mother: Naumie Stidham   a citizen of the   Choctaw   Nation.

Postoffice   Alma, I.T.

AFFIDAVIT OF MOTHER.

UNITED STATES OF AMERICA, Indian Territory, ⎱
   Southern   DISTRICT. ⎰

I,   Naumie Stidham   , on oath state that I am   32   years of age and a citizen by   Intermarriage   , of the   Choctaw   Nation; that I am the lawful wife of Jessie Stidham   , who is a citizen, by blood   of the   Choctaw   Nation;

207

that a   male   child was born to me on 23   day of December   , 1904; that said child has been named   William Harvey Stidham   , and was living March 4, 1905.

Naumie Stidham

Witnesses To Mark:

Subscribed and sworn to before me this 31 day of   March   , 1905

J.E. Harbison
Notary Public.
My Commission
expires Dec 6-08

AFFIDAVIT OF ATTENDING PHYSICIAN OR MID-WIFE.

UNITED STATES OF AMERICA, Indian Territory, ⎱
Southern   DISTRICT. ⎰

I,   J.E. Harbison M.D.   , a Physician   , on oath state that I attended on Mrs. Naumie Stidham   , wife of Jessie Stidham   on the 23 day of Dec   , 1904; that there was born to her on said date a   male   child; that said child was living March 4, 1905, and is said to have been named William Harvey Stidham

J.E. Harbison MD

Witnesses To Mark:

Subscribed and sworn to before me this 31 day of   March   , 1905

J.P. Bodard
Notary Public.

My commission
expires March 8/1908

Choc New Born 1028
Virgia Lucile[sic] Clark
(Born Jan. 30, 1905)

BIRTH AFFIDAVIT.

DEPARTMENT OF THE INTERIOR.
COMMISSION TO THE FIVE CIVILIZED TRIBES.

IN RE APPLICATION FOR ENROLLMENT, as a citizen of the   Choctaw   Nation, of
Virgia Lucile[sic] Clark   , born on the 30th   day of   Jan , 1905

Name of Father: Thomas A Clark   a citizen of the   Choctaw   Nation.
Name of Mother: Burnetta Anna Clark   a citizen of the   Choctaw   Nation.

Postoffice   Bennington I.T.

AFFIDAVIT OF MOTHER.

UNITED STATES OF AMERICA, Indian Territory, ⎱
   Cent   DISTRICT. ⎰

I,   Burnetta Anna Clark   , on oath state that I am   26   years of age and a
citizen by   blood   , of the   Choctaw   Nation; that I am the lawful wife of
Thos A Clark   , who is a citizen, by   marriage   of the   Choctaw   Nation;
that a   Female   child was born to me on   30th   day of   January   , 1905; that
said child has been named   Virgia Lucill Clark   , and was living March 4, 1905.

Burnetta A. Clark

Witnesses To Mark:
   {

Subscribed and sworn to before me this 25th day of   Mch   , 1905

B.W. Williams
Notary Public.

AFFIDAVIT OF ATTENDING PHYSICIAN OR MID-WIFE.

UNITED STATES OF AMERICA, Indian Territory, ⎱
   Cent   DISTRICT. ⎰

I,   Mollie Caruthers   , a   Midwife   , on oath state that I attended on
Mrs.   Burnetta A. Clark   , wife of Thos. A. Clark   on the 30th day of Jan ,
1905; that there was born to her on said date a   Female   child; that said child was
living March 4, 1905, and is said to have been named Virgia Lucill Clark

Mollie Caruthers

Witnesses To Mark:
   {

Subscribed and sworn to before me this 25th   day of   Mch   , 1905

B.W. Williams
Notary Public.

Muskogee, Indian Territory, April 6, 1905.

Thomas A. Clark,
Bennington, Indian Territory.

Dear Sir:

Receipt is hereby acknowledged of the affidavits of Burnetta A. Clark and Mollie Carruthers[sic] to the birth of Virgie[sic] Lucill Clark, daughter of Thomas A. and Burnetta Anna Clark, January 30, 1905.

It appears from the affidavit of the mother that she is a citizen by blood of the Choctaw Nation. If this is correct you are requested to state when, where and under what name she was listed for enrollment, the names of her parents and any other information which will enable us to identify her upon our records. This matter should receive your immediate attention in order that proper disposition may be made of the application for the enrollment of this child.

Respectfully,

Commissioner in Charge.

7-4553

Muskogee, Indian Territory, April 19, 1905.

Thomas A. Clark,
Bennington, Indian Territory.

Dear Sir:

Receipt is hereby acknowledged of your letter of April 10, 1905, replying to our communication of April 6, 1905, in which you give information relative to the enrollment of Burnetta Anna Clark which has enabled us to identify her upon our records as an enrolled citizen by blood of the Choctaw Nation.

The affidavits of Burnetta A. Clark and Mollie Caruthers to the birth of Virgia Lucile Clark, daughter of Thomas A. and Burnetta Anna Clark January 30, 1905, have been filed with our records as an application for the enrollment of said child.

210

Applications for Enrollment of Choctaw Newborn
Act of 1905   Volume XIV

Respectfully,

Chairman.

Choc New Born 1029
   Willie Wade
   (Born Jan 12, 1904)

BIRTH AFFIDAVIT.

DEPARTMENT OF THE INTERIOR.
COMMISSION TO THE FIVE CIVILIZED TRIBES.

IN RE APPLICATION FOR ENROLLMENT, as a citizen of the   Choctaw   Nation, of
Willie Wade   , born on the 12th day of   January   , 1904

Name of Father: Scott Wade   a citizen of the   U.S.A.   Nation.
Name of Mother: Mary Wade - nee Heavener   a citizen of the   Choctaw   Nation.

Postoffice   Reichert, Ind. Ter.

AFFIDAVIT OF MOTHER.

UNITED STATES OF AMERICA, Indian Territory,
.... DISTRICT.

   I,   Mary Wade - nee Heavener   , on oath state that I am   19   years of age
and a citizen by   blood   , of the   Choctaw   Nation; that I am the lawful wife of
Scott Wade   , who is a citizen, by ——— of the   U. S. A.   Nation; that a   male
child was born to me on   12th day of   January   , 1904; that said child has been
named   Willie Wade   , and was living March 4, 1905.

                                   Mary Wade
Witnesses To Mark:

   Subscribed and sworn to before me this   7th day of   April   , 1905

                         Lacey P Bobo
                              Notary Public.

211

AFFIDAVIT OF ATTENDING PHYSICIAN OR MID-WIFE.

UNITED STATES OF AMERICA, Indian Territory, ⎫
    Central   DISTRICT. ⎰

I, Gussie Ward , a midwife , on oath state that I attended on Mrs. Mary Wade - nee Heavener , wife of Scott Wade on the 12th day of January , 1904; that there was born to her on said date a male child; that said child was living March 4, 1905, and is said to have been named Willie Wade

Gussie Ward

Witnesses To Mark:

⎰

Subscribed and sworn to before me this 7th day of April , 1905

Lacey P Bobo
Notary Public.

NEW BORN AFFIDAVIT

No ....

CHOCTAW ENROLLING COMMISSION

IN THE MATTER OF THE APPLICATION FOR ENROLLMENT as a citizen of the Choctaw Nation, of Willie Wade born on the 12 day of January 190 4

Name of father Scott Wade a citizen of non Nation, final enrollment No. ——
Name of mother Mary Wade (nee Heavener) a citizen of Choctaw Nation, final enrollment No. 6415

Reichert I.T. Postoffice.

AFFIDAVIT OF MOTHER

UNITED STATES OF AMERICA ⎫
    INDIAN TERRITORY ⎬
DISTRICT   Central ⎭

I Mary Wade (nee Heavener) , on oath state that I am 19 years of age and a citizen by blood of the Choctaw Nation, and as such have been placed upon the final roll of the   Choctaw   Nation, by the Honorable Secretary of the Interior my final enrollment number being   6415   ; that I am the lawful wife of   Scott Wade   , who is a citizen of the   non   Nation, and as such has been placed upon the final roll of said Nation by the Honorable Secretary of the Interior, his final enrollment number being   — and that a   Male   child was born to me on the   12   day of   January   190 4; that said child has been named Willie Wade   , and is now living.

WITNESSETH: Mary Wade

Must be two witnesses ⎰ David Ward
who are citizens   ⎱ John Folsom

Subscribed and sworn to before me this, the   16 day of   February   , 190 5

James Bower
Notary Public.

My Commission Expires:
Sept 23-1907

Affidavit of Attending Physician or Midwife

UNITED STATES OF AMERICA, ⎫
    INDIAN TERRITORY,   ⎬
  Central   DISTRICT ⎭

I,   M A Stewart   a   Practicing Physician on oath state that I attended on Mrs. Mary Wade (nee Heavener)   wife of   Scott Wade on the   12   day of   January , 190 4, that there was born to her on said date a   male child, that said child is now living, and is said to have been named Willie Wade

MA Stewart   M. D.

Subscribed and sworn to before me this the   16   day of   February   1905

James Bower
Notary Public.

WITNESSETH:

Must be two witnesses ⎰ David Ward
who are citizens and   ⎬
know the child.   ⎱ John Folsom

We hereby certify that we are well acquainted with   M.A. Stewart a   Practicing Physician   and know   him   to be reputable and of good standing in the community.

Must be two citizen ⎰ David Ward
witnesses.   ⎱ John Folsom

Applications for Enrollment of Choctaw Newborn
Act of 1905   Volume XIV

Choc New Born 1030
>   Crystal May Askew
>   (Born Oct. 11, 1904)

BIRTH AFFIDAVIT.

DEPARTMENT OF THE INTERIOR.
COMMISSION TO THE FIVE CIVILIZED TRIBES.

IN RE APPLICATION FOR ENROLLMENT, as a citizen of the　　　Choctaw　　　Nation, of
Crystal May Askew　　　, born on the 11th　day of　October　, 1904

Name of Father: Bolden Askew　　　　　　a citizen of the　Choctaw　Nation.
Name of Mother: Lelia Ethel Askew　　　　a citizen of the　Arkansas　Nation.

Postoffice　　Stockton, Calif

AFFIDAVIT OF MOTHER.

UNITED STATES OF AMERICA, Indian Territory, ⎱ s. s.
State of California,　　　　　　DISTRICT. ⎰
County of San Joaquin.

I,　Lelia Ethel Askew　　, on oath state that I am　twenty　years of age and a
citizen by　birth　, of the　State of Arkansas　Nation; that I am the lawful wife of
Bolden Askew　　, who is a citizen, by　Blood　of the　Choctaw　Nation;
that a　Female　child was born to me on　Eleventh　day of　October　, 1904;
that said child has been named　Crystal May Askew　, and was living March 4, 1905.

Lelia Ethel Askew

Witnesses To Mark:
>   ⎰ Arthur L. Levices Ky
>   ⎱ M. Kreider

Subscribed and sworn to before me this　Third　day of　April　, 1905

Arthur L Levices Ky
Notary Public.
**In and for the County of San Joaquin,
State of California.**

214

AFFIDAVIT OF ATTENDING PHYSICIAN OR MID-WIFE.

UNITED STATES OF AMERICA, ~~Indian Territory~~, ⎫
State of California,　　　　DISTRICT. ⎬
County of Yuba.　　　　　　　　　　⎭

　　　I,　C.W. Lund　　　　, a　Physician　　, on oath state that I attended on
Mrs.　Lelia Ethel Askew　　, wife of　Bolden Askew　　on the　11th　day of
October　　, 1904; that there was born to her on said date a　Female　　child; that said
child was living March 4, 1905, and is said to have been named　Crystal May Askew

　　　　　　　　　　　　　　　　　　　C.W. Lund M.D.

Witnesses To Mark:
　　⎧ Minnie Anderson
　　⎩ C.T. Manwell

　　　　Subscribed and sworn to before me this　5th day of　　April　　, 1905

　　　　　　　　　　　　　　　Minnie Anderson
　　　　　　　　　　　　　　　　　　Notary Public.

CERTIFICATE OF RECORD.

United States of America, ⎫
　INDIAN TERRITORY,　　　⎬ ss.
　Western District.　　　　⎭

　　　I, ROBERT P. HARRISON, Clerk of the United States Court in the Western District,
Indian Territory, do hereby certify that the instrument hereto attached was filed for record in my
office the　16　day of　Sept　　1903 at ....M., and duly recorded in Book　P　,
Marriage Record, Page　128

　　　　　WITNESS my hand and seal of said Court at Muscogee, in said Territory,
　　　　　this　16　　day of　Sept　　A. D. 1903

　　　　　　　　　　　　　　　R P Harrison　　　　Clerk.
By　J Harlan　　　Deputy.

𝕸ARRIAGE 𝕷ICENSE.
••••••••

𝖀niteb 𝕾tates of 𝖆merica,
    INDIAN TERRITORY, } *ss.*   *No.* **236**
    Western District.

To Any Person Authorized by Law to Solemnize Marriage---Greeting:

𝖄**ou are** 𝕳**ereby** 𝕮**ommanded** *to Solemnize the Rite and Publish the Banns of Matrimony between Mr.*   J.B. Askew   *of*   Wagoner   *, in the Indian Territory, aged* 23   *years and* M*iss* Ethel Rowley   *of*   Wagoner   *in the Indian Territory aged*   18 *years according to law, and do you officially sign and return this License to the parties therein named.*

WITNESS my hand and official seal at Muscogee Indian Territory this   10th   *day of* September   *A.D. 190* 3

                          R.P. Harrison
                               Clerk of the U.S. Court

By   A.J. Byons   *Deputy*

CERTIFICATE OF MARRIAGE.
•••••

𝖀niteb 𝕾tates of 𝖆merica,
    INDIAN TERRITORY, } *ss.*
    Western District.

I,   Henry R Walling   *, a Minister of the Gospel, DO HEREBY CERTIFY that on the* 10   *day of*   September.   *A. D. 1903, I did duly and according to law as commanded in the foregoing License, solemnize the Rite and publish the Banns of Matrimony between the parties therein named.*

WITNESS my hand this 15 *day of*   September   *A. D. 1903*

My credentials are recorded in the office of the Clerk of the United States Court, Indian Territory, Western District, Book   C   *, Page*   224   *.*

                          Henry R Walling
                          A Minister of the Gospel

Note—This License and Certificate of Marriage must be returned to the Office of the Clerk of the United States Court in the Northern District, Indian Territory, from whence it was issued, within sixty days from the date thereof, or the party to whom the license was issued will be liable in the amount of the One Hundred Dollars ($100.00)

Applications for Enrollment of Choctaw Newborn
Act of 1905   Volume XIV

Choctaw N.B. 1030.

Muskogee, Indian Territory, May 2, 1905.

J. Bolden Askew,
     Stockton, California.

Dear Sir:

     Receipt is hereby acknowledged of your letter of April 25, transmitting certified copy of the marriage license and certificate between J. D. Askew and Ethel Rowley, which you offer in support of the application for the enrollment of Crystal May Askew, and the same has been filed with the records in this case. In the event further evidence is necessary to enable us to determine the right of this child to enrollment you will be duly notified.

                      Respectfully,

                                Chairman.

Choc New Born 1031
     Emma Dickinson
     (Born December 31, 1904)

BIRTH AFFIDAVIT.

DEPARTMENT OF THE INTERIOR.
COMMISSION TO THE FIVE CIVILIZED TRIBES.

IN RE APPLICATION FOR ENROLLMENT, as a citizen of the   Choctaw   Nation, of
Emma Dickinson   , born on the 31st day of   December   , 1904

Name of Father: William A. Dickinson   a citizen of the   Choctaw   Nation.
Name of Mother: Belle Dickinson   a citizen of the   Choctaw   Nation.

             Postoffice   Albany I.T.

AFFIDAVIT OF MOTHER.

UNITED STATES OF AMERICA, Indian Territory, ⎫
    Central   DISTRICT. ⎭

     I,   Belle Dickinson   , on oath state that I am 28 years of age and a citizen
by   blood   , of the   Choctaw   Nation; that I am the lawful wife of   William A.

Dickinson   , who is a citizen, by marriage   of the   Choctaw   Nation; that a   female   child was born to me on 31st day of   December   , 1904; that said child has been named   Emma Dickinson   , and was living March 4, 1905.

Belle Dickinson

Witnesses To Mark:

Subscribed and sworn to before me this 7th day of   April   , 1905

W.J. ODonby
Notary Public.

AFFIDAVIT OF ATTENDING PHYSICIAN OR MID-WIFE.

UNITED STATES OF AMERICA, Indian Territory,
   Central   **DISTRICT.**

I,   A.J. Wells   , a Physician   , on oath state that I attended on Mrs. Belle Dickinson   , wife of   William A. Dickinson   on the 31st day of December   , 1904; that there was born to her on said date a   female   child; that said child was living March 4, 1905, and is said to have been named Emma Dickinson

A.J. Wells M.D.

Witnesses To Mark:

Subscribed and sworn to before me this 4th day of   April   , 1905

W.J. O'Donby
Notary Public.

NEW-BORN AFFIDAVIT.

Number *7- 3499*
Roll - 9958

Choctaw Enrolling Commission.

IN THE MATTER OF THE APPLICATION FOR ENROLLMENT, as a citizen of the Choctaw   Nation, of   Emma Dickinson

born on the   31st day of   Dec   190 4

Name of father   W A Dickinson   a citizen of
Nation final enrollment No

Name of mother   Belle Dickinson   a citizen of   Choctaw
Nation final enrollment No   9958

Postoffice   Albany I.T.

AFFIDAVIT OF MOTHER.

UNITED STATES OF AMERICA,
   INDIAN TERRITORY,
  Central   DISTRICT

I   Belle Dickinson   on oath state that
I am   27 years of age and a citizen by   blood   of the   Choctaw   Nation, and as
such have been placed upon the final roll of the   Choctaw   Nation, by the Honorable
Secretary of the Interior my final enrollment number being   9958   ; that I am the lawful
wife of   W.A. Dickinson , who is a citizen of the   Choctaw by Marriage   Nation,
and as such has been placed upon the final roll of said Nation by the Honorable Secretary of the
Interior, his final enrollment number being — and that a   female   child was born to me
on the   31st   day of   December   190 4 ; that said child has been named   Emma
Dickinson   , and is now living.

Belle Dickinson

WITNESSETH:
  Must be two   H. G. Vanzant
  Witnesses who
  are Citizens.   Thomas T Beal

Subscribed and sworn to before me this   17th   day of   Jan   190 5

W.J. O'Donby
Notary Public.

My commission expires   Dec the 17th AD 1905

Affidavit of Attending Physician or Midwife.

UNITED STATES OF AMERICA
INDIAN TERRITORY
  Central   DISTRICT

I,   A.J. Wells   a   Physician
on oath state that I attended on Mrs.   Belle Dickinson   wife of   W. A. Dickinson
on the   31st   day of   December   , 190 4, that there was born to her on said date a
Female   child, that said child is now living, and is said to have been named   Emma
Dickinson

A.J. Wells   M.D.

Subscribed and sworn to before me this, the   16th   day of   Jan   190 5

W.J. O'Donby

Notary Public.

WITNESSETH:

Must be two witnesses
who are citizens and
know the child.

{ H. G. Vanzant

Thomas T Beal

We hereby certify that we are well acquainted with   A.J. Wells
a   Physician   and know   him   to be reputable and of good standing in the community.

{ H. G. Vanzant

Thomas T. Beal

_____

(The letter below typed as given.)

(Copy)

Albany, I. T. 4-10-1905.

Commission to the five civilized tribes

I enclose one application for enrollment of Infant Children   If it is not filled our correct notifie at once.

Respectfully,

Belle Dickinson

on roll

Belle Hughes

Roll no
        9958

_____

Chickasaw[sic] 3499.

Muskogee, Indian Territory, April 19, 1905.

Belle Dickinson,
    Albany, Indian Territory.

Dear Madam:

    Receipt is hereby acknowledged of your letter of April 10, transmitting your affidavit and that of A. J. Wells to the birth of Emma Dickinson, daughter of William A. and Belle Dickinson, December 31, 1904, and the same have been filed with our records as an application for the enrollment of said child.

Respectfully,

Chairman.

Choc New Born 1032
    Dudley Pitchlynn Lester
    (Born October 12, 1904)

BIRTH AFFIDAVIT.

DEPARTMENT OF THE INTERIOR.
COMMISSION TO THE FIVE CIVILIZED TRIBES.

IN RE APPLICATION FOR ENROLLMENT, as a citizen of the   Choctaw   Nation, of
Dudley Pitchlynn Lester   , born on the 12th   day of   October   , 1904

Name of Father: Preston S Lester   a citizen of the   Choctaw   Nation.
Name of Mother: Alice Pitchlynn Lester   a citizen of the   Choctaw   Nation.

Postoffice   South McAlester I T

AFFIDAVIT OF MOTHER.

UNITED STATES OF AMERICA, Indian Territory,
    Central   DISTRICT.

    I,   Alice P Lester   , on oath state that I am   30   years of age and a citizen
by   blood   , of the   Choctaw   Nation; that I am the lawful wife of   Preston S

221

Lester   , who is a citizen, by intermarriage   of the   Choctaw   Nation; that a   male   child was born to me on   12th   day of   October   , 1904; that said child has been named   Dudley Pitchlynn Lester   , and was living March 4, 1905.

Alice P Lester

Witnesses To Mark:

{

April

Subscribed and sworn to before me this   11th   day of   ~~October~~   , 1905

H L Haynes
Notary Public.

My commission expires July 27 1906

AFFIDAVIT OF ATTENDING PHYSICIAN OR MID-WIFE.

UNITED STATES OF AMERICA, Indian Territory,
Central   DISTRICT.

I,   J M Lester   , a   physician   , on oath state that I attended on Mrs.   Alice P Lester   , wife of   Preston S Lester   on the 12th   day of October, 1904; that there was born to her on said date a   male   child; that said child was living March 4, 1905, and is said to have been named   Dudley Pitchlynn Lester

J.M. Lester, M.D.

Witnesses To Mark:

{

Subscribed and sworn to before me this   11th   day of   April   , 1905

My commission expires July 27 1906   H L Haynes
Notary Public.

7-5601

Muskogee, Indian Territory, April 19, 1905.

Preston S. Lester,
          South McAlester, Indian Territory.

Dear Sir:

Receipt is hereby acknowledged of your letter of April 11, 1905, transmitting the affidavits of Alice P. Lester and J. M. Lester to the birth of Sudley[sic] Pitchlynn

222

Lester, son of Preston S. and Alice Pitchlynn Lester October 12, 1904, and the same have been filed with our records as an application for the enrollment of said child.

Respectfully,

Chairman.

Choc New Born 1033
   Ellis Johnson
   (Born Aug. 1, 1903)

BIRTH AFFIDAVIT.

DEPARTMENT OF THE INTERIOR.
COMMISSION TO THE FIVE CIVILIZED TRIBES.

IN RE APPLICATION FOR ENROLLMENT, as a citizen of the   Choctaw   Nation, of
Ellis Johnson   , born on the 1st   day of August   , 1903

Name of Father: Joseph Johnson   a citizen of the   Choctaw   Nation.
Name of Mother: Adeline Johnson   a citizen of the   Choctaw   Nation.

Postoffice   Smithville, Ind. Ter.

AFFIDAVIT OF MOTHER.

UNITED STATES OF AMERICA, Indian Territory,
   Central   DISTRICT.

I,   Joseph Johnson   , on oath state that I am   about 55   years of age and a citizen by   blood   , of the   Choctaw   Nation; that I ~~am~~ was the lawful ~~wife~~ husband of   Adeline Johnson, deceased   , who ~~is~~ was a citizen, by   blood   of the Choctaw   Nation; that a   male   child was born to ~~me~~ us on   1st   day of August   , 1903; that said child has been named   Ellis Johnson   , and was living March 4, 1905.

                                   his
                        Joseph x Johnson
Witnesses To Mark: mark
   { Robert Anderson
   { Vester Rose

223

Subscribed and sworn to before me this   6th day of   April   , 1905

Wirt Franklin
Notary Public.

AFFIDAVIT OF ATTENDING PHYSICIAN OR MID-WIFE.

UNITED STATES OF AMERICA, Indian Territory, ⎱
   Central   **DISTRICT.** ⎰

I,   Sallie Hudson   , a   mid-wife   , on oath state that I attended on
Mrs.   Adeline Johnson   , wife of   Joseph Johnson   on the 1st day of   August,
1903; that there was born to her on said date a   male   child; that said child was living
March 4, 1905, and is said to have been named Ellis Johnson

her

Sallie x Hudson

mark

Witnesses To Mark:
  ⎰ Robert Anderson
  ⎱ Vester Rose

Subscribed and sworn to before me this   6th day of   April   , 1905

Wirt Franklin
Notary Public.

-------------------- AFFIDAVIT   -------------------------------

UNITED STATES OF AMERICA.

Indian Territory --Central District.

In the matter of the birth of   male child   of   Adeline Johnson   and
~~Joseph Johnson~~   citizen of the   Choctaw   Nation of   Smithville   Ind.
Ter., and that the said   male   child was born on the   1st   day of   August   190 3.

I   Albert Carney   , on oath state that I am   50   years of age a citizen by
blood   of the   Choctaw   Nation, that my post office address is   Smithville   Ind.
Ter., that I was personally acquainted with Adeline Johnson wife of Joseph Johnson of
Smithville, Ind. Terr., and that I have personal knowledge that a male child was born to
Adeline Johnson on   1st   day of   August   190 3 , and that the said child has been
named   Ellis Johnson   and was living on the 4th day of March 1905 and is now living.

Albert Carney

224

Subscribed and sworn to before me this 9th day of June   1905

Wm H McKinney
Notary Public.

My commission expires   March 30 1909

-------------------- AFFIDAVIT   ------------------------------

UNITED STATES OF AMERICA.

Indian Territory --Central District.

In the matter of the birth of   male child   of   Adeline Johnson   and
~~Joseph Johnson~~   citizen of the   Choctaw   Nation of   Smithville   Ind.
Ter., and that the said   male   child was born on the   1st   day of   August   190 3.

     I   Wickles McCoy   , on oath state that I am   51   years of age a citizen by
blood   of the   Choctaw   Nation, that my post office address is   Smithville   Ind.
Ter., that I was personally acquainted with Adeline Johnson wife of Joseph Johnson of
Smithville, Ind. Terr., and that I have personal knowledge that a male child was born to
Adeline Johnson on   1st   day of   August   190 3 , and that the said child has been
named   Ellis Johnson   and was living on the 4th day of March 1905 and is now living.

Wickles McCoy

Subscribed and sworn to before me this 9th day of June   1905

Wm H McKinney
Notary Public.

My commission expires   March 30 1909

225

$W^m O.B.$

COMMISSIONERS:
TAMS BIXBY,
THOMAS B. NEEDLES,
C.R. BRECKINBRIDGE.

WM. O. BEALL
Secretary

DEPARTMENT OF THE INTERIOR,
COMMISSIONER TO THE FIVE CIVILIZED TRIBES.

REFER IN REPLY TO THE FOLLOWING:

7--NB--1033

ADDRESS ONLY THE
COMMISSION TO THE FIVE CIVILIZED TRIBES.

Muskogee, Indian Territory, June 2, 1905.

Joseph Johnson,
　　　Smithville, Indian Territory.

Dear Sir:

Referring to the application for the enrollment of your infant child, Ellis Johnson, born August 1, 1903, it is noted from the affidavits heretofore filed in this office that the mother of the child is dead.

In this event it will be necessary that the affidavits of two persons, who are disinterested and not related to the applicant, who have actual knowledge of the facts that the child was born, the date of his birth; that he was living on March 4, 1905, and that Adeline Johnson was his mother be filed with the Commission.

This matter should receive your immediate attention as no further action can be taken relative to the enrollment of said child until the Commission has been furnished these affidavits.

Respectfully,
T.B. Needles
Commissioner in Charge.

---

7 NB 1033

Muskogee, Indian Territory, June 14, 1905.

Joseph Johnson,
　　　Smithville, Indian Territory.

Dear Sir:

Receipt is hereby acknowledged of the affidavits of Albert Carney and Wickles McCoy to the birth of Ellis Johnson, son of Adeline Johnson, August 1, 1903, and the same have been filed in the matter of the enrollment of said child.

Respectfully,

Chairman.

226

Choc New Born 1034
    Marie Hudson
    (Born Feb. 11, 1905)

---

7 - 711

BIRTH AFFIDAVIT.   *5673*

DEPARTMENT OF THE INTERIOR.
COMMISSION TO THE FIVE CIVILIZED TRIBES.

IN RE APPLICATION FOR ENROLLMENT, as a citizen of the   Choctaw   Nation, of
Marie Hudson   , born on the 11   day of   February   , 1905

Name of Father: Peter W. Hudson   a citizen of the   Choctaw   Nation.
Name of Mother: Myrtle Hudson   a citizen of the   Choctaw   Nation.

Postoffice   Tuskahoma

AFFIDAVIT OF MOTHER.

UNITED STATES OF AMERICA, Indian Territory,
    Central   **DISTRICT.**

    I,   Myrtle Hudson   , on oath state that I am 23   years of age and a citizen
by   intermarriage   , of the   Choctaw   Nation; that I am the lawful wife of
Peter W Hudson   , who is a citizen, by blood   of the   Choctaw   Nation;
that a   female   child was born to me on 11   day of   February   , 1905; that
said child has been named Marie Hudson   , and was living March 4, 1905.

        Myrtle Hudson
Witnesses To Mark:

    Subscribed and sworn to before me this 11 day of   April   , 1905

        OL Johnson
           Notary Public.

Applications for Enrollment of Choctaw Newborn
Act of 1905   Volume XIV

AFFIDAVIT OF ATTENDING PHYSICIAN OR MID-WIFE.

UNITED STATES OF AMERICA, Indian Territory, ⎫
.... DISTRICT. ⎭

   I,   L.P. McCustion   , a   Physician   , on oath state that I attended on
Mrs.   Myrtle Hudson   , wife of   Peter W Hudson   on the 11th   day of   Feby ,
1905; that there was born to her on said date a   Female   child; that said child was
living March 4, 1905, and is said to have been named   Marie Hudson

                                        L.P. McCustion
Witnesses To Mark:

   {

   Subscribed and sworn to before me this 13th   day of   April   , 1905

                              Maud Osborne
                                 Notary Public.

                      _____

                                    7-1980

                  Muskogee, Indian Territory, April 19, 1905.

Peter W. Hudson,
      Tuskahoma, Indian Territory.

Dear Sir:

      Receipt is hereby acknowledged of the affidavits of Myrtle Hudson and L. P.
McCustion to the birth of Marie Hudson, daughter of Peter W. and Myrtle Hudson,
February 11, 1905, and the same have been filed with our records as an application for
the enrollment of said child.
                              Respectfully,

                                    Chairman.

_____

Choc New Born 1035
      Tarie E. Harris
      (Born Oct. 12, 1903)

                      _____

                                228

BIRTH AFFIDAVIT.

DEPARTMENT OF THE INTERIOR.
COMMISSION TO THE FIVE CIVILIZED TRIBES.

IN RE APPLICATION FOR ENROLLMENT, as a citizen of the   Chocktaw[sic]   Nation, of   Tarie E. Harris   , born on the 12 day of   Oct , 1903

Name of Father: Calvin Q Harris   a citizen of the   Chocktaw   Nation.
Name of Mother: Susan Harris   a citizen of the   Chocktaw   Nation.

Postoffice   Pontotoc, I.T.

Father
AFFIDAVIT OF ~~MOTHER~~.

The mother is Dead

UNITED STATES OF AMERICA, Indian Territory, ⎫
    Southern   DISTRICT. ⎭

I,   Calvin Q Harris   , on oath state that I am   27   years of age and a citizen by   Intermarige[sic]   , of the   Chocktaw   Nation; that I am the lawful ~~wife~~ *Husband* of   Susan Harris   , who is a citizen, by   Blood   of the Chocktaw   Nation; that a   female   child was born to ~~me~~ *my wife* on   12 day of   Oct   , 1903; that said child has been named   Tarie E. Harris   , and was living March 4, 1905.

                                        Calvin Q. Harris
Witnesses To Mark:
    {

Subscribed and sworn to before me this 3 day of   April   , 1905

                            M.S. Bradford
                                Notary Public.

AFFIDAVIT OF ATTENDING PHYSICIAN OR MID-WIFE.

UNITED STATES OF AMERICA, Indian Territory, ⎫
    Southern   DISTRICT. ⎭

I,   W. James   , a   Physician   , on oath state that I attended on Mrs.   Susan Harris   , wife of   Calvin Q Harris   on the 12 day of   Oct   , 1903; that there was born to her on said date a   female   child; that said child was living March 4, 1905, and is said to have been named   Tarie E Harris

                            W. James M.D.
Witnesses To Mark:
    {

229

Subscribed and sworn to before me this 3 day of   April   , 1905

M.S. Bradford
Notary Public.

_____

Lady Present

AFFIDAVIT OF ATTENDING ~~PHYSICIAN OR MID-WIFE~~.

UNITED STATES OF AMERICA, Indian Territory, ⎫
Southern   **DISTRICT.** ⎭

I, Mrs. J. D. Harbin   , a   —————— , on oath state that I attended on
Mrs. Susan Harris   , wife of   Calvin Q Harris   on the 12   day of   Oct   ,
1903; that there was born to her on said date a   female   child; that said child was
living March 4, 1905, and is said to have been named   Tarie E Harris

Mrs. J.D. Harbin

Witnesses To Mark:

{
⎱ Subscribed and sworn to before me this 3 day of   April   , 1905

M.S. Bradford
Notary Public.

_____

AFFIDAVIT OF ATTENDING ~~PHYSICIAN OR MID-WIFE~~.

A Disinterested Person

UNITED STATES OF AMERICA, Indian Territory, ⎫
Southern   **DISTRICT.** ⎭

visited

I, C. J. Bradford   , a   Lady   , on oath state that I ~~attended on~~
Mrs. Susan Harris   , wife of   Calvin Q Harris   on the 12   day of   Oct   ,
1903; that there was born to her on said date a   female   child; that said child was
living March 4, 1905, and is said to have been named   Tarie E Harris

C. J. Bradford

Witnesses To Mark:

{
⎱ Subscribed and sworn to before me this 10th day of   June   , 1905

M.S. Bradford
Notary Public.

_____

Choctaw 3537.

Muskogee, Indian Territory, April 19, 1905.

Calvin Q. Harris,
Pontotoc, Indian Territory.

Dear Sir:

Receipt is hereby acknowledged of your letter of April 11, transmitting the affidavits of Calvin Q. Harris, W. James, M.D., and Mrs. J. D. Harbin to the birth of Tarie E. Harris, daughter of Calvin Q. and Susan Harris, October 12, 1903, and the same have been filed with our records as an application for the enrollment of said child.

Respectfully,

Chairman.

WᵐO.B.

| COMMISSIONERS:
TAMS BIXBY,
THOMAS B. NEEDLES,
C.R. BRECKINBRIDGE.

WM. O. BEALL
Secretary | **DEPARTMENT OF THE INTERIOR,**
COMMISSIONER TO THE FIVE CIVILIZED TRIBES. | REFER IN REPLY TO THE FOLLOWING:
_____
7-NB-1035. |

ADDRESS ONLY THE
COMMISSION TO THE FIVE CIVILIZED TRIBES.

Muskogee, Indian Territory, June 2, 1905.

Calvin Q. Harris,
Pontotoc, Indian Territory.

Dear Sir:

Referring to the application for the enrollment of your infant child, Tarie E. Harris, born October 12, 1903, it is noted from the affidavits heretofore filed in this office that the mother of the applicant is dead.

In this event it will be necessary that the affidavits of two persons, who are disinterested and not related to the applicant, who have actual knowledge of the facts that the child was born, the date of her birth; that she was living on March 4, 1905, and that Susan Harris was her mother, be filed in this office.

The affidavit of Mrs. J. D. Harbin, to the above facts, is on file in this office. It will, therefore, be necessary that you secure a similar affidavit from another person.

This matter should receive your immediate attention, as no further action can be taken relative to the enrollment of your infant child, until this affidavit is furnished the Commission.

Respectfully,

T.B. Needles

Commissioner in Charge.

---

7 NB 1035

Muskogee, Indian Territory, June 16, 1905.

Calvin Q. Harris,
Pontotoc, Indian Territory.

Dear Sir:

Receipt is hereby acknowledged of the affidavit of C. J. Bradford, to the birth of Tarrie[sic] E. Harris, daughter of Calvin Q. and Susan Harris, October 12, 1903, and the same has been filed in the matter of the enrollment of said child.

Respectfully,

Chairman.

Choc New Born 1036
   Clem Y. Hull
   (Born July 15, 1904)

BIRTH AFFIDAVIT.

DEPARTMENT OF THE INTERIOR.
COMMISSION TO THE FIVE CIVILIZED TRIBES.

IN RE APPLICATION FOR ENROLLMENT, as a citizen of the   Choctaw   Nation, of
Clem Y Hull   , born on the 15th   day of   July   , 1904

Name of Father: Tipp Hull   a citizen of the   U.S.   Nation.
Name of Mother: Mary M. Hull   a citizen of the   Choctaw   Nation.

Postoffice   Matoy Ind. Ter.

Applications for Enrollment of Choctaw Newborn
Act of 1905   Volume XIV

AFFIDAVIT OF MOTHER.

UNITED STATES OF AMERICA, Indian Territory, ⎰
    Central   DISTRICT. ⎱

    I,   Mary M. Hull (Battiest)   , on oath state that I am 19   years of age and a citizen by   blood   , of the   Choctaw   Nation; that I am the lawful wife of Tipp Hull   , who is a citizen, *of the U. S.*   of the   ~~Choctaw~~ *US*   Nation; that a   male   child was born to me on 15th day of   July   , 1904; that said child has been named Clem Y Hull   , and was living March 4, 1905.

                                  Mary M Hull

Witnesses To Mark:

    Subscribed and sworn to before me this 10th day of   April   , 1905

                        JL Rappolee
                            Notary Public.

AFFIDAVIT OF ATTENDING PHYSICIAN OR MID-WIFE.

UNITED STATES OF AMERICA, Indian Territory, ⎰
    Central   DISTRICT. ⎱

    I,   W. J. Lindsey   , a Physician   , on oath state that I attended on Mrs. Mary M. Hull (Battiest)   , wife of Tipp Hull   on the 15th day of July , 1904; that there was born to her on said date a   male   child; that said child was living March 4, 1905, and is said to have been named Clem Y Hull

                            Dr. W. J. Lindsey

Witnesses To Mark:

    Subscribed and sworn to before me this 12 day of   Apr   , 1905

                        T.H.P. Smith
                            Notary Public.

No. 339

Certificate of Record of Marriages.

DEPARTMENT OF THE INTERIOR,
Commission to the Five Civilized Tribes.

FILED

APR 18 1905

Thos Ryley CHAIRMAN.

UNITED STATES OF AMERICA,
  INDIAN TERRITORY, } SCT:
Central   DISTRICT.

I,   E.J. Fannin   , Clerk of the United States Court in the Indian Territory and District aforesaid, do hereby CERTIFY, that the License for and Certificate of the Marriage of

Mr.   Tip Hull   and

Miss Mary M Battiest   was

filed in my office in said Territory and District the
   17   day of   August   A.D., 190 3
and duly recorded in Book I   of Marriage Record, Page 170

WITNESS my hand and seal of said Court, at   Durant   , this   17
day of   Aug   , A.D. 190 3

E.J. Fannin
                        Clerk.

By   WB Stone   *Deputy.*

No. 339

FORM NO. 598.

MARRIAGE LICENSE.

UNITES STATES OF AMERICA,
  THE INDIAN TERRITORY, } ss:
Central   DISTRICT.

To any Person Authorized by Law to Solemnize Marriage—Greeting:

234

Applications for Enrollment of Choctaw Newborn
Act of 1905   Volume XIV

You are hereby commanded to solemnize the Rite and publish the Banns of Matrimony *between* Mr. Tip Hull *of* Caddo *in the Indian Territory, aged* 22 *years, and* Miss Mary M. Battiest *of* Caddo *in the Indian Territory, aged* 18 *years, according to law, and do you officially sign and return this License to the parties therein named.*

WITNESS *my hand and official seal, this* 10th *day of* August   A. D. 190 3

E J Fannin
> Clerk of the United States Court.

WB Stone   *Deputy*

CERTIFICATE OF MARRIAGE.

UNITES STATES OF AMERICA, ⎤
THE INDIAN TERRITORY, ⎬ ss:
_____DISTRICT. ⎦

I,   W J B Lloyd
a   Minister of the Gospel

do hereby CERTIFY, *that on the* 12 *day of* August   A, D. 190 3 ; *I did duly and according to law, as commanded in the foregoing License, solemnize the Rite and publish the* BANNS OF MATRIMONY *between the parties therein named.*

Witness my hand this 12 *day of* August , A. D. 190 3

My credentials are recorded in the office of the Clerk of the United States Court in the Indian Territory, Central District, Book A   *Page* 101

W.J.B. Lloyd

a   Minister of the Gospel

Applications for Enrollment of Choctaw Newborn
Act of 1905   Volume XIV

Choctaw 3676.

Muskogee, Indian Territory, April 19, 1905.

Tipp Hull,
    Matoy, Indian Territory.

Dear Sir:

    Receipt is hereby acknowledged of the affidavits of Mary M. Hull and Dr. W. T. Lindsey to the birth of Clem Y. Hull, son of Tipp and Mary M. Hull (Battiest), July 15, 1904; receipt is also acknowledged of the marriage license and certificate between Tip Hull and Miss Mary M. Battiest, and the same have been filed with our records in the matter of the enrollment of said child.

Respectfully,

Chairman.

Choc New Born 1037
    Florence LeFlore
    (Born June 17, 1904)

BIRTH AFFIDAVIT.
DEPARTMENT OF THE INTERIOR.
COMMISSION TO THE FIVE CIVILIZED TRIBES.

IN RE APPLICATION FOR ENROLLMENT, as a citizen of the   Choctaw   Nation, of
Florence Leflore   , born on the   17   day of   June   , 1904

Name of Father: James Leflore   a citizen of the   Choctaw   Nation.
Name of Mother: Susan Leflore   a citizen of the   Choctaw   Nation.

Postoffice   Garvin Ind Ter

AFFIDAVIT OF MOTHER.

UNITED STATES OF AMERICA, Indian Territory, ⎱
    Central   DISTRICT. ⎰

    I,   Susan Leflore   , on oath state that I am   18   years of age and a citizen by Blood   , of the   Choctaw   Nation; that I am the lawful wife of   James Leflore   , who is a citizen, by   Blood   of the   Choctaw   Nation; that a   Female

236

child was born to me on   18th[sic]   day of   June   , 1904; that said child has been named   Florence Leflore   , and was living March 4, 1905.

her
Susan x Leflore
mark

Witnesses To Mark:
 { Ephraim McKinney
 { Melvina Taylor

Subscribed and sworn to before me this   14 day of   April   , 1905

Simon Taylor
Notary Public.

AFFIDAVIT OF ATTENDING PHYSICIAN OR MID-WIFE.

UNITED STATES OF AMERICA, Indian Territory, }
 Central   DISTRICT. }

 I,   Nellie Hall   , a   Midwife   , on oath state that I attended on Mrs.   Susan Leflore   , wife of   James Leflore   on the   18[sic] day of   June   , 1904; that there was born to her on said date a   Female   child; that said child was living March 4, 1905, and is said to have been named   Florence Leflore

her
Nellie x Hall
mark

Witnesses To Mark:
 { Ephraim McKinney
 { Melvina Taylor

Subscribed and sworn to before me this   14 day of   April   , 1905

Simon Taylor
Notary Public.

BIRTH AFFIDAVIT.

DEPARTMENT OF THE INTERIOR.
COMMISSION TO THE FIVE CIVILIZED TRIBES.

IN RE APPLICATION FOR ENROLLMENT, as a citizen of the   Choctaw   Nation, of Florence LeFlore   , born on the   17th   day of   June   , 1904

Name of Father: James LeFlore Roll 2775   a citizen of the   Choctaw   Nation.
Name of Mother: Susan LeFlore nee Austin   a citizen of the   Choctaw   Nation.

Roll 2543
Postoffice   Garvin I.T.

237

Applications for Enrollment of Choctaw Newborn
Act of 1905   Volume XIV

AFFIDAVIT OF MOTHER.

UNITED STATES OF AMERICA, Indian Territory, ⎫
.... DISTRICT. ⎭

I,   Susan LeFlore nee Austin   , on oath state that I am   18   years of age and
a citizen by   blood   , of the   Choctaw   Nation; that I am the lawful wife of
James LeFlore   , who is a citizen, by blood   of the   Choctaw   Nation; that a
Female   child was born to me on 17ᵗʰ   day of   June AD   , 1904; that said child
has been named   Florence LeFlore   , and was living March 4, 1905.

Susan Leflore

Witnesses To Mark:

⎧
⎩

Subscribed and sworn to before me this   17ᵗʰ   day of   June   , 1905

Simon Taylor
Notary Public.

AFFIDAVIT OF ATTENDING PHYSICIAN OR MID-WIFE.

UNITED STATES OF AMERICA, Indian Territory, ⎫
    Central   DISTRICT. ⎭

I,   Nellie Hall   , a   mid wife   , on oath state that I attended on
Mrs.   Susan Leflore   , wife of   James Leflore   on the 17ᵗʰ   day of   June AD ,
1904; that there was born to her on said date a   female   child; that said child was
living March 4, 1905, and is said to have been named   Florence LeFlore
her
Nellie x Hall
Witnesses To Mark: mark
⎧ Melvina Taylor
⎩ Allie Hannah

Subscribed and sworn to before me this   17ᵗʰ   day of   June AD   , 1905

Simon Taylor
Notary Public.

238

NEW BORN AFFIDAVIT

No ....

CHOCTAW ENROLLING COMMISSION

IN THE MATTER OF THE APPLICATION FOR ENROLLMENT as a citizen of the Choctaw
Nation, of   Florence LeFlore   born on the 17th   day
of   June   190 4

Name of father   James LeFlore   a citizen of   Choctaw   Nation,
final enrollment No.   2775
Name of mother   Susan Austin   a citizen of   Choctaw   Nation,
final enrollment No.   2543

Garvin I.T.   Postoffice.

AFFIDAVIT OF MOTHER

UNITED STATES OF AMERICA ⎫
   INDIAN TERRITORY ⎬
DISTRICT   Central ⎭

   I   Susan Austin   , on oath state that I am   18   years of age and a
citizen by   blood   of the   Choctaw   Nation, and as such have been placed upon
the final roll of the   Choctaw   Nation, by the Honorable Secretary of the Interior my final
enrollment number being   2543   ; that I am the lawful wife of   James LeFlore   , who
is a citizen of the   Choctaw   Nation, and as such has been placed upon the final roll
of said Nation by the Honorable Secretary of the Interior, his final enrollment number being
2775   and that a   female   child was born to me on the   17th   day of   June   190 4;
that said child has been named   Florence LeFlore   , and is now living.

WITNESSETH: Susan Austin
  Must be two witnesses ⎧ L.M. LeFlore
  who are citizens   ⎩ Abner Williams

Subscribed and sworn to before me this, the   16th   day of   Feb.   , 190 5

W.A. Shoney
Notary Public.

My Commission Expires:
    Jan 10, 1909

239

Applications for Enrollment of Choctaw Newborn
Act of 1905   Volume XIV

Affidavit of Attending Physician or Midwife

———

UNITED STATES OF AMERICA, ⎫
INDIAN TERRITORY, ⎬
Central   DISTRICT ⎭

I,   Nellie Hall   a   midwife
on oath state that I attended on Mrs. Susan Austin   wife of James LeFlore
on the   17th   day of   June   , 190 4, that there was born to her on said date a   female
child, that said child is now living, and is said to have been named   Florence LeFlore

her
Nellie x Hall   ~~M. D~~.
mark

Subscribed and sworn to before me this the   16th   day of   Feb   1905

W.A. Shoney
Notary Public.

WITNESSETH:

Must be two witnesses ⎧ L.M. LeFlore
who are citizens and ⎨
know the child. ⎩ Abner Williams

We hereby certify that we are well acquainted with   Nellie Hall
a   midwife   and know   her   to be reputable and of good standing in the
community.

Must be two citizen ⎧ L.M. LeFlore
witnesses. ⎩ Abner Williams

———

(Copy)

Garvin, I. T.   April 14, 1905.

Commission to the Five Civilized Tribes,
Muskogee, Ind. Ter.

Sir:

Enclosed please birth affidavits of Florence Leflore, child of James and Susan
Leflore.

Very respectfully,

James Leflore

Adam Austin father of Susan Austin (Leflore)
Mary Austin Mother of Susan Austin (L3flore)[sic]
Father and Mother both deceased-- of Garvin, Ind. Ter.

———

7-NB-1037.

Muskogee, Indian Territory, June 2, 1905.

James LeFlore,
    Garvin, Indian Territory.

Dear Sir:

There is enclosed you herewith for execution application for the enrollment of your infant child, Florence Leflore.

In the affidavits of February 16, 1905, heretofore filed in this office, the date of the applicant's birth is given as June 17, 1904, while the affidavits of April 14, 1905, give the date as June 18, 1904. In the enclosed application the date of birth is left blank. Please insert the correct date and, when the affidavits are properly executed, return them to this office.

In having these affidavits executed care should be exercised to see that all names are written in full, as they appear in the body of the affidavit, and in the event that either of the persons signing the affidavit are unable to write, signatures by mark must be attested by two witnesses. Each affidavit must be executed before a Notary Public and the notarial seal and signature of the officer must be attached to each separate affidavit.

Respectfully,

VR 2-2.   [sic]

---

7 NB 1037

Muskogee, Indian Territory, June 21, 1905.

James LeFlore,
    Garvin, Indian Territory.

Dear Sir:

Receipt is hereby acknowledged of your letter of June 18, 1905, enclosing affidavits of Susan LeFlore and Nellie Hall to the birth of Florence LeFlore, daughter of James and Susan LeFlore, June 17, 1904, and the same have been [sic] with our records in the matter of the enrollment of said child.

Respectfully,

Chairman.

Applications for Enrollment of Choctaw Newborn
Act of 1905 Volume XIV

<u>Choc New Born 1038</u>
   Catherine Isabelle Garrison
   (Born Feb. 15, 1904)

BIRTH AFFIDAVIT.

DEPARTMENT OF THE INTERIOR.
COMMISSION TO THE FIVE CIVILIZED TRIBES.

IN RE APPLICATION FOR ENROLLMENT, as a citizen of the   Choctaw   Nation, of
Catherine Isabelle Garrison   , born on the   15th day of   February   , 1904

Name of Father: J.E.S. Garrison   a citizen of the   US   Nation.
Name of Mother: Isabelle Pernell Garrison   a citizen of the   Choctaw   Nation.

Postoffice

AFFIDAVIT OF MOTHER.

UNITED STATES OF AMERICA, Indian Territory, ⎞
     Southern   DISTRICT. ⎠

     I,   Isabelle Pernell Garrison   , on oath state that I am   20   years of age and
a citizen by   blood   , of the   Choctaw   Nation; that I am the lawful wife of
J.E.S. Garrison   , who is a citizen, by birth   of the   United States ~~Nation~~; that
a   female   child was born to me on   the 15th day of   February   , 1904; that
said child has been named   Catherine Isabelle Garrison   , and was living March 4,
1905.

            Isabell[sic] Pernell Garrison

Witnesses To Mark:
   {

     Subscribed and sworn to before me this   11th day of   April   , 1905

             JE Williams
                 Notary Public.

Applications for Enrollment of Choctaw Newborn
Act of 1905   Volume XIV

AFFIDAVIT OF ATTENDING PHYSICIAN OR MID-WIFE.

UNITED STATES OF AMERICA, Indian Territory, }
  Southern   DISTRICT. }

I,   J B Morgan   , a   physician   , on oath state that I attended on
Mrs. Isabelle Pernell Garrison   , wife of J E S Garrison   on the 15th day of
February   , 1904; that there was born to her on said date a   female   child; that said
child was living March 4, 1905, and is said to have been named ~~Isabelle Pe~~ Catherine
Isabelle Garrison

Jno B Morgan M.D.
Witnesses To Mark:

{

Subscribed and sworn to before me this 12   day of   April   , 1905

WW Howerton
Notary Public.
My commission expires Feb 15, 1906

Choc New Born 1039
    Etna Sampson
    (Born Feb. 13, 1903)

BIRTH AFFIDAVIT.

DEPARTMENT OF THE INTERIOR.
COMMISSION TO THE FIVE CIVILIZED TRIBES.

IN RE APPLICATION FOR ENROLLMENT, as a citizen of the   Choctaw   Nation, of
Etna Sampson   , born on the 13th   day of Feb   , 1903

Name of Father: Noel Sampson   a citizen of the   Choctaw   Nation.
Name of Mother: Lucy Sampson   a citizen of the   Choctaw   Nation.

Postoffice   Goodwater I.T.

243

Applications for Enrollment of Choctaw Newborn
Act of 1905   Volume XIV

AFFIDAVIT OF MOTHER.

UNITED STATES OF AMERICA, Indian Territory, ⎱
Central   DISTRICT. ⎰

I,   Lucy Sampson   , on oath state that I am   about 30   years of age and a citizen by   Blood   , of the   Choctaw   Nation; that I am the lawful wife of Noel Sampson   , who is a citizen, by Blood   of the   Choctaw   Nation; that a   Female   child was born to me on 13th day of   February   , 1903; that said child has been named   Etna Sampson   , and was living March 4, 1905.

her
Lucy x Sampson
mark

Witnesses To Mark:
⎰ L.G. Battiest
⎱ Wilkin Billy

Subscribed and sworn to before me this 12th day of   April   , 1905

(Name Illegible)
Notary Public.

AFFIDAVIT OF ATTENDING PHYSICIAN OR MID-WIFE.

UNITED STATES OF AMERICA, Indian Territory, ⎱
Central   DISTRICT. ⎰

I,   Yahoke Sampson   , a   mid-wife   , on oath state that I attended on Mrs.   Lucy Sampson   , wife of   Noel Sampson   on the 13th day of February, 1903; that there was born to her on said date a   Female   child; that said child was living March 4, 1905, and is said to have been named   Etna Sampson

her
Yahoke x Sampson
mark

Witnesses To Mark:
⎰ L.G. Battiest
⎱ Wilkin Billy

Subscribed and sworn to before me this 12th day of   April   , 1905

(Name Illegible)
Notary Public.

Choc New Born 1040
     Annie Johnson
     (Born Jan. 17, 1904)

BIRTH AFFIDAVIT.

DEPARTMENT OF THE INTERIOR.
COMMISSION TO THE FIVE CIVILIZED TRIBES.

IN RE APPLICATION FOR ENROLLMENT, as a citizen of the   Choctaw   Nation, of
Annie Johnson   , born on the 17th day of   January   , 1904

Name of Father: William Johnson   a citizen of the   Choctaw   Nation.
Name of Mother: Sophia Johnson   a citizen of the   Choctaw   Nation.

Postoffice   **LUKPATA[sic] IND TER**

AFFIDAVIT OF MOTHER.

UNITED STATES OF AMERICA, Indian Territory, ⎱
     Central   **DISTRICT.** ⎰

I,   Sophia Johnson   , on oath state that I am 35   years of age and a citizen
by   Blood   , of the   Choctaw   Nation; that I am the lawful wife of   William
Johnson   , who is a citizen, by Inter Marriage   of the   Choctaw   Nation;
that a   Female   child was born to me on   17th   day of   January   , 1904; that
said child has been named   Annie Johnson   , and was living March 4, 1905.
                                        her
                          Sophia x Johnson
Witnesses To Mark: mark
  ⎰ Jno. James
  ⎱ W.A. Julian

Subscribed and sworn to before me this 11th day of   April   , 1905

J.W. Costelow
Notary Public.

AFFIDAVIT OF ATTENDING PHYSICIAN OR MID-WIFE.

UNITED STATES OF AMERICA, Indian Territory, ⎤
Central   DISTRICT. ⎦

I,   Jane Butler   , a midwife   , on oath state that I attended on
Mrs. Sophia Johnson   , wife of William Johnson   on the 17th   day of
January   , 1904; that there was born to her on said date a   Female   child; that said
child was living March 4, 1905, and is said to have been named   Annie Johnson

her
Jane x Butler
mark

Witnesses To Mark:
⎰ Jno. James
⎱ W.A. Julian

Subscribed and sworn to before me this 11th day of   April   , 1905

J.W. Costelow
Notary Public.

Choc New Born 1041
Jessie James Bickle
(Born Nov. 28, 1903)

BIRTH AFFIDAVIT.
DEPARTMENT OF THE INTERIOR.
COMMISSION TO THE FIVE CIVILIZED TRIBES.

IN RE APPLICATION FOR ENROLLMENT, as a citizen of the   Choctaw   Nation, of
Jessie James Bickle   , born on the 28   day of November   , 1903

Name of Father: James A. Bickle   a citizen of the   Choctaw   Nation.
    by In#termarriage[sic]
Name of Mother: Susan Bickle   a citizen of the   Choctaw   Nation.

Postoffice   Quinton, Ind. T.

246

Applications for Enrollment of Choctaw Newborn
Act of 1905   Volume XIV

AFFIDAVIT OF MOTHER.

UNITED STATES OF AMERICA, Indian Territory, ⎱
   Western   DISTRICT. ⎰

      I,   Susan Bickle   , on oath state that I am.................years of age and a citizen by Blood   , of the   Choctaw   Nation; that I am the lawful wife of   James A. Bickle, who is a citizen, by In=termarriage[sic]   of the   Choctaw   Nation; that a Male   child was born to me on 28   day of   November   , 1903; that said child has been named   Jessie James Bickle   , and was living March 4, 1905.

her
Susan x Bickle
mark

Witnesses To Mark:
  ⎰ J.A. Nation
  ⎱ J.N. Dunn

     Subscribed and sworn to before me this 3 day of   April   , 1905

J. M. White
Notary Public.

AFFIDAVIT OF ATTENDING PHYSICIAN OR MID-WIFE.

UNITED STATES OF AMERICA, Indian Territory, ⎱
   Central   DISTRICT. ⎰

      I,   J. M. Turner   , a physician   , on oath state that I attended on Mrs.   Susan Bickle   , wife of   James A Bickle   on the 28th day of November   , 1903; that there was born to her on said date a   male   child; that said child was living March 4, 1905, and is said to have been named Jessie James Bickle

J.M. Turner

Witnesses To Mark:
  ⎰

     Subscribed and sworn to before me this 14th   day of   April   , 1905

Edwin O. Clark
Notary Public.

NEW-BORN AFFIDAVIT.

Number............

...Choctaw Enrolling Commission...

IN THE MATTER OF THE APPLICATION FOR ENROLLMENT, as a citizen of the
Choctaw　　　　　Nation, of　　　　　Jessie James Bickle

born on the 28th day of __November__ 190 3

Name of father James A. Bickle	a citizen of Choctaw
Nation final enrollment No. 916	
Name of mother Susan Bickle	a citizen of Choctaw
Nation final enrollment No. 8616	

Postoffice　　Quinton I.T.

AFFIDAVIT OF MOTHER.

UNITED STATES OF AMERICA
INDIAN TERRITORY
　Western　　　DISTRICT

　　　　　I　　Susan Bickle　　　　　　　, on oath state that I am
　38　　　years of age and a citizen by blood of the　Choctaw　　　　Nation,
and as such have been placed upon the final roll of the　Choctaw　Nation, by the Honorable
Secretary of the Interior my final enrollment number being　8616 ; that I am the lawful wife
of　James A Bickle　, who is a citizen of the　Choctaw　　Nation, and as such has
been placed upon the final roll of said Nation by the Honorable Secretary of the Interior, his
final enrollment number being　916　and that a　Male　child was born to me on the
28th　day of　November　190 3; that said child has been named Jessie James Bickle ,
and is now living.

　　　　　　　　　　　　Susan Bickle

Witnesseth.

Must be two ⎫　Jess Walls
Witnesses who ⎬
are Citizens. ⎭　T.J. Walls

　　　Subscribed and sworn to before me this　5　day of　Jan　　190 5

　　　　　　　　　　　John M Lenz
　　　　　　　　　　　　　　Notary Public.
My commission expires: Nov 27 1907

248

AFFIDAVIT OF ATTENDING PHYSICIAN OR MIDWIFE

UNITED STATES OF AMERICA
INDIAN TERRITORY
Western   DISTRICT

I,   J M Turner   a   practicing physician
on oath state that I attended on Mrs. Susan Bickle   wife of James A Bickle
on the   28th   day of   November , 190 3 , that there was born to her on said date a   male
child, that said child is now living, and is said to have been named   Jessie James Bickle

J.M. Turner

Subscribed and sworn to before me this, the   3rd   day of
February   190 5

WITNESSETH: J.F. Griffin   Notary Public.

Must be two witnesses ⎰ Jess Walls   *My commission expires Jan 26.1907*
who are citizens   ⎱ T.J. Walls

We hereby certify that we are well acquainted with   J.M. Turner M.D.
a   practicing physician   and know   him   to be reputable and of good standing in
the community.

Jess Walls   _____

T.J. Walls   _____

_____

7-2930

Muskogee, Indian Territory, April 19, 1905.

James A. Bickle,
    Quinton, Indian Territory.

Dear Sir:

Receipt is hereby acknowledged of the affidavits of Susan Bickle and J. M.
Turner to the birth of Jessie James Bickle, son of James A. and Susan Bickle November
28, 1903, and the same have been filed with our records as an application for the
enrollment of said child.

Respectfully,

Chairman.

Choc New Born 1042
Coleman Crawford
(Born Aug. 15, 1903)

_____

BIRTH AFFIDAVIT.

DEPARTMENT OF THE INTERIOR.
COMMISSION TO THE FIVE CIVILIZED TRIBES.

_____

IN RE APPLICATION FOR ENROLLMENT, as a citizen of the   Choctaw   Nation, of
Coleman Crawford   , born on the 15th   day of August   , 1903

Name of Father: Frank Crawford   a citizen of the   Choctaw   Nation.
Name of Mother: Minnie Crawford   a citizen of the   Choctaw   Nation.

Postoffice   Durant, Indian Territory.

_____

AFFIDAVIT OF MOTHER.

UNITED STATES OF AMERICA, Indian Territory, ⎫
      Central   DISTRICT. ⎰

I,   Minnie Crawford   , on oath state that I am   27   years of age and a
citizen by   blood   , of the   Choctaw   Nation; that I am the lawful wife of
Frank Crawford   , who is a citizen, by   intermarriage   of the   Choctaw
Nation; that a   male   child was born to me on   15th   day of   August   , 1903;
that said child has been named   Coleman Crawford   , and was living March 4, 1905.

Minnie Crawford
Witnesses To Mark:
⎰

Subscribed and sworn to before me this 8th day of   April   , 1905

Jno W. Hampton
Notary Public.

_____

AFFIDAVIT OF ATTENDING PHYSICIAN OR MID-WIFE.

UNITED STATES OF AMERICA, Indian Territory, ⎫
      Central   DISTRICT. ⎰

I,   A.B. Strange M.D.   , a   physician   , on oath state that I attended on
Mrs.   Minnie Crawford   , wife of   Frank Crawford   on the   15th   day of

August   , 1903; that there was born to her on said date a   male   child; that said child was living March 4, 1905, and is said to have been named Coleman Crawford

A.B. Strange M.D.

Witnesses To Mark:

{

Subscribed and sworn to before me this 13th day of   April   , 1905

J.P. Ward

Notary Public.

NEW-BORN AFFIDAVIT.

Number...........

...Choctaw Enrolling Commission...

IN THE MATTER OF THE APPLICATION FOR ENROLLMENT, as a citizen of the Choctaw   Nation, of   Coleman Crawford

born on the   15 day of ___August___ 190 3

Name of father Frank Crawford   a citizen of   white
Nation final enrollment No. ——
Name of mother   Minnie Crawford   a citizen of   Choctaw
Nation final enrollment No. 9834

Postoffice   Caddo I.T.

AFFIDAVIT OF MOTHER.

UNITED STATES OF AMERICA
INDIAN TERRITORY
 Central   DISTRICT

I   Minnie Crawford   , on oath state that I am 27   years of age and a citizen by blood   of the   Choctaw   Nation, and as such have been placed upon the final roll of the   Choctaw   Nation, by the Honorable Secretary of the Interior my final enrollment number being   9834 ; that I am the lawful wife of   Frank Crawford   , who is a citizen of the   *white* ~~Choctaw~~   Nation, and as such has been placed upon the final roll of said Nation by the Honorable Secretary of the Interior, his final enrollment number being —— and that a   Male   child was born to me on the   15 day of   August   190 3; that said child has been named Coleman Crawford   , and is now living.

Minnie Crawford

Witnesseth.

Must be two
Witnesses who
are Citizens.

John Owens

C.D. Robinson

Subscribed and sworn to before me this 16 day of Jan   190 5

W A Shoney

Notary Public.

My commission expires:
Jan 10-1909

Affidavit of Attending Physician or Midwife

UNITED STATES OF AMERICA,
INDIAN TERRITORY,
Central   DISTRICT

I,   A.B. Strange   a   Physician
on oath state that I attended on Mrs. Minnie Crawford   wife of Frank Crawford
on the   15th   day of August   , 190 3, that there was born to her on said date a   male
child, that said child is now living, and is said to have been named Coleman Crawford

A.B. Strange   M. D.

Subscribed and sworn to before me this the   17 day of   Jany   1905

JM Routh

Notary Public.

WITNESSETH:

Must be two witnesses
who are citizens and
know the child.

(Name Illegible)

HB Hayes

We hereby certify that we are well acquainted with   Dr A B Strange
a   Physician   and know   him   to be reputable and of good standing in the
community.

Must be two citizen
witnesses.

(Name Illegible)

HB Hayes

7-3452

Muskogee, Indian Territory, April 19, 1905.

Frank Crawford,
Durant, Indian Territory.

Dear Sir:

Receipt is hereby acknowledged of the affidavits of Minnie Crawford and A. B. Strange to the birth of Coleman Crawford, son of Frank and Minnie Crawford August 15, 1903, and the same have been filed with our records as an application for the enrollment of said child.

Respectfully,

Chairman.

7-N.B. 1042
7-3452

Muskogee, Indian Territory, May 2, 1905.

L. D. Horton,
Boswell, Indian Territory.

Dear Sir:

Receipt is hereby acknowledged of your letters of April 25 and 26, enclosing the affidavits of Minnie Durant (formerly Minnie Crawford), V. T. Stephens and J. S. Durant, Indian Territory to the birth of Ruby Gertrude Crawford, daughter of Barney and Minnie Crawford, October 18, 1902:   receipt is also acknowledged of the marriage license and certificate between Barney Crawford and Minnie Burnes and the same have been filed with our records in the matter of the enrollment of the child herein named.

Respectfully,

Chairman.

<u>Choc New Born 1043</u>
     Thomas Beal
     (Born Nov. 9, 1903)

NEW-BORN AFFIDAVIT.

Number..............

Choctaw Enrolling Commission.

IN THE MATTER OF THE APPLICATION FOR ENROLLMENT, as a citizen of the Choctaw   Nation, of   Thomas Beal

born on the 9th day of November   190 3

Name of father   Thomas T. Beal   a citizen of   Choctaw
Nation final enrollment No 9935
Name of mother   Verdie Beal   a citizen of   white
Nation final enrollment No..............

Postoffice   Albany I.T.

AFFIDAVIT OF MOTHER.

UNITED STATES OF AMERICA, ⎫
    INDIAN TERRITORY, ⎬
  Central   DISTRICT ⎭

I   Verdie Beal   on oath state that I am 30 years of age and a citizen by white   of the ....Nation, and as such have been placed upon the final roll of the ....Nation, by the Honorable Secretary of the Interior my final enrollment number being ....; that I am the lawful wife of Thomas T. Beal   , who is a citizen of the Choctaw   Nation, and as such has been placed upon the final roll of said Nation by the Honorable Secretary of the Interior, his final enrollment number being 9935 and that a male child was born to me on the ninth day of November   190 3; that said child has been named Thomas Beal   , and is now living.

Verdie Beal

WITNESSETH:
  Must be two ⎫ Andrew P Beal
  Witnesses who ⎬
  are Citizens. ⎭ Pinkney Beal

Subscribed and sworn to before me this 16 day of Jan   190 5

J M Reasor
Notary Public.

My commission expires May 1908

254

Affidavit of Attending Physician or Midwife.

UNITED STATES OF AMERICA ⎫
INDIAN TERRITORY   ⎬
  Central   DISTRICT ⎭

    I,   P. L. Cain   a   Physician
on oath state that I attended on Mrs.   Verdie   wife of   Thomas T. Beal
on the ninth day of November , 190 3 , that there was born to her on said date a
Male child, that said child is now living, and is said to have been named Thomas Beal

P.L. Cain   M.D.

Subscribed and sworn to before me this, the 16th day of   January   190 5

J.M. Reasor
Notary Public.

WITNESSETH:

Must be two witnesses ⎧ Andrew P Beal
who are citizens and   ⎨
know the child.   ⎩ Pinkney Beal

    We hereby certify that we are well acquainted with   P.L. Cain
a Physician   and know him   to be reputable and of good standing in the
community.

⎧ Andrew P Beal
⎨
⎩ Pinkney Beal

BIRTH AFFIDAVIT.

DEPARTMENT OF THE INTERIOR.
COMMISSION TO THE FIVE CIVILIZED TRIBES.

IN RE APPLICATION FOR ENROLLMENT, as a citizen of the   Choctaw   Nation, of
Thomas Beal   , born on the 9th day of November , 1903

Name of Father: Thomas T. Beal   a citizen of the Choctaw   Nation.
Name of Mother: Virdie[sic] Beal   a citizen of the   U.S.   Nation.

Postoffice   Albany I.T.

Applications for Enrollment of Choctaw Newborn
Act of 1905   Volume XIV

AFFIDAVIT OF MOTHER.

UNITED STATES OF AMERICA, Indian Territory, }
Central   DISTRICT.

I,   Virdie Beal   , on oath state that I am   30   years of age and a citizen by marriage   , of the   Choctaw   Nation; that I am the lawful wife of   Thomas T Beal, who is a citizen, by   blood   of the   Choctaw   Nation; that a   male child was born to me on   ninth   day of   November   , 1903; that said child has been named   Thomas Beal   , and was living March 4, 1905.

                                        Virdie Beal

Witnesses To Mark:
{

Subscribed and sworn to before me this   12   day of   April   , 1905

                                J.M. Reasor
                                        Notary Public.

AFFIDAVIT OF ATTENDING PHYSICIAN OR MID-WIFE.

UNITED STATES OF AMERICA, Indian Territory, }
Central   DISTRICT.

I,   P.L. Cain   , a   Physician   , on oath state that I attended on Mrs.   Virdie Beal   , wife of   Thomas T. Beal   on the 9th   day of   November, 1903; that there was born to her on said date a   male   child; that said child was living March 4, 1905, and is said to have been named Thomas Beal

                                P.L. Cain

Witnesses To Mark:
{

Subscribed and sworn to before me this   12th   day of   April   , 1905

                                J.M. Reasor
                                        Notary Public.

7-3490

Muskogee, Indian Territory, April 19, 1905.

Thomas F. Beal,
    Albany, Indian Territory.

Dear Sir:

Receipt is hereby acknowledged of the affidavits of Virdie Beal and P. L. Cain to the birth of Thomas Beal, son of Thomas F. and Virdie Beal November 9, 1903, and the same have been filed with our records as an application for the enrollment of said child.

Respectfully,

Chairman.

Choc New Born 1044
    Laurence E. Arnote
    (Born April 1, 1904)

Affidavit of Attending Physician or Midwife

UNITED STATES OF AMERICA, ⎤
    INDIAN TERRITORY, ⎬
Central   DISTRICT ⎦

I,   W.N. John   a   Physician
on oath state that I attended on Mrs. Annie T. Arnote   wife of   Andrew J Arnote
on the   First   day of   April   , 190 4, that there was born to her on said date a   male   child,
that said child is now living, and is said to have been named   Laurence E. Arnote

W.N. John   M. D.

Subscribed and sworn to before me this the   13   day of   February   1905

M.P. Stewart
                    Notary Public.

WITNESSETH:

Must be two witnesses ⎱ Jno G Farr
who are citizens and
know the child. ⎰ Inez Farr

257

We hereby certify that we are well acquainted with   W. N. John
a   Physician   and know   him   to be reputable and of good standing in the community.

Must be two citizen⎰ Jno G Farr
witnesses.   ⎱ Inez Farr

NEW BORN AFFIDAVIT

No ....

CHOCTAW ENROLLING COMMISSION

IN THE MATTER OF THE APPLICATION FOR ENROLLMENT as a citizen of the Choctaw
Nation, of   Laurence E. Arnote   born on the First   day
of April   190 4

     Name of father   Andrew J Arnote   a citizen of   Choctaw   Nation,
final enrollment No.   483
     Name of mother   Annie T. Arnote   a citizen of   Choctaw   Nation,
final enrollment No.   13140

        Antlers, Ind Ter   Postoffice.

AFFIDAVIT OF MOTHER

UNITED STATES OF AMERICA ⎱
    INDIAN TERRITORY   ⎰
DISTRICT   Central

    I   Annie T. Arnote   , on oath state that I am   33   years of age and
a citizen by   blood   of the   Choctaw   Nation, and as such have been placed
upon the final roll of the   Choctaw   Nation, by the Honorable Secretary of the Interior my
final enrollment number being   13140   ; that I am the lawful wife of   Andrew J Arnote   ,
who is a citizen of the   Choctaw   Nation, and as such has been placed upon the final
roll of said Nation by the Honorable Secretary of the Interior, his final enrollment number
being   483   and that a   Male   child was born to me on the   First   day of   April
190 4; that said child has been named   Laurence E. Arnote   , and is now living.

WITNESSETH: Annie T. Arnote
   Must be two witnesses ⎰ Jno G Farr
     who are citizens   ⎱ Inez Farr

258

Applications for Enrollment of Choctaw Newborn
Act of 1905   Volume XIV

Subscribed and sworn to before me this, the   13 day of   February   , 190 5

W.P. Stewart
Notary Public.

My Commission Expires: April 21, 1907

BIRTH AFFIDAVIT.

DEPARTMENT OF THE INTERIOR.
COMMISSION TO THE FIVE CIVILIZED TRIBES.

IN RE APPLICATION FOR ENROLLMENT, as a citizen of the   Choctaw   Nation, of
Laurence E Arnote   , born on the 1st day of   April   , 1904

Name of Father: Andrew J. Arnote   a citizen of the   Choctaw   Nation.
Name of Mother: Annie T. Arnote   a citizen of the   Choctaw   Nation.

Postoffice   Antlers I.T.

AFFIDAVIT OF MOTHER.

UNITED STATES OF AMERICA, Indian Territory, ⎫
    Central   DISTRICT. ⎭

I,   Annie T. Arnote   , on oath state that I am .... years of age and a
citizen by   blood   , of the   Choctaw   Nation; that I am the lawful wife of
Andrew J. Arnote   , who is a citizen, by Intermarriage   of the   Choctaw
Nation; that a   male   child was born to me on   1st day of   April   , 1904; that
said child has been named   Laurence E. Arnote   , and was living March 4, 1905.

Annie T. Arnote

Witnesses To Mark:
  ⎰ S.P. Davenport
  ⎱ H.C. Noah

Subscribed and sworn to before me this 12 day of   April   , 1905

W.P. Stewart
Notary Public.

259

AFFIDAVIT OF ATTENDING PHYSICIAN OR MID-WIFE.

UNITED STATES OF AMERICA, Indian Territory, ⎫
   Central   **DISTRICT.** ⎭

    I,   W. N. John   , a Physician   , on oath state that I attended on
Mrs.   Annie T. Arnote   , wife of Andrew J. Arnote   on the 1st day of April,
1904; that there was born to her on said date a   male   child; that said child was living
March 4, 1905, and is said to have been named Laurence E. Arnote

W. N. John M.D.

Witnesses To Mark:
  ⎰ Peter J Hudson
  ⎱ J.M. Ennis

    Subscribed and sworn to before me this 12 day of   April   , 1905

W.P. Stewart
Notary Public.

7-NB-1044

Muskogee, Indian Territory, August 15, 1905.

Andrew J. Arnote,
    Antlers, Indian Territory.

Dear Sir:

    Receipt is hereby acknowledged of the affidavits of Annie T. Arnote and John G. Farr to the death of your child, Lawrence E. Arnote, a citizen by blood of the Choctaw Nation of the Choctaw Nation, which occurred March 18, 1905, and the same have been filed with the records as evidence of the death of the above named citizen.

Respectfully,

Acting Commissioner.

<u>Choc New Born 1045</u>
>   Spencer Jefferson
>   (Born May 19, 1904)

BIRTH AFFIDAVIT.

   IN RE-APPLICATION FOR ENROLLMENT, as a citizen of the   Chocktaw[sic]   Nation,
of Spencer Jefferson , born on the 19th   day of May , 190 4

Name of Father: Swiney[sic] Jefferson   a citizen of the   Chocktaw   Nation.
Name of Mother: Rosa Jefferson   a citizen of the   Chocktaw   Nation.

   Postoffice   Pontotoc Ind. Ter.

AFFIDAVIT OF MOTHER.

UNITED STATES OF AMERICA, INDIAN TERRITORY,
   Southern   District.

   I,   Rosa Jefferson   , on oath state that I am 20   years of age and a citizen by
Blood , of the   Chocktaw   Nation; that I am the lawful wife of   Swiney Jefferson ,
who is a citizen, by   Blood   of the   Chocktaw   Nation; that a   male   child was born
to me on 19th   day of May   , 1904, that said child has been named Spencer Jefferson ,
and is now living.

                Rosa Jefferson
Witnesses To Mark:

   Subscribed and sworn to before me this   24 day of   Feb , 1905.

                M.S. Bradford
                   Notary Public.

AFFIDAVIT OF ATTENDING PHYSICIAN OR MID-WIFE.

UNITED STATES OF AMERICA, INDIAN TERRITORY,
   Southern   District.

   I,   Elsie Anderson   , a   Midwife   , on oath state that I attended on
Mrs. Rosa Jefferson , wife of Swiney Jefferson on the 19th   day of May   , 190 5[sic];
that there was born to her on said date a   male   child; that said child is now living and is said to
have been named Spencer Jefferson   her
                Elsie x Anderson
Witnesses To Mark: mark
   J A Stamps
   M.D. Anderson

Applications for Enrollment of Choctaw Newborn
Act of 1905   Volume XIV

Subscribed and sworn to before me this   24   day of   Feb   , 1905.

M.S. Bradford
Notary Public.

BIRTH AFFIDAVIT.

DEPARTMENT OF THE INTERIOR.
COMMISSION TO THE FIVE CIVILIZED TRIBES.

IN RE APPLICATION FOR ENROLLMENT, as a citizen of the   Choctaw   Nation, of
Spencer Jefferson   , born on the   19   day of   May   , 1904

Roll

Name of Father: Sweeny[sic] Jefferson   *12554*   a citizen of the   Choctaw   Nation.

Roll

Name of Mother: Rosa Jefferson   *12594*   a citizen of the   Choctaw   Nation.

Postoffice   Pontotoc I.T.

AFFIDAVIT OF MOTHER.

UNITED STATES OF AMERICA, Indian Territory, ⎫
        Southern   **DISTRICT.** ⎬

I,   Rosa Jefferson   , on oath state that I am   20   years of age and a citizen
by   blood   , of the   Choctaw   Nation; that I am the lawful wife of   Sweeny
Jefferson   , who is a citizen, by   blood   of the   Choctaw   Nation; that a
male   child was born to me on   19   day of   May   , 1904; that said child has
been named   Spencer Jefferson   , and was living March 4, 1905.

Rosa Jefferson
Witnesses To Mark:
⎰
⎱

Subscribed and sworn to before me this   12   day of   June   , 1905

M.S. Bradford
Notary Public.

262

Applications for Enrollment of Choctaw Newborn
Act of 1905   Volume XIV

AFFIDAVIT OF ATTENDING PHYSICIAN OR MID-WIFE.

UNITED STATES OF AMERICA, Indian Territory, ⎱
  Southern   DISTRICT. ⎰

I,   Dora Whistler   , a midwife   , on oath state that I attended on
Mrs. Rosa Jefferson   , wife of Sweeny Jefferson   on the 19 day of May   ,
1904; that there was born to her on said date a   male   child; that said child was living
March 4, 1905, and is said to have been named   Spencer Jefferson

                                    Dora Whistler
Witnesses To Mark:

{

Subscribed and sworn to before me this 12 day of   June   , 1905

                        M.S. Bradford
                            Notary Public.

BIRTH AFFIDAVIT.
DEPARTMENT OF THE INTERIOR.
COMMISSION TO THE FIVE CIVILIZED TRIBES.

IN RE APPLICATION FOR ENROLLMENT, as a citizen of the   Chocktaw [sic]   Nation,
of   Spencer Jefferson   , born on the 19   day of   May   , 1904

Name of Father: Swiney Jefferson   a citizen of the   Chocktaw   Nation.
Name of Mother: Rosa Jefferson   a citizen of the   Chocktaw   Nation.

          Postoffice   Pontotoc I.T.

AFFIDAVIT OF MOTHER.

UNITED STATES OF AMERICA, Indian Territory, ⎱
  Southern   DISTRICT. ⎰

I,   Rosa Jefferson   , on oath state that I am   22   years of age and a citizen
by   Blood   , of the   Chocktaw   Nation; that I am the lawful wife of   Swiney
Jefferson   , who is a citizen, by Blood   of the   Chocktaw   Nation; that a
male   child was born to me on   19   day of   May   , 1904; that said child has
been named   Spencer Jefferson   , and was living March 4, 1905.

                        Rosa Jefferson
Witnesses To Mark:

{

Subscribed and sworn to before me this 12   day of   June   , 1905

M.S. Bradford
Notary Public.

_____

AFFIDAVIT OF ATTENDING PHYSICIAN OR MID-WIFE.

UNITED STATES OF AMERICA, Indian Territory, ⎫
   Southern   DISTRICT. ⎬
                       ⎭

    I,   Dora Whistler   , a mid wife   , on oath state that I attended on
Mrs. Rosa Jefferson   , wife of Swiney Jefferson   on the 19 day of May ,
1904; that there was born to her on said date a   male   child; that said child was living
March 4, 1905, and is said to have been named   Spencer Jefferson

Dora Whistler

Witnesses To Mark:

   ⎰
   ⎱

    Subscribed and sworn to before me this 12   day of   June   , 1905

M.S. Bradford
Notary Public.

_____

Choctaw 5374.

Muskogee, Indian Territory, April 19, 1905.

Swiney Jefferson,
      Pontotoc, Indian Territory.

Dear Sir:

    Receipt is hereby acknowledged of the affidavits of Rosa Jefferson and Dora Whistler to the birth of Spencer Jefferson, son of Swiney and Rosa Jefferson, May 19, 1904, and the same have been filed with our records as an application for the enrollment of said child.

                Respectfully,

Chairman.

_____

7 NB 1045

Muskogee, Indian Territory, June 17, 1905.

Sweeney Jefferson,
Pontotoc, Indian Territory.

Dear Sir:

Receipt is hereby acknowledged of the affidavits of Rosa Jefferson and Dora Whistler to the birth of Spencer Jefferson, son of Sweeney and Rosa Jefferson, May 19, 1904, and the same have been filed with our records in the matter of the enrollment of said child.

Respectfully,

Chairman.

---

7 NB 1045.

Muskogee, Indian Territory, June 2, 1905.

Sweeney Jefferson,
Pontotoc, Indian Territory.

Dear Sir:

There is enclosed you herewith for execution application for the enrollment of your infant child, Spencer Jefferson.

The midwife in her affidavit of February 24, 1905, gave the date of the applicant's birth as May 19, 1905, while the mother, in her affidavit of the same date, gives it as May 19, 1904. In the affidavits of April 12, 1905, the date of birth is given as May 19, 1904. In the enclosed application the date of birth is left blank. Please insert the correct date and, when the affidavits are properly executed, return them to this office.

In having these affidavits executed care should be exercised to see that all names are written in full, as they appear in the body of the affidavit, and in the event that either of the persons signing the affidavit are unable to write, signatures by mark must be attested by two witnesses. Each affidavit must be executed before a Notary Public and the notarial seal and signature of the officer must be attached to each separate affidavit.

Respectfully,

VR 2-3.   [sic]

Choc New Born 1046
      Earl Going[sic]
      (Born Feb. 1, 1903)

BIRTH AFFIDAVIT.

DEPARTMENT OF THE INTERIOR.
COMMISSION TO THE FIVE CIVILIZED TRIBES.

IN RE APPLICATION FOR ENROLLMENT, as a citizen of the   Choctaw   Nation, of
Earl Goins   , born on the   1st   day of   February   , 1903

Name of Father: Jim Goins   a citizen of the   Choctaw   Nation.
Name of Mother: Zarabell Goins   a citizen of the   Choctaw   Nation.

             Postoffice   Boswell I.T.

AFFIDAVIT OF MOTHER.

UNITED STATES OF AMERICA, Indian Territory,⎫
     Central   **DISTRICT.** ⎬

I,   Zarabell Goins   , on oath state that I am   37   years of age and a citizen
by   blood   , of the   Choctaw   Nation; that I am the lawful wife of   Jim Goins ,
who is a citizen, by blood   of the   Choctaw   Nation; that a   male   child
was born to me on   1st   day of   February   , 1903; that said child has been named
Earl Goins   , and was living March 4, 1905.

                       her
                Zarabell x Goins
Witnesses To Mark: mark
    ⎧ L.A. Riddle
    ⎩ Elizabeth Riddle

Subscribed and sworn to before me this   15" day of   April   , 1905

                SH Downing
                   Notary Public.

Applications for Enrollment of Choctaw Newborn
Act of 1905 Volume XIV

UNITED STATES OF AMERICA, Indian Territory, ⎫
 Central   DISTRICT. ⎰

I,   Elizabeth Durant   , a   Midwife   , on oath state that I attended on
Mrs.   Zarabell Goins   , wife of   Jim Goins   on the 1st day of   February   ,
1903; that there was born to her on said date a   male   child; that said child was living
March 4, 1905, and is said to have been named Earl Goins

her
Elizabeth x Durant
mark

Witnesses To Mark:
 ⎧ L.A. Riddle
 ⎩ Elizabeth Riddle

Subscribed and sworn to before me this 15" day of   April   , 1905

SH Downing
Notary Public.

Choc New Born 1047
        James Billy
        (Born July 19, 1904)

BIRTH AFFIDAVIT.
DEPARTMENT OF THE INTERIOR.
COMMISSION TO THE FIVE CIVILIZED TRIBES.

IN RE APPLICATION FOR ENROLLMENT, as a citizen of the   Choctaw   Nation, of
James Billy   , born on the   19th day of   July , 1904

Name of Father: Walton Billy   a citizen of the   Choctaw   Nation.
Name of Mother: Louisa Billy (nee Leflore)   a citizen of the   Choctaw   Nation.

Postoffice   Bennington I.T.

Applications for Enrollment of Choctaw Newborn
Act of 1905   Volume XIV

AFFIDAVIT OF MOTHER.

UNITED STATES OF AMERICA, Indian Territory, ⎫
Cent   DISTRICT. ⎰

I,   Louisa Billy   , on oath state that I am   22   years of age and a citizen by blood   , of the   Choctaw   Nation; that I am the lawful wife of   Walton Billy   , who is a citizen, by   blood   of the   Choctaw   Nation; that a   male   child was born to me on   19th   day of   July   , 1904; that said child has been named James Billy   , and was living March 4, 1905.

Louisa Billy

Witnesses To Mark:
{

Subscribed and sworn to before me this 15th   day of   April   , 1905

BW Williams
Notary Public.

AFFIDAVIT OF ATTENDING PHYSICIAN OR MID-WIFE.

UNITED STATES OF AMERICA, Indian Territory, ⎫
Cent   DISTRICT. ⎰

I,   R M Parish   , a   Physician   , on oath state that I attended on Mrs. Louisa Billy   , wife of   Walton Billy   on the 19th   day of   July   , 1904; that there was born to her on said date a   male   child; that said child was living March 4, 1905, and is said to have been named   James Billy

R M Parish M.D.

Witnesses To Mark:
{

Subscribed and sworn to before me this 15th   day of   April   , 1905

BW Williams
Notary Public.

NEW-BORN AFFIDAVIT.

Number.................

Choctaw Enrolling Commission.

IN THE MATTER OF THE APPLICATION FOR ENROLLMENT, as a citizen of the Choctaw   Nation, of   James Billy

born on the   19th   day of   July   190 4

Name of father   Walton Billy   a citizen of   Choctaw
Nation final enrollment No   9863
Name of mother   Louisa Leflore - now Billy   a citizen of   Choctaw
Nation final enrollment No   13347

Postoffice   Bennington I.T.

AFFIDAVIT OF MOTHER.

UNITED STATES OF AMERICA, ⎫
   INDIAN TERRITORY, ⎬
  Central   DISTRICT ⎭

   I   Louisa Leflore - now Billy   on oath state that I am   23   years of age and a citizen by   blood   of the   Choctaw   Nation, and as such have been placed upon the final roll of the   Choctaw   Nation, by the Honorable Secretary of the Interior my final enrollment number being   13347   ; that I am the lawful wife of   Waltor[sic] Billy   , who is a citizen of the   Choctaw Nation, and as such has been placed upon the final roll of said Nation by the Honorable Secretary of the Interior, his final enrollment number being   9863   and that a   male child was born to me on the   19th   day of   July   190 4 ; that said child has been named James Billy   , and is now living.

Louisa Billy

WITNESSETH:

Must be two ⎫   Eli Julius
Witnesses who ⎬
are Citizens. ⎭   Eliza Julius

Subscribed and sworn to before me this   16   day of   Jan   190 5

W A Shoney
Notary Public.

My commission expires   Jan 10, 1909

269

Affidavit of Attending Physician or Midwife.

UNITED STATES OF AMERICA ⎫
INDIAN TERRITORY   ⎬
..................................DISTRICT ⎭

I,   J H Hargrove   a   Physician
on oath state that I attended on Mrs. Louisa Leflore now Billy   wife of   Walter Billy
on the 19ᵗʰ   day of   July   , 190 4 , that there was born to her on said date a   Male
child, that said child is now living, and is said to have been named   James Billy

J H Hargrove   M.D.

Subscribed and sworn to before me this, the 17 day of January   190 5

Thomas H Bayass
Notary Public.

WITNESSETH:

Must be two witnesses ⎰ Eli Julius
who are citizens and ⎱
know the child.   Eliza Julius

We hereby certify that we are well acquainted with ....
a   Physician   and know   him   to be reputable and of good standing in the
community.

Eli Julius
⎰
⎱ Eliza Julius

Choctaw N B 1047
Choctaw 4835

Muskogee, Indian Territory, May 20, 1905.

W. J. Billy,
Bennington, Indian Territory.

Dear Sir:

Receipt is hereby acknowledged of your letter of May 12, asking when you can file for your children, Rose and James Billy.

In reply to your letter you are advised that the name of your daughter, Rossie Billy, has been placed upon a schedule of citizens by blood of the Choctaw Nation prepared for forwarding to the Secretary of the Interior.   The affidavits heretofore forwarded to the birth of your son, James Billy, have been filed with our records as an application for the enrollment of said child, but his name has not been placed upon a schedule of citizens by blood of the Choctaw Nation for forwarding to the Secretary of the Interior Pending the approval of the enrollment of these children by the Secretary of the Interior, no selection of allotment can be made in their behalf.

Respectfully,

Chairman.

Choc New Born 1048
> George Johnson Perkins
> (Born Jan. 14, 1904)

BIRTH AFFIDAVIT.

DEPARTMENT OF THE INTERIOR,
COMMISSION TO THE FIVE CIVILIZED TRIBES.

IN RE Application for Enrollment, as a citizen of the   Choctaw   Nation, of   George Johnson Perkins , born on the   14   day of   Jan   , 1904

Name of Father: L. H. Perkins   a citizen of the   Choctaw   Nation.
Name of Mother: Hattie A Perkins   a citizen of the   Choctaw   Nation.

Post-Office: Indianola I.T.

AFFIDAVIT OF MOTHER.

UNITED STATES OF AMERICA,
  INDIAN TERRITORY.
  Western   District.

I,   Hattie A Perkins   , on oath state that I am   39   years of age and a citizen by   intermarriage   , of the Choctaw   Nation; that I am the lawful wife of L.H. Perkins   , who is a citizen, by   Blood   of the Choctaw   Nation; that a   male child was born to me on   14   day of   January   , 1904, that said child has been named George Johnson Perkins   , and is now living.

Hattie A Perkins

WITNESSES TO MARK:

271

Subscribed and sworn to before me this 14 *day of* April , 1905.

T.J. Rice

NOTARY PUBLIC.

AFFIDAVIT OF ATTENDING PHYSICIAN OR MID-WIFE.

UNITED STATES OF AMERICA, ⎫
  INDIAN TERRITORY. ⎬
Western   District. ⎭

I, J. A. Eubank , a Physician , on oath state that I attended on Mrs. Hattie A Perkins , wife of L. H. Perkins on the 14 day of January , 1904 ; that there was born to her on said date a male child; that said child is now living and is said to have been named George Johnson Perkins

JA Eubanks M.D.

WITNESSES TO MARK:

{

Subscribed and sworn to before me this 14 *day of* April , 1905.

T.J. Rice

NOTARY PUBLIC.

NEW-BORN AFFIDAVIT.

Number................

...Choctaw Enrolling Commission...

IN THE MATTER OF THE APPLICATION FOR ENROLLMENT, as a citizen of the Choctaw   Nation, of   George Johnston[sic] Perkins

born on the 14 day of ____January____ 190 4

Name of father L. H. Perkins   a citizen of   Choctaw
Nation final enrollment No. 12701
Name of mother Hattie A Perkins   a citizen of   Choctaw
Nation final enrollment No. ....

Postoffice   Indianola I.T.

Applications for Enrollment of Choctaw Newborn
Act of 1905   Volume XIV

AFFIDAVIT OF MOTHER.

United States of America
Indian Territory Western District

I   Hattie A Perkins   , on oath state that I am
38   years of age and a citizen by   intermarriage   of the   Choctaw
Nation, and as such have been placed upon the final roll of the   Choctaw   Nation, by the
Honorable Secretary of the Interior my final enrollment number being   none ; that I am the
lawful wife of   L.H. Perkins   , who is a citizen of the   Choctaw   Nation, and as
such has been placed upon the final roll of said Nation by the Honorable Secretary of the
Interior, his final enrollment number being   12701   and that a   Male   child was born
to me on the   14th   day of   January   190 4; that said child has been named   George
Johnston[sic] Perkins   , and is now living.

Hattie A Perkins

Witnesseth.

Must be two ⎫ John F Bolling
Witnesses who ⎬
are Citizens. ⎭ Robert T Pearson

Subscribed and sworn to before me this   12   day of   Jan   190 5

DM Crawford
Notary Public.

My commission expires:
Sept 19 1907

AFFIDAVIT OF ATTENDING PHYSICIAN OR MIDWIFE

United States of America
Indian Territory Western District

J A Eubank

I,   P.S. Johnston   a   Physician
on oath state that I attended on Mrs.   Hattie A Perkins   wife of   L. H. Perkins
on the   14th   day of   January , 190 4 , that there was born to her on said date a   male
child, that said child is now living, and is said to have been named   George Johnston Perkins
P. S. Johnston
JA Eubank   *M.D.*

Subscribed and sworn to before me this, the   12   day of
Jan   190 5

WITNESSETH: DM Crawford   Notary Public.
Must be two witnesses ⎰ John F Bolling
who are citizens ⎱
Robert T Pearson

273

We hereby certify that we are well acquainted with..
a .... and know................................. to be reputable and of good standing in the
community.

7-4591

Muskogee, Indian Territory, April 19, 1905.

L. H. Perkins,
     Indianola, Indian Territory.

Dear Sir:

    Receipt is hereby acknowledged of the affidavits of Hattie A. Perkins and J. A. Eubanks to the birth of George Johnson Perkins son of L. H. and Hattie A. Perkins January 14, 1904, and the same have been filed with the records of our office as an application for the enrollment of said child.

Respectfully,

Chairman.

Choc New Born 1049
     Addie Jennings
     Born Feb. 21, 1905
     Lota Jennings
     (Born July 13, 1903)

BIRTH AFFIDAVIT.

DEPARTMENT OF THE INTERIOR.
COMMISSION TO THE FIVE CIVILIZED TRIBES.

IN RE APPLICATION FOR ENROLLMENT, as a citizen of the   Choctaw   Nation, of
Addie Jennings   , born on the 21st   day of   February   , 1905

Name of Father: Nathaniel F. Jennings   a citizen of the   Choctaw   Nation.
Name of Mother: Crotia A. Jennings   a citizen of the   Choctaw   Nation.

Postoffice   Purcell, Indian Territory.

AFFIDAVIT OF MOTHER.

UNITED STATES OF AMERICA, Indian Territory, ⎱
   Southern   DISTRICT. ⎰

I,   Crotia A. Jennings   , on oath state that I am   24   years of age and a
citizen by   inter-marriage   , of the   Choctaw   Nation; that I am the lawful wife
of   Nathaniel F. Jennings   , who is a citizen, by Blood   of the   Choctaw
Nation; that a   Female   child was born to me on   21st   day of   February   ,
1905; that said child has been named   Addie Jennings   , and was living March 4,
1905.

Crotia A. Jennings

Witnesses To Mark:
⎧ I W William
⎩ S P Steward

Subscribed and sworn to before me this   13th day of   April   , 1905

WH Downard
Notary Public.

AFFIDAVIT OF ATTENDING PHYSICIAN OR MID-WIFE.

UNITED STATES OF AMERICA, Indian Territory, ⎱
   Southern   DISTRICT. ⎰

I,   Nancy C. Trower   , a   Mid- Wife   , on oath state that I attended on
Mrs.   Crotia A. Jennings   , wife of   Nathaniel F. Jennings   on the 21st day of
February   , 1905; that there was born to her on said date a   female   child; that
said child was living March 4, 1905, and is said to have been named Addie Jennings

Nancy C Trower

Witnesses To Mark:
{ I W William
{ S P Steward

Subscribed and sworn to before me this 13th day of April   , 1905
My commission
expires Feby 29-1908   WH Downard
                                                    Notary Public.

BIRTH AFFIDAVIT.

DEPARTMENT OF THE INTERIOR.
COMMISSION TO THE FIVE CIVILIZED TRIBES.

IN RE APPLICATION FOR ENROLLMENT, as a citizen of the   Choctaw   Nation, of
Lota Jennings   , born on the 13th   day of July , 1903

Name of Father: Nathaniel F. Jennings   a citizen of the   Choctaw   Nation.
Name of Mother: Crotia A. Jennings   a citizen of the   Choctaw   Nation.

Postoffice   Purcell, Indian Territory.

AFFIDAVIT OF MOTHER.

UNITED STATES OF AMERICA, Indian Territory, }
    Southern   **DISTRICT.** }

I,   Crotia A. Jennings   , on oath state that I am   24   years of age and a
citizen by   inter-marriage   , of the   Choctaw   Nation; that I am the lawful wife
of   Nathaniel F. Jennings   , who is a citizen, by Blood   of the   Choctaw
Nation; that a   Female   child was born to me on 13th   day of July   , 1903;
that said child has been named   Lota Jennings   , and was living March 4, 1905.

Crotia A. Jennings

Witnesses To Mark:
{ I W William
{ S P Steward

Subscribed and sworn to before me this 13th day of April   , 1905

WH Downard
Notary Public.

AFFIDAVIT OF ATTENDING PHYSICIAN OR MID-WIFE.

UNITED STATES OF AMERICA, Indian Territory, ⎱
   Southern   DISTRICT. ⎰

I,   Nancy C. Trower   , a   Mid Wife   , on oath state that I attended on Mrs.   Crotia A. Jennings   , wife of   Nathaniel F. Jennings   on the 13th day of July   , 1903; that there was born to her on said date a   female   child; that said child was living March 4, 1905, and is said to have been named Lota Jennings

Nancy C Trower

Witnesses To Mark:
  ⎰ I W William
  ⎱ S P Steward

Subscribed and sworn to before me this   13th day of   April   , 1905
My commission
expires Feby 29-1908   WH Downard
                           Notary Public.

7-5628

Muskogee, Indian Territory, April 19, 1905.

Nathaniel F. Jennings,
      Purcell, Indian Territory.

Dear Sir:

Receipt is hereby acknowledged of the affidavits of Crotia A. Jennings and Nancy C. Trower to the birth of Lota Jennings and Addie Jennings children of Nathaniel F. and Crotia A. Jennings July 13, 1903 and February 21, 1905, respectively, and the same have been filed with our records as an application for the enrollment of said children.

Respectfully,

Chairman.

Choc New Born 1050
    John D. Folsom
    (Born Feb. 26, 1904)

DEPARTMENT OF THE INTERIOR,
COMMISSIONER TO THE FIVE CIVILIZED TRIBES.

Record in the matter of the application for enrollment as a citizen by blood of the Choctaw Nation of:

JOHN D. FOLSOM   7-NB-1050.

BIRTH AFFIDAVIT.

DEPARTMENT OF THE INTERIOR.
COMMISSION TO THE FIVE CIVILIZED TRIBES.

IN RE APPLICATION FOR ENROLLMENT, as a citizen of the   Choctaw   Nation, of
John D. Folsom   , born on the 26 day of February , 1904

Name of Father: John Folsom   a citizen of the Choctaw Nation.
Name of Mother: Sarah Folsom   *Intermarried* a citizen of the Choctaw Nation.

Postoffice   Enterprise Ind Ter

AFFIDAVIT OF MOTHER.

UNITED STATES OF AMERICA, Indian Territory,
    Western   **DISTRICT.**

    I, Sarah Folsom   , on oath state that I am 43 years of age and a citizen by Intermarriage , of the Choct Nation; that I am the lawful wife of John Folsom, who is a citizen, by Blood of the Choctaw Nation; that a male child was born to me on 26 day of February , 1904; that said child has been named John D Folsom , and ~~was living March 4, 1905~~. *Died March 9, 1904*

                        her
                   Sarah x Folsom
Witnesses To Mark: mark
    { Thomas J Walls   Enterprise IT
    { John Barber   Enterprise IT

Subscribed and sworn to before me this 14   day of   April   , 1905
My commission
expires Nov 27 1907   John M Lenz
                                                Notary Public.

_____

AFFIDAVIT OF ATTENDING PHYSICIAN OR MID-WIFE.

UNITED STATES OF AMERICA, Indian Territory, ⎤
   Western   DISTRICT. ⎦

     I,   D.S. Billington   , a   Physician   , on oath state that I attended on Mrs.   Sarah Folsom   , wife of John Folsom   on the 26 day of   February   , 1904; that there was born to her on said date a   male   child; that said child ~~was living~~ *Died* March 4 ~~9~~, 1905, and is said to have been named John D. Folsom

                                   Dr D S Billington
Witnesses To Mark:
   ⎰ *(Name Illegible)*
   ⎱ S H Matthews

     Subscribed and sworn to before me this 14   day of   April   , 1905
My commission
expires Nov 27 1907   John M Lenz
                                                Notary Public.

_____

W.F.
7-NB-1050.
DEPARTMENT OF THE INTERIOR,
COMMISSIONER TO THE FIVE CIVILIZED TRIBES.

     In the matter of the application for the enrollment of John D. Folsom as a citizen by blood of the Choctaw Nation.

----oOo----

     It appears from the record herein that on April 20, 1905, there was filed with the Commission to the Five Civilized Tribes an application for the enrollment of John D. Folsom as a citizen by blood of the Choctaw Nation.

     It further appears from the record herein and the records of this office that the applicant was born February 26, 1904; that he is a son of John Folsom, a recognized and enrolled citizen by blood of the Choctaw Nation whose name appears opposite number 7446 upon the final roll of citizens by blood of said nation, approved by the Secretary of the Interior January 17, 1903, and Sarah Folsom, a recognized and enrolled citizen by intermarriage of the Choctaw Nation; and that said applicant died March 9, 1904.

Applications for Enrollment of Choctaw Newborn
Act of 1905   Volume XIV

The Act of Congress approved March 3, 1905 (Public No. 212) among other things provided:

"That the Commission to the Five Civilized Tribes is authorized for sixty days after the date of the approval of this act to receive and consider applications for enrollment of children born subsequent to September twenty-fifth, nineteen hundred and two, and prior to March fourth, nineteen hundred and five, and who were living on said latter date, to citizens by blood of the Choctaw and Chickasaw tribes of Indians whose enrollment has been approved by the Secretary of the Interior prior to the date of the approval of this act; and to enroll and make allotments to such children."

It is, therefore, hereby ordered that the application for the enrollment of John D. Folsom as a citizen by blood of the Choctaw Nation be dismissed.

Tams Bixby   Commissioner.

Muskogee, Indian Territory.
OCT 6- 1905

7-NB-1050

Muskogee, Indian Territory, October 5[sic], 1905.

COPY

John Folsom,
Enterprise, Indian Territory.

Dear Sir:

Inclosed herewith you will find a copy of the order of the Commissioner to the Five Civilized Tribes, dated October 6, 1905, dismissing the application for the enrollment of your minor son John D. Folsom as a citizen by blood of the Choctaw Nation.

Respectfully
SIGNED

Tams Bixby
Commissioner.

Register.
7-1050-NB

Applications for Enrollment of Choctaw Newborn
Act of 1905   Volume XIV

7-NB-1050

Muskogee, Indian Territory, October 6, 1905.

COPY

Mansfield, McMurray & Cornish,
    Attorneys for Choctaw and Chickasaw Nations,
        South McAlester, Indian Territory.

Gentlemen:

    Inclosed herewith you will find a copy of the order of the Commissioner to the Five Civilized Tribes, dated October 6, 1905, dismissing the application for the enrollment of John D. Folsom as a citizen by blood of the Choctaw Nation.

Respectfully
SIGNED

Tams Bixby
Commissioner.

7-1050-NB

Choc New Born 1051
    Norman Scott
    (Born May 20, 1903)

BIRTH AFFIDAVIT.
DEPARTMENT OF THE INTERIOR.
COMMISSION TO THE FIVE CIVILIZED TRIBES.

IN RE APPLICATION FOR ENROLLMENT, as a citizen of the   Choctaw   Nation, of
Norman Scott   , born on the 20th   day of May   , 1903

Name of Father: Willie Scott   a citizen of the Choctaw   Nation.
Name of Mother: Elizabeth Scott   a citizen of the Choctaw   Nation.

Postoffice   Higgins, Ind. Ter

Applications for Enrollment of Choctaw Newborn
Act of 1905   Volume XIV

AFFIDAVIT OF MOTHER.

UNITED STATES OF AMERICA, Indian Territory, }
Central   DISTRICT. }

I,   Elizabeth Scott   , on oath state that I am   35   years of age and a citizen by   blood   , of the   Choctaw   Nation; that I am the lawful wife of   Willie Scott, who is a citizen, by   blood   of the   Choctaw   Nation; that a   male child was born to me on   20th   day of   May   , 1903; that said child has been named Norman Scott   , and was living March 4, 1905.

her
Elizabeth x Scott
mark

Witnesses To Mark:
{ John Pulcher
{ Stephen Cooper

Subscribed and sworn to before me this 15th   day of   April   , 1905

Wm J. Hulsey
Notary Public.

AFFIDAVIT OF ATTENDING PHYSICIAN OR MID-WIFE.

UNITED STATES OF AMERICA, Indian Territory, }
Central   DISTRICT. }

I,   Willie Scott   , a attendant   , on oath state that I attended on Mrs. Elizabeth Scott   , wife of   *myself*   on the 20th   day of   May   , 1903; that there was born to her on said date a   male   child; that said child was living March 4, 1905, and is said to have been named   Norman Scott *that at the time of birth of said child we did not have time to get a physician or midwife*

her
Willie x Scott
mark

Witnesses To Mark:
{ John Pulcher
{ Stephen Cooper

Subscribed and sworn to before me this 15th   day of   April   , 1905

Wm J. Hulsey
Notary Public.

NEW-BORN AFFIDAVIT.

Number............

...Choctaw Enrolling Commission...

IN THE MATTER OF THE APPLICATION FOR ENROLLMENT, as a citizen of the
Choctaw   Nation, of   Norman Scott

born on the   30   day of __May__ 190 3

Name of father   Willie Scott   a citizen of   Choctaw
Nation final enrollment No. 9110
Name of mother   Elizabeth Scott   a citizen of   Choctaw
Nation final enrollment No. 9111

Postoffice   Higgins, Ind. Ter.

AFFIDAVIT OF MOTHER.

UNITED STATES OF AMERICA
INDIAN TERRITORY
   Central   DISTRICT

I   Elizabeth Scott   , on oath state that I am
   35   years of age and a citizen by   blood   of the   Choctaw   Nation,
and as such have been placed upon the final roll of the   Choctaw   Nation, by the Honorable
Secretary of the Interior my final enrollment number being   9111 ; that I am the lawful wife
of   Willie Scott   , who is a citizen of the   Choctaw   Nation, and as such has been
placed upon the final roll of said Nation by the Honorable Secretary of the Interior, his final
enrollment number being   9110   and that a   Male   child was born to me on the   20
day of   May   190 3; that said child has been named   Norman Scott   , and is now living.

Witnesses to mark   her
JW White   Elizabeth x Scott
Stephen Cooper   mark

Witnesseth.

Must be two   ⎫   J.W. White
Witnesses who ⎬
are Citizens. ⎭   Stephen Cooper

Subscribed and sworn to before me this   11th   day of   Feb   190 5

Wm J Hulsey
Notary Public.
My commission expires: 1908

283

AFFIDAVIT OF ATTENDING PHYSICIAN OR MIDWIFE

UNITED STATES OF AMERICA
INDIAN TERRITORY
Central   DISTRICT

I,   Willie Scott   a ....
on oath state that I attended on Mrs.   Elizabeth Scott   wife of   *myself*
on the 20th   day of   May , 190 3, that there was born to her on said date a   male   child,
that said child is now living, and is said to have been named   Norman Scott

Witnesses to mark   his
JW White   Willie x Scott   M.D.
Stephen Cooper   mark

WITNESSETH:

Must be two witnesses   { J.W. White
who are citizens and
know the child.   { Stephen Cooper

Subscribed and sworn to before me this, the   11th   day of
February   190 5

Wm J. Hulsey   Notary Public.

We hereby certify that we are well acquainted with   Willie Scott
a   attendant   and know   him   to be reputable and of good standing in the
community.

{ J.W. White

{ Stephen Cooper

HARTSHORNE, INDIAN TERRITORY, |
                                |
   CENTRAL DISTRICT. |

I, John B. Pulcher, being duly sworn on oath state that I am forty-five years of
age, a resident of Ti, Indian Territory, and a citizen of the Choctaw Nation, Indian
Territory, by blood; that to my personal knowledge a male child was born to Willie Scott
and his wife Elizabeth Scott on the 20th day of May, 1903; that the said male child was
living on the 4th day of March, 1905 and is still living, and has been named Norman
Scott.

John B. Pulcher

Subscribed and sworn to before me at Hartshorne, Indian Territory, this the 14th
day of June, 1905.

Wm J. Hulsey
Notary Public.

Applications for Enrollment of Choctaw Newborn
Act of 1905   Volume XIV

HARTSHORNE, INDIAN TERRITORY, |
|
CENTRAL DISTRICT. |

    I, J. D. Chastain, being duly sworn on oath state that I am 45 years of age, and a resident of Hartshorne, Indian Territory; that to my personal knowledge a male child was born to Willie and Elizabeth Scott on or about the 20th day of May, 1903; that the said male child was living on the 4th day of March, 1905, and has been named Norman Scott.

J.D. Chastain

    Subscribed and sworn to before me at Hartshorne, Indian Territory, this the 14th day of May, 1905.

Wm J. Hulsey
Notary Public.

7-NB-1051

Muskogee, Indian Territory, September 12, 1905.

Hulsey & Patterson,
    Attorneys at Law,
        Hartshorne, Indian Territory.

Gentlemen:

    Your letter of the 2nd instant, addressed to the United States Indian Agent has by him been referred to this office for appropriate action.

    Replying thereto you are advised that on August 22, 1905, the Secretary of the Interior approved the enrollment of Norman Scott as a citizen by blood of the Choctaw Nation and the name of said child appears upon the roll of new-born citizens by blood of the Choctaw Nation opposite number 1410.

    The child is now entitled to an allotment and selection thereof should be made without delay at the land office for the nation in which the prospective allotment is located.

Respectfully,

Acting Commissioner.

7-3145

Muskogee, Indian Territory, April 19, 1905.

Willie Scott,
      Higgins, Indian Territory.

Dear Sir:

    Receipt is hereby acknowledged of the affidavits of Elizabeth Scott and Willie Scott to the birth of Norman Scott, son of Willie and Elizabeth Scott May 20, 1903, and the same have been filed with the records of this office as an application for the enrollment of said child.

                    Respectfully,

                              Chairman.

7--NB--1051

Muskogee, Indian Territory, June 2, 1905.

Willie Scott,
      Higgins, Indian Territory.

Dear Sir:

    Referring to the application for the enrollment of your infant child, Norman Scott, born May 20, 1903, it is noted from the affidavits heretofore filed in this office that you were the only one in attendance upon your wife at the time of the birth of the applicant.

    In this event it will be necessary that the affidavits of two persons, who are disinterested and not related to the applicant, who have actual knowledge of the facts that the child was born, the date of his birth; that he was living on March 4, 1905, and that Elizabeth Scott is his mother be filed in this office.

    This matter should receive your immediate attention as no further action can be taken relative to the enrollment of this applicant until the Commission has been furnished these affidavits.

                    Respectfully,

                              [sic]

7-NB-1051

Muskogee, Indian Territory, June 16, 1905.

Willie Scott,
    Higgins, Indian Territory.

Dear Sir:

Receipt is hereby acknowledged of the affidavits of John B. Pulcher and J. D. Chastain to the birth of Norman Scott, son of Willie and Elizabeth Scott, May 20, 1903, and the same have been filed with our records in the matter of the enrollment of said child.

Respectfully,

Chairman.

Choc New Born 1052
    Ester May Jones
    (Born Aug. 8, 1903)

BIRTH AFFIDAVIT.

DEPARTMENT OF THE INTERIOR.
COMMISSION TO THE FIVE CIVILIZED TRIBES.

IN RE APPLICATION FOR ENROLLMENT, as a citizen of the   Choctaw   Nation, of
Ester May Jones   , born on the 8" day of August , 1903

Name of Father: David Jones   a citizen of the   Choctaw   Nation.
Name of Mother: Almeda Jones   a citizen of the   Choctaw   Nation.

Postoffice   Boswell I.T.

AFFIDAVIT OF MOTHER.

UNITED STATES OF AMERICA, Indian Territory,
    Central   DISTRICT.

I, Almeda Jones   , on oath state that I am 26   years of age and a citizen by blood   , of the   Choctaw   Nation; that I am the lawful wife of   David Jones   , who is a citizen, by blood   of the   Choctaw   Nation; that a   Female

287

child was born to me on 8" day of   August   , 1903; that said child has been named
Ester May Jones   , and was living March 4, 1905.

Almeda Jones

Witnesses To Mark:

{

Subscribed and sworn to before me this 15" day of   April   , 1905

S.H. Downing
Notary Public.

AFFIDAVIT OF ATTENDING PHYSICIAN OR MID-WIFE.

UNITED STATES OF AMERICA, Indian Territory, }
  Central   **DISTRICT.** }

    I,   Eliza Bacon   , a   Mid-Wife   , on oath state that I attended on
Mrs. Almeda Jones   , wife of David Jones   on the 8" day of   August   ,
1903; that there was born to her on said date a   Female   child; that said child was
living March 4, 1905, and is said to have been named Ester May Jones

her
Eliza x Bacon
mark

Witnesses To Mark:
{ Sophie Leflore
{ A F Leflore

Subscribed and sworn to before me this 15" day of   April   , 1905

S.H. Downing
Notary Public.

7-1851

Muskogee, Indian Territory, April 19, 1905.

David Jones,
    Boswell, Indian Territory.

Dear Sir:

    Receipt is hereby acknowledged of the affidavits of Almeda Jones and Eliza
Bacon to the birth of Ester May Jones, child of David and Almeda Jones August 8, 1903,
and the same have been filed with the records of this office as an application for the
enrollment of said child.

Respectfully,

Chairman.

<u>Choc New Born 1053</u>
Robert L. Cochneuer
(Born Feb. 12, 1905)

NEW-BORN AFFIDAVIT.

Number.............

...Choctaw Enrolling Commission...

IN THE MATTER OF THE APPLICATION FOR ENROLLMENT, as a citizen of the Choctaw   Nation, of   Robert L. Cochneuer

born on the 12   day of __February__ 190 5

Name of father   David J Cochneuer   a citizen of   Choctaw
Nation final enrollment No. 10077
Name of mother   Tallow Cochneuer   a citizen of ....
Nation final enrollment No...................

Postoffice   Bokchito I.T.

AFFIDAVIT OF MOTHER.

UNITED STATES OF AMERICA
INDIAN TERRITORY
Central   DISTRICT

I   Tallow Cochneuer   , on oath state that I am 18   years of age and a citizen by marriage   of the   ———— Nation, and as such have been placed upon the final roll of the ———— Nation, by the Honorable Secretary of the Interior my final enrollment number being   —— —; that I am the lawful wife of   David J Cochneuer   , who is a citizen of the   Choctaw   Nation, and as such has been placed upon the final roll of said Nation by the Honorable Secretary of the Interior, his final enrollment number being................. and that a   Male   child was born to me on the   12th day of   February   190 5; that said child has been named   Robert L Cochneuer   , and is now living.

Tallow Cochneuer

289

Witnesseth.

Must be two
Witnesses who
are Citizens.   } James Boland

W.D. Impson

Subscribed and sworn to before me this   13   day of   Mar   190 5

F A McAllen
Notary Public.

My commission expires:

_____

BIRTH AFFIDAVIT.

DEPARTMENT OF THE INTERIOR.
COMMISSION TO THE FIVE CIVILIZED TRIBES.

_____

IN RE APPLICATION FOR ENROLLMENT, as a citizen of the   Choctaw   Nation, of
a male child   , born on the Twelfth   day of   Feb   , 1903

Name of Father: David J Cochneuer   a citizen of the Chocktaw[sic]Nation.
Name of Mother: Tallow Cochneuer   a citizen of the United States Nation.

Postoffice   Bokchito

_____

AFFIDAVIT OF MOTHER.

UNITED STATES OF AMERICA, Indian Territory, }
Central Judicial   **DISTRICT.** }

I,   Tallow Cochneuer   , on oath state that I am   18   years of age and a
citizen by   Birth   , of the   United States   Nation; that I am the lawful wife of
David J Cochneuer   , who is a citizen, by   Birth   of the   Chocktaw
Nation; that a   male   child was born to me on   12   day of   Feb   , 1905; that
said child has been named   Robert L Cochneuer   , and was living March 4, 1905.

Tallow Cochneuer

Witnesses To Mark:
{

Subscribed and sworn to before me this   15 day of   Apr   , 1905

J M Moore
Notary Public.

_____

290

AFFIDAVIT OF ATTENDING PHYSICIAN OR MID-WIFE.

UNITED STATES OF AMERICA, Indian Territory, ⎫
  Central Judicial   **DISTRICT.** ⎭

I, Montie Sargent   , a Midwife   , on oath state that I attended on Mrs. Tallow Cochneuer   , wife of David J Cochneuer   on the Twelfth day of Feb   , 1905; that there was born to her on said date a   male   child; that said child was living March 4, 1905, and is said to have been named Robert L Cochneuer

                                        Montie Sargent

Witnesses To Mark:

  {

Subscribed and sworn to before me this 15 day of   Apr , 1905

                             J M Moore
                                 Notary Public.

AFFIDAVIT OF ATTENDING PHYSICIAN OR MIDWIFE

UNITED STATES OF AMERICA
INDIAN TERRITORY
  Central   DISTRICT

I,   Maud Lowery   a   mid wife
on oath state that I attended on Mrs.   Tallow Cochneuer   wife of   David J Cochneuer on the 12th day of   February , 190 5, that there was born to her on said date a   male child, that said child is now living, and is said to have been named Robert L Cochneuer

                                           midwife
                        Maud Lowery   ~~M.D.~~

WITNESSETH:

Must be two witnesses   { James Boland
who are citizens and
know the child.   W.D. Impson

               Subscribed and sworn to before me this, the   13   day of
        March   190 5

                           F A McAllen   Notary Public.

We hereby certify that we are well acquainted with   Maud Lowery
a   Mid Wife   and know   her   to be reputable and of good standing in the community.

                        { James Boland
                        { W D Impson

7-3556

Muskogee, Indian Territory, April 19, 1905.

David J. Cochneuer,
  Bokchito, Indian Territory.

Dear Sir:

Receipt is hereby acknowledged of the affidavits of Tallow Cochneuer and Montie Sargent to the birth of Robert L. Cochneuer, son of David J. and Tallow Cochneuer February 12, 1905, and the same have been filed with our records as an application for the enrollment of said child.

Respectfully,

Chairman.

7--NB--1053

Muskogee, Indian Territory, June 1, 1905.

David J. Cochneuer,
  Bokchito, Indian Territory.

Dear Sir:

Referring to your application for the enrollment of your infant child Robert L. Cochneuer, born February 12, 1905, it is noted from the affidavits heretofore filed in this office that the applicant claims through you.

In this event it will be necessary that you file in this office, either the original, or a certified copy of the license and certificate of your marriage to the applicant's mother, Tallow Cochneuer

Respectfully,

Chairman.

Applications for Enrollment of Choctaw Newborn
Act of 1905   Volume XIV

7 NB 1053

Muskogee, Indian Territory, June 17, 1905.

Davis[sic] J. Cochneuer,
　　Bokchito, Indian Territory.

Dear Sir:

　　Receipt is hereby acknowledged of your letter of June 13, 1905, in which you state that you filed your marriage license with the Commission at Tishomingo, when you filed on your allotment.

　　In reply to your letter you are advised that it appears that evidence of your marriage has been filed with the records of the Commission and it will not therefore be necessary for you to furnish additional evidence thereof in the matter of the enrollment of your child Robert L. Cochneuer.

Respectfully,

Chairman.

Choc New Born 1054
　　William B. Sanders
　　(Born Feb. 3, 1905)

BIRTH AFFIDAVIT.

DEPARTMENT OF THE INTERIOR.

COMMISSION TO THE FIVE CIVILIZED TRIBES.

IN RE APPLICATION FOR ENROLLMENT, as a citizen of the　　Choctaw　　Nation, of
William B. Sanders　　, born on the　3rd　day of　Feb. 1905　, 1......

Name of Father:　William Sanders　　　　　a citizen of the　Choctaw　Nation.
Name of Mother:　Ada Sanders　　　　　　　a citizen of the　Choctaw　Nation.

Postoffice　　Boswell, I. T.

293

AFFIDAVIT OF MOTHER.

UNITED STATES OF AMERICA, Indian Territory, }
   Central   DISTRICT. }

I,   Ada Sanders , on oath state that I am   30   years of age and a citizen by intermarriage , of the   Choctaw   Nation; that I am the lawful wife of   William Sanders , who is a citizen, by blood   of the   Choctaw   Nation; that a male   child was born to me on   3rd   day of   Feb, 1905 , 1......; that said child has been named   William B. Sanders , and was living March 4, 1905.

Ada Sanders

Witnesses To Mark:
{

   Subscribed and sworn to before me this   12th   day of   April,1905.   , 190......

Perry M Clark
Notary Public.

AFFIDAVIT OF ATTENDING PHYSICIAN OR MID-WIFE.

UNITED STATES OF AMERICA, Indian Territory, }
   Central   DISTRICT. }

I,   W.M. Sanders , a   midwife , on oath state that I attended on Mrs.   Ada Sanders , wife of   William Sanders   on the   3rd   day of   February,1905 , 1......; that there was born to her on said date a   male   child; that said child was living March 4, 1905, and is said to have been named   William B. Sanders

W. M. Sanders

Witnesses To Mark:
{

   Subscribed and sworn to before me this   12th   day of   April,1905.   , 190......

Perry M Clark
Notary Public.

My Commission Expires 2/27/09

7-3609

Muskogee, Indian Territory, April 19, 1905.

William Sanders,
  Boswell, Indian Territory.

Dear Sir:

Receipt is hereby acknowledged of the affidavits of Ada Sanders and W. M. Sanders to the birth of William B. Sanders, son of William and Ada Sanders February 3, 1905, and the same have been filed with our records as an application for the enrollment of said child.

Respectfully,

Chairman.

Choc New Born 1055
  Bertha Perry
  (Born Nov. 17, 1904)

DEPARTMENT OF THE INTERIOR,
COMMISSIONER TO THE FIVE CIVILIZED TRIBES,
CHOCTAW LAND OFFICE.
---:---
Atoka, Indian Territory, March 2, 1906.
---:---

In the matter of the enrollment of Bertha Perry, Choctaw New Born, Card No. 1055, Approved Roll No. 1412.

DANIEL PERRY, being first duly sworn, testified as follows:-

--::EXAMINATION BY THE COMMISSIONER::--

Q What is your name? A Daniel Perry.
Q How old are you? A About 29 or 30 years old.
Q What is your post office address? A Stigler.
Q What is your father's name? A Lyman Perry.
Q What is your mother's name, do you know? A Charlotte.
Q How many times have you been married? A This is the third time.
Q What was the name of your first wife? A Jane.
Q Do you know her father's name? A No, I don't know it.

Q Do you know her mother's name? A Yes sir, they used to call Munsey or Narcy.
Q What was her last name? A She has married a fellow by the name of White.
Q What was you second wife's name? A Jane.
Q What was this wife's father's name? A I don't know her -- Aleck Cooper.
Q Do you know her mother's name? A I have heard it, but I forgot. She has been died[sic] a good while.
Q Do you know whether it was Elsie? A Yes sir, that is it.
Q Your first two wives were both named Jane? A Yes sir.
Q Your second wife was the daughter of Aleck and Elsie Cooper? A Yes sir.

Witness is identified as Daniel Perry upon the approved Choctaw Roll by blood, No. 9254, Card No. 3198.

Q What is your present wife's name? A Eliza.
Q What was her father's name? A Simon Isaac.
Q Your present wife's maiden name then was Eliza Isaac? A Yes sir.
Q How old is she? A 18 - may be 19 or 20.
Q What is her mother's name? A I have forgotten her name, she died good while.
Q Do you know her brothers and sisters names? A Yes sir.
Q What are they? A One Kizzie, one Alice, one James Isaac and Ida.
Q Is your wife, Eliza, living? A Yes sir.
Q Do you appear at the land office to-day to select land in allotment for your new born child, Bertha Perry? A Yes sir.
Q Is Bertha Perry living? A Yes sir.
Q What is her mother's name? A Eliza.
Q Is that your wife to whom you have referred as Eliza Isaac? A Yes sir.
Q Is Bertha Perry living? A Yes sir.
Q You are the father of Bertha Perry? A Yes sir.
Q Do you know one Daniel Perry, son of Hampton Perry and Peggy Perry? A I don't know Peggy.
Q Do you know Hampton Perry? A Yes sir.
Q Do you know that he has a son named Daniel Perry? A Yes sir.
Q The name of Bertha Perry appears at No. 1412 upon the approved Choctaw new born roll. Her father's name is given as Daniel Perry enrolled at No. 6866 upon the approved roll of citizens by blood of the Choctaw Nation, and it appears that his father's name is Hampton Perry, and that her mother's name is Peggy Perry. Is it a mistake that Daniel Perry the father of this child, Bertha Perry, is given as the son of Hampton Perry an Peggy Perry? A Yes sir, that is a mistake.
Q You are the father of Bertha Perry? A Yes sir.
Q And the mother of this child, Eliza Perry, whose maiden name was Eliza Isaac, is your wife? A Yes sir.
Q If the records of this office show the father of Bertha Perry to be Daniel Perry the son of Hampton Perry and Peggy Perry, is that an error? A Yes sir, my father was Lyman.
Q Do you know whether this other Daniel Perry, the son of Hampton Perry, is married? A No sir.
Q You don't know whether he has any children? A No sir.
Q Do you know about how old he is? A No, I do not.

Q Is he somewhat younger that you are? A Yes sir, he is younger than me.
Q Do you know how much younger than you? A No sir.

Witness excused.

Wm. L. Martin, stenographer to the Commissioner to the Five Civilized Tribes, upon oath states that the above and foregoing is a full, true and correct transcript of his stenographic notes taken in said cause on said date.

Wm L Martin

Subscribed and sworn to before me this the 9th day of March, 1906.

W.H. Angell
Notary Public.

BIRTH AFFIDAVIT.

DEPARTMENT OF THE INTERIOR.
COMMISSION TO THE FIVE CIVILIZED TRIBES.

IN RE APPLICATION FOR ENROLLMENT, as a citizen of the   Choctaw   Nation, of
Bertha Perry   , born on the 17th   day of November   , 1904

Name of Father: Daniel Perry   a citizen of the   Choctaw   Nation.
Name of Mother: Eliza Perry   a citizen of the   Choctaw   Nation.

Postoffice   Stigler, I.T.

AFFIDAVIT OF MOTHER.

UNITED STATES OF AMERICA, Indian Territory, ⎱
      Central   **DISTRICT.** ⎰

I,   Eliza Perry   , on oath state that I am   19   years of age and a citizen by blood   , of the   Choctaw   Nation; that I am the lawful wife of   Daniel Perry   , who is a citizen, by blood   of the   Choctaw   Nation; that a   female   child was born to me on 17th   day of November   , 1904; that said child has been named Bertha Perry   , and was living March 4, 1905.

Eliza Perry

Witnesses To Mark:

297

Subscribed and sworn to before me this first day of   March   , 1905

Edwin O. Clark
Notary Public.

AFFIDAVIT OF ATTENDING PHYSICIAN OR MID-WIFE.

UNITED STATES OF AMERICA, Indian Territory, ⎱
Central   DISTRICT. ⎰

I,   R.F. Terrell   , a   Physician   , on oath state that I attended on
Mrs.   Eliza Perry   , wife of   Daniel Perry   on the 17th day of   November ,
1904; that there was born to her on said date a   female   child; that said child was
living March 4, 1905, and is said to have been named Bertha Perry

R.F. Terrell, M.D.

Witnesses To Mark:

{

Subscribed and sworn to before me this   sixth day of   March   , 1905

Edwin O. Clark
Notary Public.

BIRTH AFFIDAVIT.
DEPARTMENT OF THE INTERIOR.
COMMISSION TO THE FIVE CIVILIZED TRIBES.

IN RE APPLICATION FOR ENROLLMENT, as a citizen of the   Choctaw   Nation, of
Bertha Perry   , born on the 17th day of November , 1904

Name of Father: Daniel Perry   Roll 6866   a citizen of the   Choctaw   Nation.
Name of Mother: Eliza Perry   Roll 7724   a citizen of the   Choctaw   Nation.

Postoffice   Stigler, I.T.

AFFIDAVIT OF MOTHER.

UNITED STATES OF AMERICA, Indian Territory, ⎱
.... DISTRICT. ⎰

I,   Eliza Perry   , on oath state that I am   19   years of age and a citizen by
blood   , of the   Choctaw   Nation; that I am the lawful wife of   Daniel Perry   ,
who is a citizen, by blood   of the   Choctaw   Nation; that a   female   child

298

was born to me on 17th day of November , 1904; that said child has been named Bertha Perry , and was living March 4, 1905.

Eliza Perry

Witnesses To Mark:

{

Subscribed and sworn to before me this 28th day of June , 1905

Edwin O. Clark
Notary Public.

AFFIDAVIT OF ATTENDING PHYSICIAN OR MID-WIFE.

UNITED STATES OF AMERICA, Indian Territory, }
    Central   DISTRICT. }

    I, R.F. Terrell , a Physician , on oath state that I attended on Mrs. Eliza Perry , wife of Daniel Perry on the 17th day of November , 1904; that there was born to her on said date a female child; that said child was living March 4, 1905, and is said to have been named Bertha Perry

R.F. Terrell

Witnesses To Mark:

{

Subscribed and sworn to before me this 29th day of June , 1905

Edwin O. Clark
Notary Public.

7-NB-1055.

Muskogee, Indian Territory, June 2, 1905.

Daniel Perry,
    Stigler, Indian Territory.

Dear Sir:

    There is enclosed you herewith for execution application for the enrollment of your infant child, Bertha Perry, born November 17, 1904.

In the mother's affidavit, heretofore filed in this office, it appears that the child was living on March 1, 1905. It is necessary, for the child to be enrolled, that she was living on March 4, 1905.

In having the affidavit executed care should be exercised to see that all names are written in full, as they appear in the body of the affidavit. Signatures by mark must be attested by two witnesses who can write. Each affidavit must be executed before a Notary Public and the notarial seal and signature of the officer must be attached to each separate affidavit.

Respectfully,

[sic]

VR 2-4.

7-2661

Muskogee, Indian Territory, April 20, 1905.

Daniel Perry,
Stigler, Indian Territory.

Dear Sir:

Receipt is hereby acknowledged of your letter of April 13, 1905, enclosing affidavits of Eliza Perry and R. F. Terrell to the birth of Bertha Perry daughter of Daniel and Eliza Perry, November 17, 1904, and the same have been filed with our records as an application for the enrollment of said child.

Respectfully,

Chairman.

7-NB 1055

Muskogee, Indian Territory, July 5, 1905.

David Perry,
Stigler, Indian Territory.

Dear Sir:

Receipt is hereby acknowledged of the affidavits of Eliza Perry and R. F. Terrell to the birth of Bertha Perry daughter of Daniel and Eliza Perry, November 17, 1904, and the same have been filed with the records of this office in the matter of the enrollment of said child.

Respectfully,

Commissioner.

_____

7-NB-1055

Muskogee, Indian Territory, March 23, 1906.

Chief Clerk,
    Chickasaw Land Office,
        Ardmore, Indian Territory

Dear Sir:

Referring to Choctaw new born roll card No. 1055, Bertha Perry, you are advised that this card has been changed so as to show, "father's roll No." 9254, and "for father's roll No. see Choctaw roll card No." 3198.

You are therefore directed to make duplicate roll card of this number in your possession conform with this information.

Respectfully,

Acting Commissioner.

_____

7-NB-1055

Muskogee, Indian Territory, March 23, 1906.

Chief Clerk,
    Choctaw Land Office,
        Atoka, Indian Territory.

Dear Sir:

Receipt is hereby acknowledged of your letter of March 14, 1906, inclosing copies of testimony in the matter of the enrollment of Bertha Perry as a new born citizen of the Choctaw Nation, from which it appears that the father of said child is Daniel Perry, whose name appears on the approved roll of citizens by blood of the Choctaw Nation at No. 9254.

You are therefore advised that Choctaw new born roll card No. 1055 has been changed so as to show, "father's roll No." 9254, and "for father's roll No. see Choctaw roll card No." 3198.

301

Applications for Enrollment of Choctaw Newborn
Act of 1905   Volume XIV

You are therefore directed to make duplicate roll card of this number in your possession conform with this information.

Respectfully,

Acting Commissioner.

Stigler, I.T. April 13, 1905.

Commission to the Five Civilized Tribes,
    Muskogee, I.T.

Dear Sirs:

Eliza Perry the mother of Bertha Perry whose application for enrollment as a citizen of the Choctaw Nation is inclosed was enrolled by the Commission under the name of Eliza Isaac which was her maiden name; her father's name was Simon Isaac, the place and time of the enrollment of the mother, Eliza Perry, is forgotten.

Yours Truly,

(signed) Dan Perry

Choc New Born 1056
    Eula Folsom
    (Born August 14, 1904)

BIRTH AFFIDAVIT.
DEPARTMENT OF THE INTERIOR.
COMMISSION TO THE FIVE CIVILIZED TRIBES.

IN RE APPLICATION FOR ENROLLMENT, as a citizen of the Choctaw Nation, of Eula Folsom , born on the 14 day of Aug , 1904

Name of Father: Elias W Folsom   a citizen of the Choctaw Nation.
Name of Mother: Delena Folsom   a citizen of the Choctaw Nation.

Postoffice   Non I.T.

302

AFFIDAVIT OF MOTHER.

UNITED STATES OF AMERICA, Indian Territory, ⎫
    Central   DISTRICT. ⎭

I,   Delena Folsom   , on oath state that I am 24 years of age and a citizen by   intermarriage   , of the   Choctaw   Nation; that I am the lawful wife of Elias W Folsom   , who is a citizen, by Blood of the   Choctaw   Nation; that a   female   child was born to me on 14 day of August   , 1904; that said child has been named Eula Folsom   , and was living March 4, 1905.

Delena Folsom

Witnesses To Mark:
{

Subscribed and sworn to before me this 11 day of Apr   , 1905

C.E. McCain
Notary Public.

AFFIDAVIT OF ATTENDING PHYSICIAN OR MID-WIFE.

UNITED STATES OF AMERICA, Indian Territory, ⎫
    Central   DISTRICT. ⎭

I,   J. E. Blackwood   , a mid wife   , on oath state that I attended on Mrs. Delena Folsom   , wife of E. W. Folsom on the 14 day of August , 1904; that there was born to her on said date a   female   child; that said child was living March 4, 1905, and is said to have been named Eula Folsom

J E Blackwood

Witnesses To Mark:
{

Subscribed and sworn to before me this 11 day of Apr   , 1905

C.E. McCain
Notary Public.

Choctaw 5395.

Muskogee, Indian Territory, April 15, 1905.

Elias W. Folsom,
Non, Indian Territory.

Dear Sir:

Receipt is hereby acknowledged of your letter of April 10, in which you state that your full name is Elias W. Folson[sic] and that of your wife, Delena Folsom, and that sometime in February you forwarded an application for your child, Eula Folsom, and have heard nothing from it and you ask if the same has been received and also if you and your wife can go to the land office at Ardmore or Atoka and have the baby enrolled and file on its land while there.

In reply to your letter you are informed that it does not appear from our records that affidavits to the birth of Eula Folsom, child of Elias and Delena Folsom, have been received, and for your convenience there is enclosed herewith blank for the enrollment of an infant child, which you should have executed and returned to this office within sixty days from March 3, 1905.

Replying to that portion of your letter in which you ask if you can go to the land office and have your child enrolled and file on its land while there, you are advised that application is made under the provisions of the Act of Congress approved March 3, 1905, until their enrollment has been approved by the Secretary of the Interior.

Respectfully,

1 B. C.   Chairman.

7-5395

Muskogee, Indian Territory, April 20, 1905.

Elias W. Folsom,
Non, Indian Territory.

Dear Sir:

Receipt is hereby acknowledged of the affidavits of Delena Folsom and J. E. Black to the birth of Eula Folsom, daughter of Elias W. and Delena Folsom, August 14, 1904, and the same have been filed with our records as an application for the enrollment of said child.

Respectfully

Chairman.

Choc New Born 1057
>Joseph Woods Everidge
>(Born May 4, 1903)
>Thomas Dudley Everidge
>(Born May 4, 1903)

BIRTH AFFIDAVIT.

DEPARTMENT OF THE INTERIOR.
COMMISSION TO THE FIVE CIVILIZED TRIBES.

IN RE APPLICATION FOR ENROLLMENT, as a citizen of the   Choctaw   Nation, of
Joseph Woods Everidge   , born on the 4th   day of May   , 1903

Name of Father: Thomas W. Everidge   a citizen of the   Choctaw   Nation.
Name of Mother: Mollie Everidge   a citizen of the   Choctaw   Nation.

Postoffice   Grant, Ind. Ter.

AFFIDAVIT OF MOTHER.

UNITED STATES OF AMERICA, Indian Territory,
Central   DISTRICT.

I,   Mollie Everidge   , on oath state that I am   31   years of age and a citizen
by   marriage   , of the   Choctaw   Nation; that I am the lawful wife of   Thomas
W. Everidge   , who is a citizen, by blood   of the   Choctaw   Nation; that
a   male   child was born to me on   4th   day of   May   , 1903; that said child
has been named   Joseph Woods Everidge   , and was living March 4, 1905.

Mollie Everidge

Witnesses To Mark:

Subscribed and sworn to before me this 17th   day of   April   , 1905

Wirt Franklin
Notary Public.

AFFIDAVIT OF ATTENDING PHYSICIAN OR MID-WIFE.

UNITED STATES OF AMERICA, Indian Territory, ⎫
Central   DISTRICT. ⎭

I,   Fannie L Nelson   , a mid-wife   , on oath state that I attended on Mrs.   Mollie Everidge   , wife of   Thomas W Everidge   on the 4th   day of May   , 1903; that there was born to her on said date a   male   child; that said child was living March 4, 1905, and is said to have been named Joseph Woods Everidge

Fannie L Nelson

Witnesses To Mark:

{

Subscribed and sworn to before me this 17th   day of   April   , 1905

Wirt Franklin
Notary Public.

BIRTH AFFIDAVIT.

DEPARTMENT OF THE INTERIOR.
COMMISSION TO THE FIVE CIVILIZED TRIBES.

IN RE APPLICATION FOR ENROLLMENT, as a citizen of the   Choctaw   Nation, of Thomas Dudley Everidge   , born on the 4th   day of   May   , 1903

Name of Father: Thomas W. Everidge   a citizen of the   Choctaw   Nation.
Name of Mother: Mollie Everidge   a citizen of the   Choctaw   Nation.

Postoffice   Grant, Ind. Ter.

AFFIDAVIT OF MOTHER.

UNITED STATES OF AMERICA, Indian Territory, ⎫
Central   DISTRICT. ⎭

I,   Mollie Everidge   , on oath state that I am   31   years of age and a citizen by   marriage   , of the   Choctaw   Nation; that I am the lawful wife of   Thomas W. Everidge   , who is a citizen, by blood   of the   Choctaw   Nation; that a   male   child was born to me on 4th   day of   May   , 1903; that said child has been named   Thomas Dudley Everidge   , and was living March 4, 1905.

Mollie Everidge

Witnesses To Mark:

{

306

Applications for Enrollment of Choctaw Newborn
Act of 1905   Volume XIV

Subscribed and sworn to before me this 17th day of   April   , 1905

Wirt Franklin
Notary Public.

AFFIDAVIT OF ATTENDING PHYSICIAN OR MID-WIFE.

UNITED STATES OF AMERICA, Indian Territory, }
    Central   DISTRICT. }

I,   Fannie L Nelson   , a mid-wife   , on oath state that I attended on Mrs.   Mollie Everidge   , wife of   Thomas W Everidge   on the 4th day of May   , 1903; that there was born to her on said date a   male   child; that said child was living March 4, 1905, and is said to have been named Thomas Dudley Everidge

Fannie L Nelson

Witnesses To Mark:

{

Subscribed and sworn to before me this 17th   day of   April   , 1905

Wirt Franklin
Notary Public.

---

7 NB 1057

Muskogee, Indian Territory, June 15, 1905.

Thomas B[sic]. Everidge,
      Grant, Indian Territory.

Dear Sir:

Receipt is hereby acknowledged of your letter of June 12, 1905, asking if the enrollment of your twin children has been approved.

In reply to your letter you are advised that the names of your children Joseph Woods and Thomas W[sic]. Everidge are being placed upon a schedule of citizens by blood of the Choctaw Nation and you will be advised when their enrollment is approved by the Secretary of the Interior.

That portion of your letter referring to the application of Tom of Thomas Dodson will be made the subject of another communication.

Respectfully,

Chairman.

307

Choc New Born 1058
Jane Collin
(Born Oct. 20, 1903)

NEW BORN AFFIDAVIT

No ....

CHOCTAW ENROLLING COMMISSION

IN THE MATTER OF THE APPLICATION FOR ENROLLMENT as a citizen of the Choctaw Nation, of Jen[sic] Collin born on the 20th day of October 190 3

Name of father Phelin Collin a citizen of Choctaw Nation,
final enrollment No. 6960
Name of mother Sibbel Collin a citizen of Choctaw Nation,
final enrollment No. 6961

Howe I.T. Postoffice.

AFFIDAVIT OF MOTHER

UNITED STATES OF AMERICA
INDIAN TERRITORY
DISTRICT Central

I Sibbel Collin , on oath state that I am 23 years of age and a citizen by blood of the Choctaw Nation, and as such have been placed upon the final roll of the Choctaw Nation, by the Honorable Secretary of the Interior my final enrollment number being 6961 ; that I am the lawful wife of Phelin Collin , who is a citizen of the Choctaw Nation, and as such has been placed upon the final roll of said Nation by the Honorable Secretary of the Interior, his final enrollment number being 6960 and that a female child was born to me on the 20 day of October 190 3; that said child has been named Jen Collin , and is now living.

WITNESSETH: Sibbel Collin
Must be two witnesses { David Ward
who are citizens { Samuel R Wilson

Subscribed and sworn to before me this, the 16 day of   February   , 190 5

James Bower
Notary Public.

My Commission Expires:
Sept 23-1907

Affidavit of Attending Physician or Midwife

UNITED STATES OF AMERICA, ⎫
   INDIAN TERRITORY, ⎬
 Central   DISTRICT ⎭

    I,   Missouri McNoel   a   midwife
on oath state that I attended on Mrs Sibbel Collin   wife of   Phelin Collin
on the   20th   day of   October , 190 3, that there was born to her on said date a   female
child, that said child is now living, and is said to have been named Jen Collin

                             her
                Missouri x McNoel   M. D.
                          mark
Subscribed and sworn to before me this the   21st   day of   Feby   1905

My com exp March 6, 1905   J.M. Young
                           Notary Public.

WITNESSETH:

Must be two witnesses ⎰   David Ward
who are citizens and ⎱
know the child.   Samuel R Wilson

    We hereby certify that we are well acquainted with   Missouri McNoel
a   midwife   and know   her   to be reputable and of good standing in the
community.

                 Must be two citizen ⎰   David Ward
                 witnesses.   ⎱   Samuel R Wilson

7- 6961- 6960

BIRTH AFFIDAVIT.

DEPARTMENT OF THE INTERIOR.
COMMISSION TO THE FIVE CIVILIZED TRIBES.

IN RE APPLICATION FOR ENROLLMENT, as a citizen of the   Choctaw   Nation, of
Jane Collin   , born on the   20   day of   October   , 1903

Name of Father: Phelin Collin   a citizen of the   Choc   Nation.
Name of Mother: Sibbel Collin   a citizen of the   Choc   Nation.

Postoffice   Howe I.T.

AFFIDAVIT OF MOTHER.

UNITED STATES OF AMERICA, Indian Territory,
   Central   **DISTRICT.**

I,   Sibbel Collin   , on oath state that I am   23   years of age and a citizen by
blood   , of the   Choctaw   Nation; that I am the lawful wife of   Phelin Collin   ,
who is a citizen, by blood   of the   Choctaw   Nation; that a   female   child
was born to me on   20   day of   October   , 1903; that said child has been named
Jane Collin   , and was living March 4, 1905.

Sibbel Collin

Witnesses To Mark:

Subscribed and sworn to before me this 17   day of   April   , 1905

OL Johnson
Notary Public.

AFFIDAVIT OF ATTENDING PHYSICIAN OR MID-WIFE.

UNITED STATES OF AMERICA, Indian Territory,
   Central   **DISTRICT.**

I,   Missouri McNoel   , a   midwife   , on oath state that I attended on
Mrs.   Sibbel Collin   , wife of   Phelin Collin   on the 20   day of   October   ,
1903; that there was born to her on said date a   female   child; that said child was
living March 4, 1905, and is said to have been named   Jane Collin
                                    her
                        Missouri x McNoel
                                   mark

310

Witnesses To Mark:
 { Chas T Difendafer
 { OL Johnson

Subscribed and sworn to before me this 17 day of   April   , 1905

OL Johnson
Notary Public.

Choc New Born 1059
Clarence H. Colbert
(Born July 29, 1903)

BIRTH AFFIDAVIT.

DEPARTMENT OF THE INTERIOR.
COMMISSION TO THE FIVE CIVILIZED TRIBES.

IN RE APPLICATION FOR ENROLLMENT, as a citizen of the   Choctaw   Nation, of
Clarence H. Colbert   , born on the 29th day of July   , 1903

Name of Father: Clarence Colbert   a citizen of the   Choctaw   Nation.
Name of Mother: Rosabelle Colbert   a citizen of the   Choctaw   Nation.

Postoffice   Nail, I.T.

AFFIDAVIT OF MOTHER.

UNITED STATES OF AMERICA, Indian Territory, }
    Central   **DISTRICT.** }

I,   Rosabelle Colbert   , on oath state that I am   37   years of age and a
citizen by   intermarriage   , of the   Choctaw   Nation; that I am the lawful wife
of   Clarence Colbert   , who is a citizen, by blood   of the   Choctaw
Nation; that a   male   child was born to me on 29th day of   July   , 1903; that
said child has been named   Clarence H Colbert   , and was living March 4, 1905.

Rosabelle Colbert
Witnesses To Mark:
 {

Applications for Enrollment of Choctaw Newborn
Act of 1905   Volume XIV

Subscribed and sworn to before me this 12th day of   April   , 1905

W.H. Angell
Notary Public.

AFFIDAVIT OF ATTENDING PHYSICIAN OR MID-WIFE.

UNITED STATES OF AMERICA, Indian Territory, ⎤
  Central   **DISTRICT.** ⎦

I,   R R Dickey   , a   physician   , on oath state that I attended on
Mrs.   Rosabelle Colbert   , wife of   Clarence Colbert   on the 29th   day of
July, 1903; that there was born to her on said date a   male   child; that said child was
living March 4, 1905, and is said to have been named   Clarence H Colbert

R R Dickey

Witnesses To Mark:

{

Subscribed and sworn to before me this........day of   Apr 10   , 1905

John R. Price
Notary Public.
My Com Expires 1909

Choctaw 3530.

Muskogee, Indian Territory, April 20, 1905.

Clarence Colbert,
    Nail, Indian Territory.

Dear Sir:

Receipt is hereby acknowledged of the affidavits of Rosabelle Colbert and R.R. Dickey to the birth of Clarence H. Colbert, son of Clarence and Rosabelle Colbert, July 29, 1903, and the same have been filed with our records as an application for the enrollment of said child.

Respectfully,

Chairman.

Choc New Born 1060
     Izroe[sic] Alice Perry
     (Born Oct. 18, 1903)

NEW BORN AFFIDAVIT

No ....

CHOCTAW ENROLLING COMMISSION

IN THE MATTER OF THE APPLICATION FOR ENROLLMENT as a citizen of the Choctaw
Nation, of   Izora Alice Perry   born on the 16   day
of   October   190 3

     Name of father   Charles T. Perry   a citizen of   Choctaw   Nation,
final enrollment No.   6912
     Name of mother   Martha Perry   a citizen of   Choctaw   Nation,
final enrollment No.   6913

             Heavener, I.T.   Postoffice.

AFFIDAVIT OF MOTHER

UNITED STATES OF AMERICA ⎫
    INDIAN TERRITORY   ⎬
DISTRICT   Central   ⎭

     I   Martha Perry   , on oath state that I am   29   years of age
and a citizen by   blood   of the   Choctaw   Nation, and as such have been placed
upon the final roll of the   Choctaw   Nation, by the Honorable Secretary of the Interior my
final enrollment number being 6913   ; that I am the lawful wife of   Charles T Perry   ,
who is a citizen of the   Choctaw   Nation, and as such has been placed upon the final
roll of said Nation by the Honorable Secretary of the Interior, his final enrollment number
being   6912   and that a   Female   child was born to me on the   16   day of   October
190 3; that said child has been named   Izora Alice Perry   , and is now living.

WITNESSETH: Martha Perry
   Must be two witnesses ⎰   Jefferson Quincy
    who are citizens   ⎱   Henry J Harris

Subscribed and sworn to before me this, the   16 day of   February   , 190 5

James Bower
Notary Public.

My Commission Expires:
Sept 23-1907

Affidavit of Attending Physician or Midwife

UNITED STATES OF AMERICA, ⎫
   INDIAN TERRITORY, ⎬
 Central   DISTRICT ⎭

    I,   J.D. Fowler   a   Practicing Physician
on oath state that I attended on Mrs. Martha Perry   wife of Charles T Perry
on the   16   day of October   , 190 3, that there was born to her on said date a   Female
child, that said child is now living, and is said to have been named Izora Alice Perry

J D Fowler   M. D.

Subscribed and sworn to before me this the   16   day of   February   1905

James Bower
Notary Public.

WITNESSETH:
   Must be two witnesses ⎧   Jefferson Quincy
   who are citizens and ⎨
   know the child.   ⎩   Henry J Harris

    We hereby certify that we are well acquainted with   J.D. Fowler
a   Practicing Physician   and know   him   to be reputable and of good
standing in the community.

             Must be two citizen⎧ Jefferson Quincy
             witnesses.   ⎩ Henry J Harris

BIRTH AFFIDAVIT.

DEPARTMENT OF THE INTERIOR.
COMMISSION TO THE FIVE CIVILIZED TRIBES.

   IN RE APPLICATION FOR ENROLLMENT, as a citizen of the   Choctaw   Nation, of
Izora Alice Perry   , born on the 16" day of Oct   , 1903

Name of Father: Charles T Perry Roll 6912   a citizen of the   Choctaw   Nation.
Name of Mother: Martha Perry   Roll 6913   a citizen of the   Choctaw   Nation.

Applications for Enrollment of Choctaw Newborn
Act of 1905   Volume XIV

Postoffice   Heavener I.T.

AFFIDAVIT OF MOTHER.

UNITED STATES OF AMERICA, Indian Territory, ⎫
Central   DISTRICT. ⎬

    I,   Martha Perry   , on oath state that I am   29   years of age and a citizen by blood   , of the   Choctaw   Nation; that I am the lawful wife of   Charles T Perry   , who is a citizen, by blood   of the   Choctaw   Nation; that a   female   child was born to me on   16"   day of   Oct   , 1903; that said child has been named   Izora Alice Perry   , and was living March 4, 1905.

                               Martha Perry

Witnesses To Mark:

    Subscribed and sworn to before me this   12 day of   June   , 1905

My com exp Mch 9 1909   J.M. Young
                                      Notary Public.

AFFIDAVIT OF ATTENDING PHYSICIAN OR MID-WIFE.

UNITED STATES OF AMERICA, Indian Territory, ⎫
Central   DISTRICT. ⎬

    I,   J D Fowler   , a Physician   , on oath state that I attended on Mrs.   Martha Perry   , wife of   Charles T. Perry   on the   16" day of   Oct   , 1903; that there was born to her on said date a   female   child; that said child was living March 4, 1905, and is said to have been named   Izora Alice Perry

                              J.D. Fowler

Witnesses To Mark:

    Subscribed and sworn to before me this   12   day of   June   , 1905

                          J. M. Young
                                Notary Public.
My com exp Mch 9 1909

Applications for Enrollment of Choctaw Newborn
Act of 1905   Volume XIV

DEPARTMENT OF THE INTERIOR.
COMMISSION TO THE FIVE CIVILIZED TRIBES.

IN RE APPLICATION FOR ENROLLMENT, as a citizen of the   Choctaw   Nation, of Izroe[sic] Alice Perry   , born on the   18"[sic]   day of   Oct   , ~~1904~~ *1903*

Name of Father: Charles T Perry   a citizen of the   Choctaw   Nation.
Name of Mother: Martha Perry   a citizen of the   Choctaw   Nation.

Postoffice   Houston I.T.

AFFIDAVIT OF MOTHER.

UNITED STATES OF AMERICA, Indian Territory, }
   Central   DISTRICT. }

I,   Martha Perry   , on oath state that I am   29   years of age and a citizen by blood   , of the   Choctaw   Nation; that I am the lawful wife of   Charles T Perry   , who is a citizen, by blood   of the   Choctaw   Nation; that a   female   child was born to me on   18"   day of   Oct   , ~~1904~~ *1903*; that said child has been named Izroe Alice Perry   , and was living March 4, 1905.

                                      Martha Perry
Witnesses To Mark:
   {

   Subscribed and sworn to before me this   15 day of   April   , 1905

My com exp Mch 9th 1909   J.M. Young
                                              Notary Public.

AFFIDAVIT OF ATTENDING PHYSICIAN OR MID-WIFE.

UNITED STATES OF AMERICA, Indian Territory, }
   Central   DISTRICT. }

I,   J D Fowler   , a Physician   , on oath state that I attended on Mrs.   Martha Perry   , wife of   Charles T. Perry   on the   18" day of   Oct   , ~~1904~~ *1903*; that there was born to her on said date a   female   child; that said child was living March 4, 1905, and is said to have been named   Izroe Alice Perry

                                      J.D. Fowler

316

Witnesses To Mark:

{

    Subscribed and sworn to before me this 31   day of   Mch   , 1905

J. M. Young

My com exp Mch 9 1909   Notary Public.

Choctaw 2385.

Muskogee, Indian Territory, April 20, 1905.

Charles T. Perry,
      Houston, Indian Territory.

Dear Sir:

    Receipt is hereby acknowledged of the affidavits of Martha Perry and J. D. Fowler to the birth of Izroe[sic] Alice Perry, daughter of Charles T. and Martha Perry, October 18[sic], 1903, and the same have been filed with our records as an application for the enrollment of said child.

Respectfully,

Chairman.

---

7 NB 1060

Muskogee, Indian Territory, June 15, 1905.

Charles T. Perry,
      Heavener, Indian Territory.

Dear Sir:

    Receipt is hereby acknowledged of the affidavits of Martha Perry and J. D. Fowler to the birth of Izora Alice Perry, daughter of Charles T. and Martha Perry, October 16, 1903, and the same have been filed in the matter of the enrollment of said child.

Respectfully,

Chairman.

317

7-NB-1060.

Muskogee, Indian Territory, June 2, 1905.

Charles T. Perry,
        Heavener, Indian Territory.

Dear Sir:

There is enclosed you herewith for execution application for the enrollment of your infant child, Izora Alice Perry.

In the affidavits of February 16, 1905, the date of the applicant's birth is given as October 16, 1903, while in those of March 31, 1905 and April 15, 1905, this date is given as October 18, 1903. In the enclosed application the date of birth is left blank. Please insert the correct date and, when the affidavits are properly executed, return them to this office.

In having these affidavits executed care should be exercised to see that all names are written in full, as they appear in the body of the affidavit, and in the event that either of the persons signing the affidavit are unable to write, signatures by mark must be attested by two witnesses. Each affidavit must be executed before a Notary Public and the notarial seal and signature of the officer must be attached to each separate affidavit.

Respectfully,

VR 2-5.   [sic]

Choc New Born 1061
        Lenora Morris
        (Born June 8, 1903)

AFFIDAVIT OF ATTENDING PHYSICIAN OR MIDWIFE

UNITED STATES OF AMERICA
INDIAN TERRITORY
   Central   DISTRICT

I,   Carrie Hampton   a   mid wife
on oath state that I attended on Mrs.   Arreathy Morris   wife of   Solon Morris
on the   8th   day of   June   , 190 3 , that there was born to her on said date a   female
child, that said child is now living, and is said to have been named   Lenora Morris

318

                                                                her
                                          Carrie Hampton x
                                                                mark
             Subscribed and sworn to before me this, the   21st   day of
             Jan   190 5

WITNESSETH: W.A. Shoney   Notary Public.

Must be two witnesses { J B McFarland
who are citizens

                         H.C. Stanford

        We hereby certify that we are well acquainted with   Carrie Hampton
a   mid wife   and know .... to be reputable and of good standing in the community.

        JB McFarland   _____

        H.C. Stanford   _____

                              _____

NEW-BORN AFFIDAVIT.

                    Number...............

...Choctaw Enrolling Commission...

                    _____

        IN THE MATTER OF THE APPLICATION FOR ENROLLMENT, as a citizen of the
Choctaw   Nation, of   Lenora Morris

born on the 8th day of ___June___190 3

Name of father   Solon Morris   a citizen of   Choctaw
Nation final enrollment No. 2967
Name of mother   Arreathy Morris   a citizen of   Choctaw
Nation final enrollment No. 65

                                    Postoffice   Idabel, I.T.

AFFIDAVIT OF MOTHER.
UNITED STATES OF AMERICA
INDIAN TERRITORY
    Central   DISTRICT

                I   Arreathy Morris   , on oath state that I am
        25   years of age and a citizen by   inter marriage   of the   Choctaw
Nation, and as such have been placed upon the final roll of the   Choctaw   Nation, by the
Honorable Secretary of the Interior my final enrollment number being   65 ; that I am the
lawful wife of Solon Morris   , who is a citizen of the   Choctaw   Nation, and as

such has been placed upon the final roll of said Nation by the Honorable Secretary of the Interior, his final enrollment number being   2967   and that a   female   child was born to me on the   8th   day of   June   190 3; that said child has been named   Lenora Morris , and is now living.

Arreathy Morris

Witnesseth.

Must be two
Witnesses who
are Citizens. }   J B McFarland

H.C. Stanford

Subscribed and sworn to before me this   21   day of   Jan   190 5

W.A. Shoney
Notary Public.

My commission expires:

BIRTH AFFIDAVIT.

DEPARTMENT OF THE INTERIOR.
COMMISSION TO THE FIVE CIVILIZED TRIBES.

IN RE APPLICATION FOR ENROLLMENT, as a citizen of the   Choctaw   Nation, of Lenora Morris   , born on the   8th   day of   June   , 1903

Name of Father: Solon Edgar Morris   a citizen of the   Choctaw   Nation.
Name of Mother: Arreathy Morris   a citizen of the   Choctaw   Nation.

Postoffice   Idabel, Ind. Ter.

AFFIDAVIT OF MOTHER.

UNITED STATES OF AMERICA, Indian Territory, }
    Central   **DISTRICT.**

I,   Arreathy Morris   , on oath state that I am   25   years of age and a citizen by   marriage   , of the   Choctaw   Nation; that I am the lawful wife of   Solon Edgar Morris   , who is a citizen, by   blood   of the   Choctaw   Nation; that a   female   child was born to me on   8th   day of   June   , 1903; that said child has been named   Lenora Morris   , and was living March 4, 1905.

Arreathy Morris

Witnesses To Mark:
{ W C Harris
{ W R Kirby

Subscribed and sworn to before me this   12th day of   April   , 1905

Wirt Franklin
Notary Public.

AFFIDAVIT OF ATTENDING PHYSICIAN OR MID-WIFE.

UNITED STATES OF AMERICA, Indian Territory, ⎤
  Central   **DISTRICT.** ⎦

I,   Carrie F Hampton   , a   midwife   , on oath state that I attended on Mrs. Arreathy Morris   , wife of Solon Edgar Morris   on the 8 day of June , 1903; that there was born to her on said date a   Female   child; that said child was living March 4, 1905, and is said to have been named Lenora Morris

Carrie F Hampton

Witnesses To Mark:
  ⎰ W C Harris
  ⎱ W. R. Kirby

Subscribed and sworn to before me this   12 day of   April   , 1905

G.G. Merry
Notary Public.

Choc New Born 1062
  Marie McCann
  (Born Nov. 11, 1904)

BIRTH AFFIDAVIT.

DEPARTMENT OF THE INTERIOR.
COMMISSION TO THE FIVE CIVILIZED TRIBES.

IN RE APPLICATION FOR ENROLLMENT, as a citizen of the   Choctaw   Nation, of Marie McCann   , born on the 11 day of Nov , 1904

Name of Father: Cornelius McCann   a citizen of the Choctaw   Nation.
Name of Mother: Leonia McCann   a citizen of the Choctaw   Nation.

Postoffice   Walls IT

321

AFFIDAVIT OF MOTHER.

UNITED STATES OF AMERICA, Indian Territory, ⎱
    Central   DISTRICT. ⎰

I,   Leonia M{c}Cann   , on oath state that I am   28   years of age and a citizen by   Marriage   , of the   Choctaw   Nation; that I am the lawful wife of Cornelius M{c}Cann   , who is a citizen, by   Blood   of the   Choctaw   Nation; that a   Female   child was born to me on   11   day of   November   , 1904; that said child has been named   Marie M{c}Cann   , and was living March 4, 1905.

Leonia M{c}Cann

Witnesses To Mark:
{

Subscribed and sworn to before me this   8   day of   April   , 1905

Leo Hunt
Notary Public.

My com expires Jan 9 1908

AFFIDAVIT OF ATTENDING PHYSICIAN OR MID-WIFE.

UNITED STATES OF AMERICA, Indian Territory, ⎱
    Central   DISTRICT. ⎰

I,   Emily Oller   , a ...., on oath state that I attended on Mrs. Leonia M{c}Cann   , wife of Cornelius M{c}Cann   on the 11   day of November   , 1904; that there was born to her on said date a   female   child; that said child was living March 4, 1905, and is said to have been named Marie M{c}Cann

Emily Oller

Witnesses To Mark:
{

Subscribed and sworn to before me this   8   day of   April   , 1905

Leo Hunt
Notary Public.

My com expires Jan 9 1908

Applications for Enrollment of Choctaw Newborn
Act of 1905   Volume XIV

Choctaw 2956.

Muskogee, Indian Territory, April 20, 1905.

Cornelius McCann,
    Lodi, Indian Territory.

Dear Sir:

    Receipt is hereby acknowledged of your letter of April 10, enclosing the affidavits of Leonia McCann and Emily Oller to the birth of Marie McCann, daughter of Cornelius and Leonia McCann, November 11, 1904, and the same have been filed with our records as an application for the enrollment of said child.

Respectfully,

Chairman.

Choc New Born 1063
    Ruby May Callaway
    (Born Sept. 4, 1904)

BIRTH AFFIDAVIT.
DEPARTMENT OF THE INTERIOR.
COMMISSION TO THE FIVE CIVILIZED TRIBES.

IN RE APPLICATION FOR ENROLLMENT, as a citizen of the   Choctaw   Nation, of
Ruby May Callaway   , born on the 4   day of Sept , 1904

Name of Father: Robert E Callaway   a citizen of the   U.S.   Nation.
Name of Mother: Elizabeth Callaway   a citizen of the   Choctaw   Nation.
Name of Mothers Father Geo W. Harkins

Name of Mothers Mother Hattie Harkins   Postoffice   Owl I.T.

Applications for Enrollment of Choctaw Newborn
Act of 1905   Volume XIV

AFFIDAVIT OF MOTHER.

UNITED STATES OF AMERICA, Indian Territory,
Central   DISTRICT.

I,   Elizabeth Callaway   , on oath state that I am   17   years of age and a citizen by   Blood   , of the   Choctaw   Nation; that I am the lawful wife of Robert E Callaway   , who is a citizen, by   U.S.   of the   ——   Nation; that a Female   child was born to me on   4   day of   Sept   , 1904; that said child has been named   Ruby May Callaway   , and was living March 4, 1905.

Elizabeth Callaway

Witnesses To Mark:

{

Subscribed and sworn to before me this   7 day of   April   , 1905

John H. Cross
Notary Public.

AFFIDAVIT OF ATTENDING PHYSICIAN OR MID-WIFE.

UNITED STATES OF AMERICA, Indian Territory,
Central   DISTRICT.

I,   J. H. Arnold   , a   Physician   , on oath state that I attended on Mrs.   Elizabeth Callaway   , wife of   Robert E. Callaway   on the 4   day of Sept   , 1904; that there was born to her on said date a   Female   child; that said child was living March 4, 1905, and is said to have been named   Ruby May Callaway

Dr. J H Arnold

Witnesses To Mark:

{

Subscribed and sworn to before me this   7 day of   April   , 1905

John H. Cross
Notary Public.

324

Choctaw 3679.

Muskogee, Indian Territory, April 20, 1905.

Robert E. Calloway[sic],
    Owl, Indian Territory.

Dear Sir:

Receipt is hereby acknowledged of the affidavits of Elizabeth Callaway and Dr. J. H. Arnold to the birth of Ruby May Callaway, daughter of Robert E. and Elizabeth Callaway, September 4, 1904, and the same have been filed with our records as an application for the enrollment of said child.

Respectfully,

Chairman.

---

7 NB 1063

Muskogee, Indian Territory, April 27, 1905.

Elizabeth Callaway,
    Owl, Indian Territory.

Dear Madam:

Receipt is hereby acknowledged of your letter of April 20, 1905, asking if application for the enrollment of your child Ruby May Callaway has been receive.

In reply to your letter you are informed that the affidavits heretofore forwarded to the birth of your child Ruby May Callaway have been filed with our records as an application for the enrollment of said child.

Respectfully,

Chairman.